EMERGENCY PLANNING AND COMMUNITY RIGHT-TO-KNOW

An Implementer's Guide to SARA Title III

EMERGENCY PLANNING AND COMMUNITY RIGHT-TO-KNOW

An Implementer's Guide to SARA Title III

Victoria Cooper Musselman
Carnow, Conibear & Associates, Ltd.

 VAN NOSTRAND REINHOLD
————————————— New York

Printed in the United States of America

Van Nostrand Reinhold
115 Fifth Avenue
New York, New York 10003

Van Nostrand Reinhold International Company Limited
11 New Fetter Lane
London EC4P 4EE, England

Van Nostrand Reinhold
480 La Trobe Street
Melbourne, Victoria 3000, Australia

Macmillan of Canada
Division of Canada Publishing Corporation
164 Commander Boulevard
Agincourt, Ontario M1S 3C7, Canada

16   15   14   13   12   11   10   9   8   7   6   5   4   3   2   1

Library of Congress Cataloging-in-Publication Data

Musselman, Victoria Cooper.
    Emergency planning and community right-to-know : an implementer's guide to SARA Title III   / Victoria Cooper Musselman.
        p.   cm.
    Includes index.
    ISBN 0-442-20555-4
    1. Hazardous substances—Law and legislation—United States.
2. Chemicals—Law and legislation—United States. 3. Disaster
relief—Law and legislation—United States. 4. Hazardous
substances—United States—Safety measures. 5. Chemicals—United
States—Safety measures. 6. Disaster relief—United States.
I. Title.
KF3958.M87   1989
344.73'0424—dc19
[347.304424]   88-13495

To
Louise and Philip Cooper, my parents,
and
Bertram W. Carnow, M.D.,
for their belief
in my ability to make a contribution
to the future

PREFACE

More than two years have passed since the Emergency Planning and Community Right-to-Know Act was approved by Congress, but confusion about this law and it implementation still exists. During that period interest among American citizens about environmental issues has continued to grow. Hopefully this book will help decision-makers create the circumstances in which the hopes and aspirations for a cleaner environment will be realized.

Implementers of this law face problems common to all those using new regulatory schemes. At first the tasks at hand seem confusing, contradictory, and more complex than necessary. This has certainly been the case with EPCRA. In fact, compliance among regulated firms, in the first two years, has been estimated to have been as low as twenty-five percent. This poor record of implementation is not surprising. It always takes a few years for the regulated to catch up with the expectations placed upon them when new government regulations are instituted.

Certain trends have emerged in the handling of toxic and hazardous materials. They can be identified as two requirements codified by this law. The first trend is planning as a cornerstone of prevention. The second trend is the understanding that public disclosure about the nature of potential hazards in communities is necessary.

Recent concern about the environmental hazards associated with the production of atomic weapons illustrates these points. A front page headline in the November 1st *Chicago Tribune,* "U.S. to Cooperate on Arms Plants' Cleanup", represents a growing custom reversing the previous standard policy not to reveal information about hazardous materials contamination. Another indicator of the increasing consideration being given to the environment is shown by the amount of time spent by the candidates during the 1988 presidential election campaign dealing with environmental issues. Clearly there is a consensus among the American public that a clean a environment is necessary.

Because of the confusion that surrounds the EPCRA law, and its implementation, one note of caution must be given when using this book. Efforts to simplify difficult compliance requirements are not always successful, and so this book attempts to look at the multiple expectations of the law from the point of view of the different groups involved. Therefore, several sections of the book review the same information in various ways. For example, the program responsibilities of firms and facilities, state governments, local planning agencies, and communities are handled separately, even though the actual activities may overlap.

Using the table of contents, list of tables, and index will aid in focussing on the particular pieces of information required. However, reading the book from beginning to end will give a complete picture of the EPCRA process.

A book that is focussed on a particular law suffers under the handicap that the law can change. Indeed there have been some indications that there may be some legislative adjustments to the EPCRA law. However, it is quite unlikely that the law will be changed significantly, because of the support for this kind of environmental protection desired by the American public. If the reader wants to get a general overview of the legislation, any minor adjustments to the law, and its regulations, will have little impact on the discussions in this book. If the reader is responsible for program implementation it will become necessary to contact officials in order to get the most recent update on program requirements. Implementers will also have to keep up with the general standard of performance expected by the EPA and the LEPC's in their locality to fully understand what is expected of them. Whatever your objective, this book will be useful for understanding EPCRA.

EPCRA is to be implemented in an evolving fashion. Too often we are resigned to letting others control the initiative. Whatever our interests it is important to stay informed about policy alternatives and play an active role in shaping those policies. Of particular note are the growing role of trade associations and professional associations in setting performance standards for industry and the community. In addition, the cost of these programs can become an important factor in shaping policy. I urge the reader to stay informed about these matters and play a role in finding solutions to our environmental problems.

Writing this book has been a rewarding task. The help provided by all the staff at Van Nostrand Reinhold has been invaluable. Without their support and their patience it would never have been completed.

Chicago, Illinois

ACKNOWLEDGMENTS

There are many dedicated people who made it possible for me to write this book. Shirley A. Conibear, M.D., and Shirley A. Ness, M.S., CIH, must be mentioned first because of their strong support and encouragement while I worked on this project. As colleagues, they provided technical and professional advice that helped me through some difficult sections. Susan Munger and Robert Esposito served as patient and thorough editors. EPA staff members were helpful and responsive to my requests. Finally, professional associates in the private sector served as willing sounding boards for my ideas and approaches to program implementation. I must also thank Janice Dunbar and the members of the word processing department at Carnow, Conibear & Associates, Ltd., for their loyal and timely work on this book. They made it possible for my ideas to appear as words on paper. Without them, this project would never have been completed. In addition, I must thank my doctoral dissertation committee for patiently waiting for my thesis while I wrote this book. And finally, my immediate and extended family must be given credit for their constant support during this time of professional and personal stress.

VCM
Chicago, IL

LIST OF TABLES

CONTENTS

EMERGENCY PLANNING AND COMMUNITY RIGHT-TO-KNOW

An Implementer's Guide
to SARA Title III

Chapter 1
THE GROWTH OF CHEMICAL
RIGHT-TO-KNOW AS A PUBLIC POLICY

SECTION 1.1. INTRODUCTION

Understanding and defining the term "chemical right-to-know" requires a definition which recognizes that employees of firms and facilities, as well as community residents, have a right to information about the potential hazards of chemicals they may be exposed to on the job or in the neighborhood. This information must include the nature and extent of the potential hazards, the control measures used to prevent these hazards, and the emergency plans in place to respond to an emergency release of chemicals if one does occur. Knowledge about the health effects of chemicals requires information about chronic, long-term potential health problems resulting from low-level toxic exposures over time in addition to acute health effects resulting from emergency spills and/or other types of emergency releases into the air and water.

The concept of chemical right-to-know was first codified in the federal Occupational Safety and Health Administration (OSHA) Hazard Communication Standard (29 CFR 1910.1200) and the multiple state Right-to-Know laws promulgated by 1985 to cover employees in the manufacturing sector of the U.S. economy. In October 1986 the U.S. Congress passed, and President Reagan signed, the Emergency Planning and Community Right-to-Know Act as the free-standing Title III of the Superfund Amendments Reauthorization Act (P.L. 99-499). Many states have also passed laws pertaining to this issue. A distinction can be made between worker and community hazard information requirements. Worker Right-to-Know is regulated by OSHA and is meant to protect employees. Community Right-to-Know is regulated by the Environmental Protection Agency (EPA) and is meant to protect the environment and the community.

The purpose of this book is to provide an implementer's guide to the Community Right-to-Know process. Developing programs responsive to the laws' requirements can be complex and difficult. Hopefully, this book will make it easier for the reader to understand the issues involved and the steps required. However, the concept of Right-to-Know is a new one and, as a result, the approaches to implementation are still evolving. Therefore, no single volume can provide total guidance. If you are responsible for programs resulting from the legislation or have an ongoing interest in their meaning and impact, you will need to continue to seek out information about these laws as we gain more experience. To understand the scope and direction of of Community Right-to-Know, it is helpful to understand the rapid growth of Worker Right-to-Know as a public policy initiative. So, first, we present a little history about Right-to-Know in the workplace and how this concept has influenced the development of Community Right-to-Know.

SECTION 1.2. HISTORY OF WORKER RIGHT-TO-KNOW LAWS

Traditionally, information about industrial processes has been considered to be trade secrets and proprietary. This was the predominant legal principle and legislative concept almost until OSHA rules began to erode this industry prerogative. As you may be aware when you enter a workplace, the Bill of Rights and the Constitution do not always apply. In fact, your rights as a citizen in the community do not apply in the workplace. However, information about chemical exposures is one area where the absolute authority of the employer has begun to disappear. For example, by the late 1970's, employees began to gain access legally to the records of medical examinations performed on them by their employer. This trend was preceded by the passage of the Freedom of Information Act in the mid-1970's. It was the result of post-Watergate, post-Vietnam era concerns, which made access to government information a political issue.

The OSHA regulation, Access to Employee Exposure and Medical Record Standard, 29 CFR 1910.20, which became effective in 1980, was extremely important because it was the first OSHA standard that required companies to provide information to employees about industrial hygiene and medical record data in the workplace. The standard did not require that companies collect such data, but it did codify the right of access by employees to the information if companies did collect that data.

This rule was developed and promulgated during the Carter presidency while Dr. Eulah Bingham was director of OSHA. Dr. Bingham also tried to promulgate a labeling standard which would have required that labels with hazard warnings be placed on almost every container, pipe stream, or vessel in an industrial setting. This proposed standard lacked the communication components included in later Right-to-Know proposals. Industries actively opposed the proposed standard because of its rigid requirements for labeling. When Ronald Reagan was sworn in as President, one of his first acts was to withdraw that standard. As a result, the OSHA labeling standard was never issued.

In response to President Reagan's efforts to halt the required disclosure of information about chemicals to employees, many labor groups lobbied state legislatures to pass state Right-to-Know laws that replaced and expanded the requirements of the OSHA labeling rule.

These laws, in general, required that employers collect and disseminate information about chemicals manufactured or used in the workplace. The information had to be provided on a Material Safety Data Sheet containing specific facts about physical properties, health hazards, and protective measures associated with the chemicals. Employers were also required to familiarize employees with the specific health and safety hazards of their chemical exposure on the job, methods used to protect them, and procedures to use in case of an emergency.

It is interesting to note that the Material Safety Data Sheet has become the required method for communicating information about chemical hazards in Community Right-to-Know laws as well. This document, developed originally as a way to transfer technical information among engineering and health professionals, has become the legally acceptable information source about toxic chemicals for all citizens. This provides yet another indication of the increasingly important role that information plays in our growing technological society.

By 1983, 20 state Hazard Communication/Worker Right-to-Know laws had been passed and many others were about to pass. Each of these laws was slightly different from and inconsistent with the others. Industry representatives, who had opposed a federal standard in the past, changed their approach because they were potentially faced with having to implement 50 separate laws nationwide. Large organizations such as the Chemical Manufacturers Association came to realize that it was in their interest to have a federal standard or rule established that would codify for the nation as a whole what the requirements of Worker Right-to-Know would be. In 1984, OSHA proposed a federal Hazard Communication Standard to be implemented in phases. By May 24, 1988, that standard, 29 CFR 1910.1200, was applied to all industries.

The precursor to Title III, the Emergency Planning and Community Right-to-Know Act (EPCRA), can be traced to some of the early state Worker Right-to-Know laws, particularly the laws in New Jersey and Pennsylvania. These laws also contained some requirements for firms and facilities to provide information to communities about the chemicals used in their operations. Some manufacturing groups challenged these laws in the courts. They were unsuccessful in stopping the implementation of the Community Right-to-Know aspects of these laws. These cases clearly established the right of communities to require firms and facilities to provide information about chemical usage.

The OSHA rule is called the "Hazard Communication Standard" and applies to the workplace. How does the standard define a hazardous chemical? To a large extent, it is the responsibility of the producer of the chemical to determine what its hazards are under the OSHA standard. To some extent, this approach has been adopted by the EPA with regard to Community Right-to-Know as well. It is an innovative approach to hazard assessment and is different from what has been attempted before, with some very interesting results.

OSHA established a baseline set of chemicals considered hazardous. This includes everything that is regulated by other OSHA standards, any chemical that is listed on the *National Toxicological Program Annual Report on Carcinogens,* all the chemicals that the International Agency for Research on Cancer (IARC) lists as carcinogens, and all chemicals listed in the latest edition of the American Conference of Government Industrial Hygienists book entitled *Threshold Limit Values for Chemical Substances and Physical Agents in the Workroom Environment with Intended Changes.* These lists include approximately 3200 chemicals; however, they do not include mixtures or new chemicals. The standard says that for all other chemicals, the producer of the chemical has to develop a method of determining the hazards by using existing scientific literature. Based on this determination, producers are expected to develop a Material Safety Data Sheet for the chemical, and it is this sheet that follows the chemical through the marketplace from producer to user to local fire departments, which collect Material Data Safety Sheets from firms as part of Community Right-to-Know compliance.

For years, representatives of industry have said that OSHA standards are too specific and that performance standards would be much better. This type of standard states, for example, that protection must exist or that there must be adequate sanitary facilities in the workplace, but the regulatory agency does not need to specify exactly how these goals are to be reached. The people at OSHA who wrote the Hazard Communication Standard decided to apply the concept of performance standards. As a result, the standard established the concept that chemical producers were responsible for determining the hazards associated with the chemicals that they manufactured.

It is important to realize the implications of this approach to standard setting. Traditionally, if OSHA says that fire extinguishers must be kept 6 inches to the left of the door and the company does so, but the fire extinguisher is not in an appropriate place to fight a fire, the company can defend its practice by saying that it did what OSHA required and complied with the standard. However, when OSHA regulations state that it is the responsibility of industry to determine how hazardous a chemical is, and someone is injured by that chemical as a result of an inappropriate or incorrect determination of the hazard, the protection of the OSHA requirement no longer exists.

Also, from the chemical producer's point of view, information on a Material Safety Data Sheet can lead to increased liability. If producers underestimate the hazards of a chemical, they are exposing themselves to potential lawsuits from those who may have been injured by the chemical. If producers overestimate the potential hazards of a chemical, they may create a problem in the marketplace. People may not buy their product if they can find a substitute that is claimed to be less hazardous. So, a performance standard for hazard determination can be very problematic for industry.

As you can see, there are pros and cons to performance standards. But this approach to hazard determination has become the basis for all of hazard communication and for Community Right-to-Know as well. The Material Safety Data Sheet, as part of the OSHA Hazard Communication Standard, has become a major method for receiving information about chemicals today. This includes the public sector, the private sector, industry, and government, as well as the community.

This approach also reflects the increased level of knowledge necessary for a citizen, employee or government official to participate in the process of safe chemical handling. It is often the case that the knowledge required to evaluate the hazards of chemicals goes beyond the educational level that most individuals have attained.

SECTION 1.3. EXPANDING CHEMICAL RIGHT-TO-KNOW TO THE COMMUNITY

Once the OSHA Hazard Communication Standard was implemented and had passed a variety of tests in the courts, Congress began to consider expanding the Right-to-Know concept to the community. The motivation for this legislative initiative came from many sources. First, the tragedy in Bhopal, India, resulting in the death and illness of thousands of residents in the neighborhood of a factory where a chemical leak occurred, created concern that similar events might occur closer to home. Second, there has been continuing concern on the part of U.S. citizens that chemical contamination of soil, air and groundwater would have a continuing impact on our quality of life. Third, social activism and lobbying efforts on the part of environmental groups focused on the Right-to-Know concept. Finally, certain sectors of industry, particularly chemical manufacturers, understood that they could influence citizens' attitudes toward chemical safety and risks through community education programs such as Community Awareness and Emergency Response (CAER). This program was established by the Chemical Manufacturers Association at least a year prior to the passage of the EPCRA.

The government also felt that programs implementing strategies to handle chemical emergencies were necessary. After the Bophal incident, the EPA and the Federal Emergency Management Agency (FEMA), as well as several other agencies, began to improve existing programs in this area. A national task force was set up to provide federal and regional emergency response programs that would later create a framework for community Right-to-Know and emergency response implementation.

As is usually the case, the language and requirements of the EPCRA reflect the various compromises made by legislators in order to pass a final law. The act clearly specifies timetables for reporting by firms and requires that they report specific information about chemicals. It also requires that communities plan emergency response programs to handle potential emergency releases. Besides emergency planning, it instructs the EPA to develop an information and data base system for all citizens about industrial chemical usage.

Once Congress passed the law, EPA was authorized to write regulations specifying how firms, facilities and communities were to implement it. While the regulations are subject to public hearing, they can be expanded and clarified as EPA sees a need. The requirements of the law itself cannot be changed without congressional action.

All of these provisions make this law and its implementation very difficult. The chapters that follow create a framework for and an approach to implementation. Whether the reader is an elected official, government or private sector employee, owner of a facility required to comply with this law or a local citizen interested in this process, this book can help clarify EPCRA programs at the local, state and federal levels.

Chapter 2
ASSESSING AND COMMUNICATING
ENVIRONMENTAL RISK

SECTION 2.1. INTRODUCTION

Milton and Rose Friedman, in their now famous book *Free to Choose,*[1] identify a fundamental democratic principle in our society: the right of an individual to make decisions about those economic, social and political issues that affect his or her life. More directly, on the subject at hand, W. Kip Viscusi's book, *Risk by Choice,*[2] also clearly articulates the fundamental concept that citizens have the right to make personal choices about the risks taken based on the most complete information available. These authors argue that the government should have a minimal role, and possibly no role at all, in regulating safety. To them, market forces provide adequate protection against increased environmental risk. However, they do not argue against the increase in information provided to citizens by Community Right-to-Know statutes.

Information, however, is only one part of the risk analysis equation. First of all, economists and political scientists point out that people must often make decisions based on imperfect or incomplete information. It is also important to note that one's concept of risk is influenced greatly not only by the information one has about these risks but also by the value one places on the benefits associated with taking the risks. Behavioral scientists speak of individuals with various levels of risk acceptance. The level of risk acceptance varies depending upon how voluntary or involuntary an individual perceives the risk to be. An environmental activist, for example, might be unwilling to accept environmental damage to national parks, but, as an individual, may find the risk associated with rock climbing to be perfectly acceptable. Another person might find it acceptable to alter a once pristine environment to build a recreational facility on a remote mountainside, so that other people can comfortably view the beauties of nature. This same individual, however, might never choose to take the personal risk associated with rock climbing.

The fact is that almost everything we do has some risk associated with it. A

---

[1] Milton Friedman and Rose Friedman, *Free to Choose,* Harcourt Brace Jovanovich, New York, 1979.
[2] W. Kip Viscusi, *Risk by Choice,* Harvard University Press, Cambridge, Mass., 1983.

problem occurs when we try to establish an acceptable level of risk. Contradictions and conflicts between risks exist all the time. For example, some people choose a vegetarian diet because they find it difficult to justify eating the flesh of a living being. Often, however, these same people do not recognize that when they wear leather belts and shoes, they violate the assumptions reflected in their dietary choices.

Indicators of the American health status, such as life expectancy tables, reveal that our health risks are being reduced, since our average life expectancy for all categories has in fact increased dramatically as our economic status has improved throughout the twentieth century. However, we are also aware that infant mortality rates for certain subpopulations, particularly children of teenage mothers and urban minorities have increased dramatically in the last few decades.

Even though we cannot exist in a risk-free society, we continue to seek an increasing life span. This results in an effort to reduce risks of all sorts even further. It is in this context that we are better able to understand the basis of Title III, the EPCRA. This act is intended to help individuals and communities to establish a framework for receiving and assessing information about chemicals in the environment. As a result of the increased access to information, communities can judge the existing risk level and the effectiveness of their controls in limiting this risk.

SECTION 2.2. DEFINING ENVIRONMENTAL RISK

It should be clear by now that we are not talking about a world of absolutes. In fact, a great deal of uncertainty pervades the consideration of risk. Given these problems, a variety of definitions of environmental risk exist. For the purposes of this chapter, environmental risk is defined as our perception of:

1. A threat to human health that may be immediate, delayed or chronic
2. A threat to the environment that affects the air, water, or land on either an immediate or a delayed basis

Knowledge and perception are the key elements of this definition. First of all, there is a fair amount of scientific uncertainty about risk. To some extent, perceptions of risk and decisions about acceptable risks are based on factual scientific information. But the scientific community, as well as the general population, responds to a societal value system that influences risk analysis. Therefore, social, political, ethical and moral issues affect the scientific community, as well as the public at large, in the perception of risk.

In spite of this uncertainty regarding the scientific tools and social value orientations that play a part in making risk decisions, various scientific disciplines can be brought to bear on the process of risk analysis. Each of these specialties will be discussed briefly.

First, there are the medical disciplines of human toxicology, epidemiology and clinical medicine. They focus on the effects of hazardous chemicals on humans, using a variety of techniques. Clinical medicine looks at the diseases induced in the individual patient as a result of exposure to chemicals. Clinical toxicology, using animals as experimental models, studies how chemicals affect human organisms. Toxicological studies are, in fact, required for the licensing of new chemicals under the law. These studies form the basis for understanding the acute and chronic effects of chemicals on the human organism.

Since toxicologists cannot directly study the effects of toxic chemicals on humans in controlled experiments for ethical reasons, we often rely on epidemiology as the basis for understanding the effects of toxins on humans. Epidemiology developed as a discipline in the nineteenth century to study the effects of epidemics such as cholera and other communicable diseases on the population. In the twentieth century, these techniques have been used to study the effects of chemicals on the human body. The most well-known area of epidemiological study is the effect of smoking on health. Using statistical methods, epidemiologists are able to identify increased health hazards directly related to increases in smoking in the population. Studies of the mass phenomenon of disease, and the general acceptance of the results of these studies by the general population, have led to the increased credibility of statistical epidemiological methodology as the scientific basis of risk analysis and assessment.

Next, environmental health effects are studied by environmental toxicologists, as well as by a range of geophysical scientists. Environmental toxicologists look at the impact of chemicals on the flora and fauna in the world. Both experimental conditions and survey methods are used to make these assessments. Geophysical scientists, including geographers, environmental engineers, hydrologists, geologists and others evaluate the effects of chemicals on the environment as well. These disciplines use direct instrumentation methods for analyzing water, soil and air. Epidemiological techniques similar to those employed by scientists studying human health are used to understand the effects of chemicals on wildlife such as fish, birds, insects and mammals.

Other researchers involved in evaluating the scientific basis of risk analysis are industrial hygienists and safety specialists. This group, as professionals in the workplace or as academic investigators, see it as their role to develop control systems for the safe use of chemicals in the environment. They are often more oriented toward applied scientific research. Since control technology can play a very important part in risk reduction, one must not underestimate the contribution to the science of risk assessment and analysis that industrial hygiene and safety professionals can provide. In fact, they have been playing an increasing role in the development of Worker and Community Right-to-know programs. Yet their contribution and recognition are minimized by those who favor an approach emphasizing pure science.

Besides the basic sciences, the medical sciences and the applied sciences, one has to consider the social sciences. They also play a role in the risk analysis and assessment process. The contribution we have become most recently aware of is the influence that economists have had in developing the methodology of cost/benefit analysis. This methodology has greatly influenced the risk assessment process in the last two decades. Cost/benefit methodology tries to embrace scientific understanding and public value perceptions about risk through economic analysis to determine "appropriate" levels of risk. Political scientists also contribute to this process through their understanding of how risk analysis and risk values are codified into law.

Finally, psychologists, educators and others involved in the communication sciences have begun to play an important role in understanding our perception of risk as part of the risk analysis and control process by studying such issues as the link between knowledge and action. They contribute to our understanding of human motivation for risk reduction.

Though it would be very convenient for the scientific community to be able to provide easy answers and simple solutions to questions about risk, the reality is that scientific understanding and its interpretation are as controversial as the issues related to values and ethics that also must be considered when risk analysis is done. Social issues related to environmental concerns reflect a variety of elements.

Various individuals and communities make different decisions based on the scientific and social values that they accept. Among the various trade-offs to be considered are those concerned with economic issues. Here, for many, keeping their job in the community is more important than any assessment of possible risk or harm. However, community decisions may not reflect the wishes of all individuals. For some, the risks to the community may outweigh the value of the jobs created because of the use of the chemicals. For example, it has been difficult to find communities willing to accept sites for facilities that store hazardous materials and nuclear wastes.

Other issues to consider are the attitudes and influence that communities have regarding how their environment should be maintained. A study conducted by the United Church of Christ[3] has indicated that there is a positive

---

[3]Commission for Racial Justice, *Toxic Wastes and Race in the United States,* United Church of Christ, New York, 1987.

and significant statistical relationship between the location of hazardous waste sites and the ethnic background of the community. Poor black and Hispanic communities contain more hazardous waste sites than white, middle-class communities. This seems to be a logical finding and provides an example of how social, economic and political issues influence our decisions about chemical risks.

In this section, some of the very complex and difficult scientific and social issues associated with risk analysis and perception have been discussed. However, these complexities should not discourage the reader from embarking on a risk analysis project. Instead, they should help the reader to understand the context in which such efforts must take place. The next section discusses how to take some of these considerations into account when developing a risk communication program for Title III compliance.

SECTION 2.3. DEVELOPING A RISK COMMUNICATION PROGRAM

Scientific knowledge about risk is just one factor involved in risk analysis. We know that smoking cigarettes when a person is also exposed to asbestos greatly increases the risk of lung cancer. However, some asbestos workers still smoke even though the law requires that they be informed of this link. Because of this apparent contradiction over the last decade, there has been great interest in the factors that influence employee and community risk perception. Efforts by such organizations as the EPA and the Chemical Manufacturers Association, as well as scholars in the communication sciences, have led to some important facts about how we perceive risk.[4] An important notion to consider is the concept of voluntary versus involuntary risk.

We appear to look more favorably on risks that we ourselves choose to take. Motorcycle riders, for example, often argue against mandatory helmet laws, even though studies clearly demonstrate that the use of helmets reduces injuries in motorcycle accidents. These motorcyclists feel that it is their right to choose whether to use helmets or not, since the risk that they take is of their own choosing.

Another important distinction is the one between natural and man-made risks. The situation in California clearly illustrates this differentiation. Many people choose to live in California even though they are aware of the threat from earthquakes as a result of the many geological faults present in the state. On the other hand, Californians are strong environmental advocates. As a result, while Californians live on a daily basis with the risk of earthquakes that could result in enormous devastation, they are unwilling to

---

[4]For further information about these issues, contact the EPA Office of Toxic Substances, Assistance Office, Washington, D.C. 20460 and the Chemical Manufacturer Association, 2501 M Street, N.W., Washington, D.C. 20037.

accept certain risks to the environment, as indicated by their strong environmental laws. The fact is that many individuals who are willing to accept risks of their own creation, or risks that they perceive as acts of god or nature, are less willing (if not unwilling under many circumstances) to accept risks created by others.

To minimize the effect that perception plays in making risk decisions at the individual level, there have been efforts over the last decade to quantify comparative risks. These efforts have often been less than successful or believable, because they do not recognize the difference between voluntary and involuntary or natural and man-made risks. For example, trying to compare the risk of getting an asbestos-related disease for children in schools to the risk of accidents when children cross the street in order to minimize the hazards associated with asbestos in schools does not work. The risk of getting an asbestos-related disease may be less than the risk of an accident when a child crosses the street. But this type of risk communication often results in a negative perception on the part of the receiver of the information because it can be seen as an excuse for inaction on the part of those responsible for the hazard. In this example, it might be a school system, but the same result could be extended to an employer or a firm.

There are three important factors which influence employee and community risk perception:

1. The believability of the messenger
2. The level of access to information
3. The content of the message

The first factor to consider is the credibility of the messenger. Credibility plays a crucial role in the communication of risk messages. The level of credibility, or believability, is based to a large extent on past experience.

In the case of the Tylenol/cyanide poisonings, the Johnson & Johnson Company, by remaining open and honest about the problem, was able to maintain its credibility. This was possible because of the public service and positive customer relations that have characterized the firm over several decades. Its reputation as a reliable consumer products firm made it much easier for Johnson & Johnson to weather the storm.

On the other hand, Union Carbide, which prior to the Bhopal incident had a positive image as a responsible chemical producer, found that image deteriorating rapidly. Therefore, when another accident occurred at Union Carbide's Institute, West Virginia, facility, shortly after the Bhopal incident, the firm's assurances were not considered credible by the public. This made it difficult for Union Carbide to establish or maintain credibility regarding its environmental control programs.

The believability of the messenger can be influenced by many factors, including standing in the community, expertise of the bearer of information, level of trust developed over time and clarity of the message. Fancy public relations campaigns designed by expensive consultants who create slick promotional material may not be very convincing. By contrast, an employee of the firm who is a local community resident with a strong public service record, and who can attest to the company's commitment to safety, may be a much better messenger. A proven track record of safety on the part of the firm also strengthens the credibility of the messenger.

The amount of free access to information is another factor that influences the community's risk perception. In industry, it is traditionally acceptable to limit access to information to a need-to-know basis. However, when one considers involuntary risks, need-to-know may not be adequate. Right-to-know and full access to information are essential in creating a favorable public attitude toward risk. Since this is one of the purposes of Title III, it is easy to treat it simply as a regulatory requirement.

Though the believability of the messenger and free access to information are important, the most critical factor influencing risk perception is the nature of the message itself. This calls for relevant information about what firms, facilities and community agencies are doing to prevent man-made risks to human health and the environment. No matter how believable the messenger or how open the information access process, if there is no prevention program in place, none of the factors that make the message more believable will really help. An appropriate prevention plan or, as codified by Title III, an emergency response plan at the local level will address community concerns.

All three factors listed above influence one another. The plan must be judged by the community to be appropriate. Such a plan can enhance the credibility of the messenger. The community's past experience with firms, facilities and community response personnel will also play a role in shaping attitudes and risk perceptions.

Since risk analysis is a relatively new discipline and is influenced by so many factors, it is necessary to recognize that risk perception and risk reality may *differ*, though this is not always the case. Risk perception may distort actual risk levels by inflating them when they are man-made, nonvoluntary risks. In the reverse situation, perceptions and attitudes may lead to an underestimation of the hazards of natural, voluntary risks. Conversely, firms may underestimate the level of risk posed by their facility, whereas individuals making risk decisions for firms may accept a higher level of personal risk. This risk trade-off problem exists not only among the public or in the firm, but also in the scientific and technical community as well. We cannot underestimate the complexity and difficulty of these risk assessment problems. It seems clear that logic and rationality are not always the primary decision rules in risk analysis. However, we do know that the EPCRA, as well as local laws, mandate that we face these issues and find workable solutions that are satisfactory to all involved.

SECTION 2.4. RISK COMMUNICATION PROGRAM ELEMENTS

The term "risk communication" is not used in the EPCRA. However, the need for risk communication programs is implied by many sections of the law. Under the law, those responsible for risk communication are, first of all, the firms and facilities that create the risk. Their responsibility includes the submission of a variety of complicated reporting forms under Sections 303, 304, 305 and 313, as well as the requirement to provide Material Safety Data Sheets to public agencies.

State and local agencies are also responsible for risk communication through the State Emergency Response Commissions (SERCs) and the Local Emergency Planning Committees (LEPCs). Other local officials also responsible for risk information include fire departments, police and other public safety officials. As stated before, the more cooperative the planning effort, the more likely that risk information will be accurate and believed by the public.

Organized environmental groups, as well as other advocacy groups, also provide information to the public. Often the information provided by these groups serves as a critique of the official efforts to protect citizens and the environment. Involving such groups in LEPCs, therefore, may make the organizing process more difficult. However, the end results may be more convincing to the general public. Involving groups with environmental concerns, rather than keeping them outside of the process and, as a result, less satisfied with the process and more able to provide conflicting information, may create a credibility problem that could be avoided.

Subsection 2.4.1. Objectives of a Risk Communication Program

The overriding objective of EPCRA implementation is reducing human and environmental risks as a result of chemical exposures. This objective must be seen as part of every aspect of the risk reduction program. Therefore, the primary objective of any risk communication program is to present information about the program. Another objective that flows from this primary objective is to build confidence on the part of the community that these risk reduction efforts are appropriate and enforceable.

Specific information objectives will vary depending upon the audience to be addressed. At the firm and facility level, the first information communication targets are the employees. The more confident employees are about the risk prevention and minimization efforts, the more likely this attitude will be communicated throughout the community.

Other communication targets are the professionals in the community. This is important in areas where mixed-use zoning is allowed, especially when manufacturing establishments and residential neighborhoods exist side by side. If one is involved in emergency planning procedures in communities where there are large numbers of residents who are technical professionals, they are likely to be more aware than the general public of the risks involved in handling chemicals. If the program is believable to them, they can provide an important credibility link to other community residents.

Elected officials are another target for risk communication. Politicians have a dynamic role in the process of risk communication, because they influence the community as well as being influenced by it. If elected officials such as state legislators or city council representatives are convinced that those responsible for emergency responses are doing a credible and acceptable job in risk reduction and emergency preparedness, they will become important communicators in response to community concern. The alternative scenario, angry legislators who grandstand about weaknesses in emergency preparedness plans, can result in sensational press reports that will only hurt the planning process.

The media is another group that deserves to be considered as a target in the risk communication process. We are all aware that it is very difficult for positive stories to be covered in the printed and electronic media. These organizations sell advertising based on readership. Readership size is often based on how sensational and controversial the information provided by any given media outlet is. Editors can be encouraged and convinced that positive press related to risk reduction is beneficial from a community service point of view. Since local planning agencies are required to include representatives from the media, this dialogue can begin in the LEPC.

Finally, the target population of primary concern is the general community. It is the community residents themselves, who may be affected by chemicals, that need to be clearly targeted as recipients of information regarding community preparedness. Dissemination of information through public service announcements, advertisements and press stories helps to build confidence in the community planning process, which is the overall objective of these programs.

Subsection 2.4.2. Assessing Risk

Risk communication objectives dovetail with overall program objectives. A risk analysis procedure must be developed that is based on a thorough and complete assessment of the possible risks. The *Hazardous Materials Emergency Planning Guide* developed by the National Response Team identifies vulnerability analysis as an important aspect of risk assessment. The EPA has published a risk analysis document entitled *Technical Guidance for*

Hazard Analysis that may be useful in this process. It is available from EPA regional offices. LEPCs need to know what hazards exist in the community through the hazard analysis process based on an understanding of the information provided by firms and facilities on the Title III forms. They must also understand who is vulnerable as a result of these potential hazards. A vulnerability analysis provides information about populations, property and the environment at risk by establishing vulnerability zones.

A particular focus of the vulnerability analysis is the special populations at risk in any given vulnerability zone, as well as the general population that might be affected by any unexpected release of potentially hazardous chemicals. Populations such as school children, the elderly in the general community or in planned communities or nursing homes, hospital populations, and people with specific health risks, such as asthmatics, heart disease patients, and populations with limited mobility such as the wheel chair-bound, the blind and the hearing impaired, must all be considered to be at special risk. A vulnerability analysis must assess the existence of these individuals. Based on this information, appropriate evacuation and notification procedures must be incorporated in the emergency plan.

Subsection 2.4.3. Assessing Perceptions of Risk

Though those involved in risk reduction efforts and emergency planning need to be aware of the existing risks in the community, it is also important to understand what the community perceives as risks. Discrepancies may exist here and must be addressed by the risk communication plan. Assessment of risk perceptions can take varying forms. Surveys of community residents are possible. Interviews with key community leaders or randomly selected community members is another method. Reviewing press reports that address community attitudes may provide another source of information. It is important that the LEPC listen to what community residents are saying about the risks they perceive. Ignoring clear messages of concern, which may or may not be valid, will diminish the credibility of any program. In order to correctly assess community perceptions about risk, it is necessary to hone skills in both asking questions and listening to answers. Knowing what people think about risks is the best guide for preparing an appropriate risk communication program.

Subsection 2.4.4. Providing Required Information and Information that Addresses Community Concerns

The EPCRA clearly outlines the information that must be made available to community residents. As mentioned in other sections of this book, it is the responsibility of SERCs and LEPCs to make that information available in an accessible and complete way. However, announcing that the local fire depart-ment now has multiple file cabinets filled with Material Safety Data Sheets that are readily available for anybody to peruse is an inadequate approach to risk communication. A much more proactive approach is essential if public credibility for emergency response preparedness is desired.

Firms and facilities can influence public attitudes by taking actions and subsequently publicizing them to demonstrate their support for community preparedness. Participation in community response teams through dona-tions of equipment, facilities and staff expertise can demonstrate commit-ment to the community's effort for emergency preparedness. Publicizing written and implemented policies related to risk reduction will also strengthen the risk communication effort at the firm and facility level. These same techniques can be used by LEPCs to create confidence in their group.

There are two types of communication to be considered. First are activi-ties that have come to be known as "media events" or photo opportunities. A good example is a press conference announcing the opening of a reading room in the library where community members can review emergency planning information. Another example is to publicize a local coordinated effort that simulates an emergency response. Though involving the press and community residents in this activity might require a lot of coordination, the publicity value and confidence that will result can be invaluable.

The second type of communication that is essential to such a program is the day-to-day ongoing provision of information at the local level. Organiza-tions such as the American Heart Association, American Cancer Society, and other public service and advocacy groups, as well as the experience of the advertising industry, indicates that regular, consistent, simple informa-tion presented in an understandable way to the general population can be effective in raising overall awareness about products and services. These lessons should not go unnoticed in the EPCRA context. LEPCs should maintain a public presence that is as complete as resources and funds will allow. Examples of such activities are LEPC booths at county fairs; partici-pation in health promotion events sponsored by health service providers such as hospitals; exhibits in libraries; inserts in tax bills; stickers with emergency numbers distributed throughout the community; and emergency response procedure guidelines distributed in local schools.

SECTION 2.5. CONCLUSION

All of the recommendations presented in this chapter are based on a public approach to risk communication. Some might argue against this policy. For example, if communities seem to lack interest in emergency planning, why bother? To support this argument, it could be pointed out that when Material

Safety Data Sheets became available to employees of firms, very few, if any of them, ever asked to see one. Strong communication programs also cost money and require resources that may be better used elsewhere. Based on these arguments and others not made here, many communities may choose to deemphasize this aspect of EPCRA.

The results of choosing to deemphasize communication about risk reduction programs may not be immediately clear. However this decision will affect how thorough emergency planning will be. It is in the interest of firms and facilities, as well as the government officials involved in this process, to work as hard as possible to make planning efforts cooperative. Without this cooperative effort, the distrust and lack of credibility that can develop will only hurt the implementation efforts. Though conflicts may arise during this process, it is important that they be resolved, or else all will suffer. Risk perception is only as good as risk prevention.

Chapter 3
UNDERSTANDING THE EMERGENCY PLANNING AND COMMUNITY RIGHT-TO-KNOW ACT AND ITS REQUIREMENTS

SECTION 3.1. INTRODUCTION

Subsection 3.1.1. What We Need to Know

Concern about environmental health and safety has resulted in the passage of laws and the issuing of regulations on the part of multiple government agencies at the federal, state and local levels. Implementing these laws requires program planning activities as well as the allocation of resources to these programs. The plans developed must be comprehensive and ongoing, with consistent implementation. One often finds that at the local, state and federal governmental levels, there are program overlaps which lead to the duplication of resources, even though the sources of funding for these programs are limited. Industry is certainly not immune to this problem either. Understanding program requirements and planning appropriately for their implementation can help eliminate some of the unnecessary expense in time and resources that hurt so many government-initiated programs.

The purpose of this chapter is to introduce the laws and their programmatic requirements for implementing environmental safety activities. Though the EPCRA will be the primary focus, other laws will be included as well. Of particular interest are the Department of Transportation's Hazardous Materials Transportation laws. Also included are the Resource Conservation and Recovery Act (RCRA) as it applies to the handling and disposal of hazardous chemicals in the environment and the Comprehensive Environmental Response Compensation and Liability Act of 1980, known as CERCLA, or Superfund, and its reauthorization, known as the Superfund Amendments and Reauthorization Act of 1986, or SARA. Both of these laws, as well as EPCRA, are administered by the EPA. OSHA also promulgates rules and laws that affect the way environmental safety programs are planned and implemented. These will also be discussed briefly in this chapter.

Another purpose of this chapter is to help the reader understand these laws in the context of program implementation. Appropriate program activities require the coordination of emergency response efforts by various groups and individuals. Whether one is involved in the government program planning aspect of this law or in private sector program implementation, it is necessary to understand your role and how all these laws interconnect or overlap. If this is not understood, resources and program development time will be wasted, resulting in uncoordinated, inefficient program implementation.

One important caveat is that, unfortunately, implementation of these laws and their regulations can never be clear-cut and straight-forward. An important reason for this is that laws and regulations are developed under the federalist system established by the U.S. Constitution. This system allows various levels of government to exist, be they municipal, regional, state or federal. The first three entities can initiate their own programs as long as they are at least as strict as the federal laws and standards. Therefore, variation is possible in state and local laws pertaining to the environment throughout the country. To describe and explain in detail every state and local law pertaining to environmental matters is beyond the scope of this or any other book. Therefore, this book will provide a general overview of and framework for developing programs responsive to these laws as they exist at the federal level. Readers must find out if there are any differences in their state and local requirements.

SECTION 3.2. HOW EPCRA IS ORGANIZED

EPCRA was passed and signed into law in October 1986. This law is often referred to as Title III because it appears as the third part of another law, SARA. SARA was passed in order to continue the Superfund Cleanup Program initiated in the early 1980's. Even though EPCRA is a part of Superfund, it is actually a law unto itself. Since there is no target date in Title III itself that requires Congress to change the law, even if SARA requires reauthorization at some later time or is repealed, EPCRA will remain intact unless it is altered by Congress. It is possible that it will remain as is into the next century.

In order to better understand the various parts of this complex law, a sense of its overall scope can help. The act is organized into three sections: Subtitle A, Subtitle B and Subtitle C. The first section, Subtitle A, covers the "Emergency Planning and Notification" aspects of this act and includes the mechanisms to be used to set up the organizational framework for government programs in response to this law. Emergency preparedness and extremely hazardous chemicals are also covered in this section, as are the requirements for developing emergency response plans. The notification of appropriate authorities in emergency situations is described, and training programs for emergency response personnel are discussed.

Subtitle B, called "Reporting Requirements," describes the responsibilities of firms and facilities using hazardous chemicals and establishes reporting requirements. These reporting requirements are closely linked to the requirements of the OSHA Hazard Communication Standard (29 CFR 1910.1200), and participation in the activities outlined in this section of the law is determined by a firm's or facility's status under the OSHA law. These requirements are often referred to by their section numbers. For example, Section 311 establishes requirements for Material Safety Data Sheets, Section 312 outlines requirements for the emergency and hazardous chemical inventory forms and Section 313 refers to toxic chemical release forms.

Subtitle C, the "General Provisions" of EPCRA, specifies how the information collected under Subtitle A and Subtitle B is to be made available to the public. It also includes the trade secrets provisions of this law, as well as the enforcement provisions.

Each section of the law as written by Congress authorizes EPA to create regulations regarding implementation of the provisions. There are five separate reporting requirements under the law and several lists of chemicals whose use may trigger specific reporting requirements. As a result, creating programs mandated by these laws can be complex and difficult. Each requirement of the law will be discussed in detail. Tables and charts are provided to make it easier to understand EPCRA and other laws that govern the use of hazardous chemicals in our community.

EPCRA is reproduced in full in Appendix A of this book. Reading it, along with the descriptions of its sections, will give the reader a good overview of its requirements. The actual regulations issued by EPA have not been included. These regulations are subject to change on a regular basis and are therefore not appropriate here. They are available from the EPA and state governments.

SECTION 3.3. EPCRA SUBTITLE A: EMERGENCY PLANNING AND NOTIFICATION

Subsection 3.3.1. EPCRA Section 301: Establishing State Commissions, Planning Districts and Local Committees

This section of the law establishes the organizational structure and its implementation by requiring each of the 50 states and the territories of the United States to set up programs of their own. The State Emergency Response Commission, or SERC, is designated as the primary body responsible for implementing the program at the state level. The members of these commissions, appointed by the governor of the state, have several specific responsibilities. First, they must appoint local emergency planning committees, or LEPCs.

These committees are responsible for developing the program at the local level. Once they are established, it is the responsibility of the SERC to coordinate the activities of all the LEPCs throughout the state. This coordination requires the establishment of procedures for receiving and processing requests for information from the public. To carry out this function, it is the responsibility of the Commission to appoint an official to serve as Coordinator for Information.

In order to appoint local committees, SERCs must first define emergency planning districts. Every state has approached this task somewhat differently. Many states have chosen to use the existing county or parish structure to establish these districts. However, there has been some variation in this procedure. For example, in some locations, several counties have been combined to create one local emergency planning district. This is particularly appropriate when individual counties, often in rural areas, have no need or resources for separate planning districts. In other cases, countywide designations are, in fact, too large. In areas where major cities span county lines, or where city and county response efforts have traditionally been separated, districts have been established to cover particular municipalities or townships. This, for example, is the case in Illinois, where the city of Chicago has been designated as a separate planning district from Cook County, even though Chicago is a part of Cook County. The law also allows emergency planning districts to be established across state lines when these emergency planning areas logically overlap state borders. Multijurisdictional planning districts must be acceptable to all of the states involved.

Once SERCs have established the local emergency planning districts, they delegate authority for EPCRA implementation by appointing LEPCs for each of these districts. The law clearly specifies what kind of representation is to be included among the membership of these emergency planning committees. Five specific categories of membership are identified. They are:

1. Elected state and local officials
2. Law enforcement, civil defense, firefighting, first-aid, health, local environmental, hospital and transportation personnel
3. Broadcast and print media
4. Community groups
5. Owners of firms and facilities subject to the requirements of the law

The membership of the LEPC must include these individuals, but may include others as well. Though changes in membership are left to the discretion of the SERC, the law specifically states that interested persons may petition the SERC to modify the membership of LEPCs.

It is interesting to note the possible implications resulting from the broad spectrum of community representation required on the LEPCs. By including members of the press, members of the community who may represent local environmental groups, and businesspersons who are affected by the requirements of these laws, as well as public health and locally elected officials, these committees establish an organized method for resolving conflicts between competing interests regarding hazardous chemicals in the community. Only time will tell whether this organizational scheme will minimize conflict and lead to a coordinated effort in local communities to respond to concerns about chemicals in the environment. Though it is impossible to predict whether they will be successful, it is certainly clear from the law that it was the intent of the Congress, when passing it, to provide for such a cooperative planning environment.

It is the main job and overall responsibility of the LEPCs to develop comprehensive emergency response plans. The law clearly establishes procedures to be used by these local committees to carry out this task. First of all, a chairperson of the committee must be appointed by the committee itself. It is the chairperson's responsibility to:

1. Establish rules about public notification of committee activities
2. Plan public meetings to discuss the emergency plan which the committee must develop
3. Receive public comments and provide a response to these comments
4. Distribute the emergency plan when it is developed

The committee must also establish procedures for receiving and processing requests from the public for information available as a result of this law and, as part of this function, must designate an official as the coordinator of information for the emergency planning district. As you can see, the requirement for an Information Coordinator at the local level parallels the structure of the SERC.

Prior to the enactment of EPCRA, in many localities committees of this sort had already been established. In those areas where a high concentration of industrial activity exists, these committees were established as a result of efforts by the Federal Emergency Management Agency (FEMA) and EPA after the hazardous chemical release incidents in Bhopal, India, and Institute, West Virginia. In localities with such past experiences, there are often individuals with appropriate knowledge who can assume a leadership role in establishing emergency response programs. In other areas, however, it has been difficult to find qualified personnel to serve on these committees. The limited number of individuals professionally trained and educated to implement and give advice regarding these programs may prove to be a major stumbling block in implementing this law. As with any new program, start-

Table 3.1. Responsibilities of SERCs (Section 301, EPCRA)

- Appoint LEPCs
- Define local emergency planning districts
- Establish procedures for disseminating information
- Appoint a Coordinator for Information

Table 3.2. Responsibilities of LEPCs (Section 301, EPCRA)

- Appoint a Chairman and a Coordinator for Information
- Establish rules about public notification
- Plan public meetings
- Receive and respond to public comments
- Create and distribute an emergency plan

up activities can be difficult, but over time, experience is gained and response activities can become more sophisticated.

Subsection 3.3.2. EPCRA Section 302: Substances and Facilities Covered and Notification

It is with this section that we begin to understand the complexity of EPCRA. There are a total of five reporting requirements under this act. Before reading the descriptions of the individual sections that follow, you may want to refer to Table 3.3.

First of all, it must be understood that Subtitle A refers to emergency planning and notification. This emergency planning requirement applies only to a list entitled "Extremely Hazardous Substances." This list, containing approximately 400 chemicals, was first identified by the EPA in November 1985. Prior to the passage of EPCRA and directly as a result of the Bhopal tragedy, the EPA developed an interim guidance for emergency preparedness programs. This guide did not have the force of law but did provide vital program concepts later used by Congress to develop the emergency planning aspects of EPCRA. The reader will soon see that this list of extremely hazardous substances is only the first list of chemicals used by firms and facilities that require attention. However, under Subtitle A, which relates to emergency planning, the list of substances includes only those that the EPA considers to be extremely hazardous. The final rule regarding this list was issued on April 22, 1987. Since the number of chemicals that appear on this list may change over time, it does not appear in this book. The current list is available from the EPA through the Chemical Emergency Preparedness Program Hotline, 1-800-535-0202. The list can also be found in EPA Rules and Regulations at 40CFR 355, Appendix A. Copies of the Code of Federal Regulations, 40 CFR 355, are available through the Government Printing Office (Superintendent of Documents, U.S. Government Printing Office, Washington, D.C. 20402).

Title III (EPCRA) as a whole places great emphasis on the planning process. In fact, the EPA has interpreted planning and organization for emergency response to be the primary purpose of Congress in creating Title III. The original CERCLA, or Superfund law, passed in 1980, was intended to develop guidelines for *responding* to emergency spills, particularly of oil and gas. Title III has expanded government authority in this area. It is meant to facilitate emergency planning which can help *prevent* accidents from occurring and to create a structure enabling a timely and effective emergency response at the local level in the event of a hazardous chemical release.

Section 302 of EPCRA specifies which firms and facilities are subject to Subtitle A. This one-time-only reporting obligation requires that if a firm or facility uses one of the substances that appear on this list, and uses it in an amount above the reporting requirement, the firm or facility must inform the SERC that it is subject to this subtitle. At this stage of the process, the firm or facility does not have to specify which of the extremely hazardous chemicals it has.

It is the responsibility of the firm or facility to make such a report to the SERC. Based on these reports, the state agency must notify the EPA of facilities subject to this requirement. It must also inform the LEPCs. This information flow provides an important first step that identifies, for all levels of government, those firms or facilities subject to this law.

This rule covering extremely hazardous substances published by the EPA lists two target quantities for each chemical. First, there is the Threshold Planning Quantity, or TPQ. This exists for each chemical and specifies the amount of that chemical that must be at a facility at any one time to trigger the report to the state. This quantity does not have to remain in one location on the site at all times to be subject to the law. Nor does it have to be maintained at all times. In fact, it is defined as the minimum total amount kept at a facility at any one time, regardless of whether it is in one location or multiple locations on the site. This TPQ varies depending upon the toxicity of the chemical involved and ranges from 1 to 10,000 lb.

The second specification for each chemical is the Total Reportable Quantity, or TRQ. This amount represents the minimum quantity of a substance that, if released, will require reporting under the emergency planning provisions. The TRQ will be discussed further when the Emergency Release Reporting requirements are outlined in detail. First, it is necessary to describe the concept of TPQ.

TPQs, expressed in pounds, are simple to understand in relation to single chemicals. However, the situation is more complicated when a facility must calculate the TPQ for both solids and mixtures. First, let's consider mixtures. The specific regulations governing mixtures, which appear at 40 CFR, Part 355.30, state that the extremely hazardous substance must be present in the mixture in an amount greater than 1% by weight to qualify as a TPQ. The weight of the total amount of the extremely hazardous substance in the mixture is to be calculated as an average. This is done by multiplying the weight in percent (greater than 1%) by the mass in pounds or the total weight of the contents of a vessel or a given quantity of mixture. This calculation will determine whether the TPQ of the extremely hazardous substance or substances has been reached.

In the case of solids, extremely hazardous substances are subject to either of two TPQs, both of which appear on the list in 40 CFR, Part 355.30. The lower of the two applies if the solid exists in a powdered form that has a particle size of less than 100 microns, or is handled in a solution or in a molten form, or meets the criteria of the National Fire Protection Association rating of 2, 3 or 4 for reactivity. If the solid does not meet any of these criteria, it is subject to the larger, or upper, TPQ, as shown in the list. Calculating these percentages for solids requires information about the chemical properties of the substances in question.

All of this may seem very complicated to the uninitiated. It is important to understand that this requirement does not affect chemical manufacturers alone. If a facility stores or uses products which it does not manufacture, and if the quantity that it stores or uses is great enough, constituents of that product may trigger the reporting requirement for extremely hazardous substances.

As an example, consider formaldehyde. It has a TPQ of 500 lb. If formaldehyde exists as a constituent of products that a firm uses, the TPQ may be reached, depending on its percentage in the mixture, when only a few 55-gallon drums of the mixture are stored. Ammonia is another example of a chemical that commonly appears in mixtures. With a TPQ of 500 lb, if it is 20% by weight of a mixture, as few as ten 55-gallon drums might be needed to meet the TPQ criterion. Nitric acid, another chemical that is commonly used in industry, having a TPQ of 1,000 lb at a 20% concentration, would require fewer than twenty 55-gallon drums at one time to trigger the notification requirement.

To summarize, each firm or facility must determine if it is subject to the extremely hazardous chemical reporting requirement. This determination is made by assessing the type and quantity of the chemicals on the site. It is the responsibility of the firm or facility that uses, stores, or manufactures such chemicals to inform the SEPC or the governor that it handles these chemicals. Failure to provide this information can result in substantial fines and penalties.

Table 3.3. Reporting Structure for Extremely Hazardous Chemicals

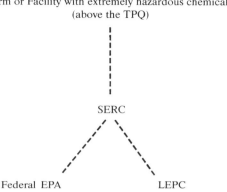

Firm or Facility with extremely hazardous chemicals
(above the TPQ)

SERC

Federal EPA   LEPC

It is important, therefore, that firms fitting the criteria as established, as well as community governing bodies responsible for this program, be aware of those operations to which this law is applicable. Once all of these facilities are identified, it is possible to begin one of the most important aspects of this program: developing comprehensive emergency response plans.

Subsection 3.3.3. EPCRA Section 303: Comprehensive Emergency Response Plans

Developing comprehensive emergency plans is the responsibility of the LEPCs. These committees, described in Subsection 3.3.1 of this chapter, are charged with the task of establishing procedures for preventing and/or containing chemical emergencies in a community. The law and the EPA regulations for emergency plans specify very broadly defined requirements in order to allow local communities to develop plans that are appropriate to their particular situation. Developing such a plan requires consideration of multiple factors. Among these factors are:

1. The quantity of chemicals stored, used or produced in the community
2. Methods of transportation into and out of the community
3. The resources available and required to implement such plans
4. Appropriate procedures such as evacuation, notification and cleanup procedures if an emergency event does occur
5. Local or state laws that apply to chemical handling or transport at the local level

Chapter 5 of this book explains how to develop such a plan. Here we will explain the parameters established by the law for such a plan. Table 3.4 presents this information in outline form.

It is very important to understand that additional requirements may be added to these rules and regulations at the state and local levels. Under this law, each community must develop a minimal plan. However, since this act does not preempt local initiative, each local community has the right to strengthen, augment and increase the basic requirements developed at the federal level.

A local emergency plan must be established by the LEPC on or before October 17, 1988. At a minimum, the plan must include the following items. First, all facilities subject to emergency planning requirements must be identified for each emergency planning district. These include, at best, all of the facilities which qualify for Section 302 reporting, as discussed in Subsection 3.3.3 of this book.

The plan must also identify transportation routes by which substances on the Extremely Hazardous Substances List are transported. Any facilities such as schools, whose occupants may be subject to additional risk because the facility is located close to operations subject to the requirements of this law, must also be identified. Another example of these types of facilities identified in the law are hospitals because of the decreased mobility and increased risk of the patients. Natural gas facilities are also mentioned in the law because of the increased risk of fire and explosion. The point here is that any facility that subjects inhabitants to special risks due to their proximity to hazardous chemicals, if they were to be released, need to be targeted. Among such institutions to consider are schools, hospitals, facilities for the elderly or infirm other than hospitals, densely populated areas, or locations with particular egress or access difficulties.

Another requirement of the emergency plan is that methods and procedures must be established by the LEPC to respond to any release of an extremely hazardous substance above the TRQ. A release is defined more clearly in Section 304 of the EPCRA and will be described in Subsection 3.3.5 of this book. The plan, however, must provide methods and procedures to follow in case such a release occurs. Facility owners and operators who store or use the extremely hazardous chemicals must be involved in this planning process. Local emergency and medical personnel, who will be required to respond to such a release if it does occur, must also be involved. Community service personnel such as firefighters, police and emergency response personnel are often called "first responders" because they are expected to be first on the scene when an emergency release occurs.

The next requirement is that both the LEPC and the facilities subject to these requirements designate emergency coordinators. It is the responsibility of these coordinators to determine when it is necessary to implement this plan.

During the planning process, the LEPC must develop procedures for providing what the law calls "reliable, effective and timely notification." It is the responsibility of facility emergency coordinators and the community emergency coordinator to provide this notification. The notification must be consistent with the Emergency Notification Requirements of Section 304, which will be discussed later. The purpose of this notification is to inform the persons designated to respond to the emergency requirements of an emergency situation.

The plan must also define or describe methods for determining the occurrence of a release. Part of this process is to identify the geographic areas or populations most likely to be affected by such a release and to develop methods for informing the public that a release has occurred.

The law requires that the LEPC describe in its emergency plan how community resources will be used to respond to an emergency release. This must include a description of emergency equipment and facilities in the community, as well as those at each facility in the community subject to the requirements of this law. Identifying the persons responsible for this equipment must also be a part of the plan. The intent here is to clarify the resources the community can use to minimize an emergency release and, if such a release does occur, to know what equipment and personnel are available to control it.

Next, the law requires that each plan contain information about a developed evacuation procedure. This should include methods for precautionary evacuation, when necessary, and should specify under which conditions this evacuation is to take place. Specifically mentioned should be the traffic routes to be used if an emergency does occur. Diagrams and maps are often used to chart out these routes.

EPCRA states that the plan must also include specific details of training programs for emergency response and medical service personnel who would be involved in responding to any emergency release that may occur. Finally, the emergency plan must specify methods and schedules for testing the plan. Each LEPC must develop regular emergency or chemical response drills to ensure that the plan can be implemented.

Firms and facilities subject to these requirements are responsible for providing information to the LEPC. They must provide the following information:

1. They must identify an individual who will serve as a facility representative and participate in the emergency planning process as a facility emergency coordinator.
2. The owner/operator of the facility subject to the emergency planning

requirements must promptly inform the LEPC of any relevant changes occurring at the facility as these changes take place or are anticipated.

3. The law also specifies that when requested by the LEPC, an owner/operator of a facility subject to this law, must promptly provide information to the committee that they may need to develop and implement an emergency plan.

This emergency response plan, when developed, is subject to review at two levels. First, the SERC must receive a copy of each LEPC plan. It is the prerogative of the SERC to review the plan. Based on that review, it may make recommendations regarding revision of the plan, if necessary, in order to ensure coordination of the plan with emergency response plans of other emergency planning districts. This provision gives the state authority to determine if emergency plans in contiguous emergency planning districts create contradictory or incompatible provisions.

A second review takes place at the regional level. The regional response team is an emergency planning program created by the original Superfund

Table 3.4: Requirements for Comprehensive Emergency Response Plans (SECTION 303, EPCRA)

1. Identify all facilities subject to emergency planning requirements
2. Identify transportation routes for substances on the Extremely Hazardous Substances List
3. Identify facilities or areas subject to additional risk because of their proximity to identified facilities, such as:
   a. Hospitals
   b. Natural gas facilities
   c. Nursing homes
   d. Densely populated areas
   e. Schools
   f. Locations with egress and access difficulties
4. Establish response procedures
5. Involve facility owners and operators in the planning process
6. Involve local emergency and medical personnel in the planning process
7. Designate emergency coordinators from the LEPC
8. Identify emergency coordinators for each facility subject to the emergency planning requirements
9. Develop "reliable, effective and timely notification" procedures
10. Identify community emergency response resources for first responders and community residents
11. Describe how these resources will be used in emergency situations
12. Develop evacuation procedures
13. Specify a training schedule for response personnel
14. Develop schedules and methods for testing the plan

Act or CERLA, which Congress passed in 1980. Under this law, a national response team and regional teams were established. They were also chartered to develop a National Contingency Plan. The regional response teams under this authority may review local emergency plans if requested to do so. They review and comment upon the plan or other issues related to preparing, implementing or testing it.

Subsection 3.3.4. EPCRA Section 304: Emergency Notification

Section 304 of EPCRA defines what constitutes a release of an extremely hazardous substance. On the surface, defining an emergency release under this act may seem simple; however, it is actually very complex. There are two reasons why the issue of notification is so complicated. First, Title III was written as a free-standing act with its own authority. However, from a legislative point of view, it is imbedded in CERCLA as Title III of the 1986 amendment to that act. CERCLA establishes its own reporting authority, separate and apart from Title III EPCRA reporting. As a result, there are actually two statutory requirements for reporting emergency releases of chemicals.

Another reason for the complexity of this section results from the substantial number of exemptions allowed, as part of this act as well as CERCLA. These exemptions complicate matters when trying to determine who has to report which releases to whom.

Now that you have been warned of the confusion, let's try to understand the requirements for hazardous chemical release reporting. An easy way to differentiate between Title III and CERCLA reporting is to know that CERCLA provided a mechanism for reporting hazardous chemical spills to a national authority, the National Response Center. However, it did not require reporting at the local level when these spills occurred. Even though local authorities would most likely respond to spills of hazardous chemicals in their communities, there was no legislative structure or community organization established to monitor, maintain records or plan for such events at the local level.

Title III, or EPCRA, was designed to provide that organization and authority at the local level. As a result, CERCLA regulates the reporting of spills to the federal government, while EPCRA creates the system for reporting spills at the local level.

This confusion would be less apparent to the program implementer if the chemicals considered hazardous under each law were the same. However, they are not. The EPCRA Extremely Hazardous Substance List (described earlier in Subsection 3.3.2 of this chapter) with specified TPQs and TPRs, was published as a final rule on April 22, 1987. This list contains approximately 406 chemicals. However, since then EPA has continued to make changes in this list.

In addition, there are two CERCLA lists; the more recent one was published on September 29, 1986, and contains 102 hazardous substances. Previously, 340 hazardous substances were identified. So, in the early phases of the implementation of Title III, there was much confusion regarding all of these lists. In the 1987 edition of the Code of Federal Regulations, the two CERCLA lists were combined. For implementation planning, it is important to realize that both lists need to be considered. It is also important to note that these lists are not identical. The CERCLA list contains more substances than the EPCRA list. In addition, these lists are subject to change. If you are involved in developing a program for Title III implementation, it is important to be aware of any changes in the list that may occur.

Now that it is understood that there is an overlap between CERCLA and EPCRA, it is appropriate to talk about the second complicating factor: the exceptions. The most important exception is for releases that result in exposure to persons solely at the site where the releases occurred. This means that a release of an extremely hazardous substance that occurs at the facility, but is contained within the facility, does not qualify as a release under either EPCRA or CERCLA.

The next exception is for releases of pesticides and herbicides. These releases are handled under the Federal Insecticide, Fungicide, Rodenticide Act, or FIFRA. Another exception applies to auto emissions. These emissions are controlled under the Clean Air Act and are not subject to either CERCLA or EPCRA.

Another important exception concerns releases that occur as a result of normal business operations. A distinction is made between normal business operation releases and abnormal emergency releases. Abnormal emergency releases in quantities above TPQs must be reported as they occur, as defined by Section 304 of EPCRA, which we are currently discussing. Releases that occur as a result of normal business operations must also be reported; however, they are reported on an annual basis and are covered under Section 313 of this law, which will be discussed later. Obviously, the definition of abnormal versus normal releases is subject to interpretation. The differences will become more clearly understood as this law is implemented and a body of experience and litigation establishes clearer definitions.

Now that we've discussed all of the exceptions to the reporting requirements, it is time to specify when emergency notification is required. Table 3.5 makes this information a little easier to understand. Emergency notification is required when:

1. A substance on the EPCRA's Extremely Hazardous Substance List is released into the community at or above its TRQ, resulting in either human or environmental exposure. The owner/operator of the facility responsible for this release must report it to the local and state authorities.

Table 3.5. Emergency Release Reporting

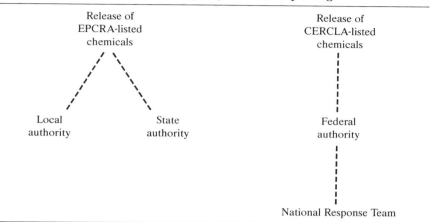

2. A substance appears on the CERCLA, but not on the EPCRA list. It is the responsibility of the owner or operator to report this release to the National Response Center in Washington, D.C. The number for the National Response Center is (800) 424-8802 or 8803. It is advisable, however, to also report the event to the LEPC and the SERC.
3. If a release occurs for a substance that appears on both the CERCLA and EPCRA lists, notification must be made to the National Response Center and also to the local and state community response organizations.

In any community, prior to a release, the owners and operators of facilities and the community response personnel, need to be aware of the hazardous materials that exist. It is obvious that if one had to figure out, which authority to notify after a release had occurred, one could become very confused. Therefore, the firms and facilities that use or store chemicals at the threshold planning level that appear on either the EPCRA or CERCLA lists must be identified during the planning process.

There is one final reporting requirement. It relates to the release of extremely hazardous substances as they are transported through a local community. Title III exempts from complete reporting any chemical release that occurs while an extremely hazardous substance is being transported through a community. A shipment of any such material that results in an incident while the substance is being transported is not subject to complete reporting requirements if the substance is still moving under active shipping papers and has not reached it ultimate consignee. In these cases, the only local reporting requirement is that the release must be reported by dialing

911 or, in the absence of this emergency telephone number, calling the operator and reporting the release.

Given these exemptions and special requirements, what kind of reporting is expected when a chemical is released into the community? Any owner or operator of a facility subject to this section, must immediately notify the community emergency response coordinator for the LEPC of any area likely to be affected by the release. A report must also be made to the SERC of any state likely to be affected. If the firm or facility is located close to the border between two or more states, this provision becomes more important.

When the release occurs, the emergency authorities must be notified verbally. All pertinent information must be readily conveyed over the phone. Since a facility holding, using or storing a reportable quantity of extremely hazardous substances under the law should have identified a emergency planning coordinator, this individual should be particularly aware of these requirements.

After giving verbal notification of a hazardous substance release, the owner or operator of the facility must also provide a written follow-up emergency notice as promptly as possible. This information described below does not need to be provided all at once; it may be given piecemeal.

The notification must include the following information. As stated above, this information may be reported verbally, but it must also be reported in written form at a later date.

1. The chemical name or identity of any substance involved in the release.
2. Whether the substance or substances is/are on the EPCRA and CERCLA lists.
3. An estimate of the quantity of any substance released into the environment.
4. The time and duration of the release.
5. The medium or media into which the release has occurred. This defines whether the release occurred on land, into the air, or in water.
6. Any known or anticipated acute or chronic health risks associated with the emergency and, where appropriate, advice regarding medical attention necessary for exposed individuals.
7. Proper precautions to be taken as a result of the release, including evacuation. Once the emergency plan is in place, this information should already be available to the LEPC.
8. The name and telephone number of person/s to be contacted for further information.
9. A written description of the actions taken to respond to and contain the release, as well as any additional information on health effects that has been gathered.

These notification requirements are subject to local discretion. This law gives local communities or states the authority to further define information required in reporting, as well as the methods of reporting releases. The intent of Congress here was to provide as much local flexibility as possible for the implementation of this law.

In conclusion, a final attempt will be made to summarize in clear language the reporting requirements for extremely hazardous substances under EPCRA. First, it is important to remember that EPCRA provides the mechanism for reporting hazardous materials incidents at the local and state levels, whereas CERCLA provides for similar reporting at the federal level. Though the extremely hazardous chemical lists and the TPQs for the two laws may be somewhat different, from a planning and implementation point of view both laws have the same impact. It is essential that facility and community planners be aware of the existence of extremely hazardous chemicals before any extremely hazardous chemical release occurs. This is, in fact, the purpose of the emergency planning aspects of both CERCLA and EPCRA.

Section 3.3.5. EPCRA Section 305: Emergency Training and Review of Emergency Systems

Many local communities lack the trained personnel, the expertise and the educational programs required to implement this law. Under Section 305, provisions were made to help provide these services at the local, state and federal levels. The law authorized the FEMA in fiscal years 1987, 1988, 1989 and 1990 to provide $5 million in grants to support research and training programs at state and local government levels. These funds were to be used to support university-sponsored programs designed to improve emergency planning preparedness, mitigation, response and recovery capabilities. This provision of the act requires cost sharing at the local level, with a maximum of 80% of the costs to be covered by federal grants. The remaining 20%, or a greater amount, are to be funded by nonfederal sources. This section of the law intended these training funds to be used to develop the following kinds of programs:

1. Hazard mitigation, or methods for reducing the possibility of emergency releases of hazardous chemicals
2. Emergency preparedness
3. Fire prevention and control
4. Disaster response
5. Long-term disaster recovery
6. National security

7. Technological and natural hazards
8. Emergency response procedures

FEMA made its initial awards in 1987. Under this granting system, the Virgin Islands received $2,000, the lowest award, while Texas received $399,466, the highest. The states, territories, and Washington, D.C., all received some financial support, as did two Regional Response Teams. Whether these funds will continue to be available, given the budget deficit in Washington, D.C. remains to be seen.

In some states, rules or laws already exist that specify the type and extent of training required for emergency response teams. This is often true with respect to firefighters. Additionally, under Section 126 E of SARA (1986), of which Title III is a part, OSHA has issued a worker protection standard for those involved in hazardous waste operations. This standard, 29 CFR 1910.120, specifically regulates employee safety and health during emergency responses to hazardous substance incidents. It includes detailed requirements for personal protective equipment, personnel training, and planning for safety and health on hazardous waste sites.

Another provision of Section 305, "Emergency Training and Review of Emergency Systems," requires the EPA administrator, with the cooperation of the states, to develop a report for Congress that evaluates existing controls for monitoring, detecting and preventing releases of extremely hazardous substances at representative domestic facilities that produce, use or store these substances. The purpose of this report is to provide information regarding the current status of emergency response technology capabilities, to monitor, detect and prevent, in a timely manner, significant releases of extremely hazardous substances. Examples of these systems include emergency response warning alarms and continuous air monitoring apparatus to determine dangerous concentrations of such chemicals in the air.

Though this report will not be completed before this book goes to press, it is clear that Congress wants to understand the warning capabilities related to hazardous chemical releases. It was intended that the report would contain recommendations for initiatives to support the development of new or improved technologies or systems that would facilitate the timely monitoring, detection and prevention of releases of extremely hazardous substances and improve devices or systems for alerting the public in a timely manner in the event of an accident or release of such substances.

It is important to understand the limitations of these types of systems. None are fail safe. They are often incorporated into the production system and have many weaknesses. Most importantly, they do not guarantee protection. Also, though they are not necessarily required by OSHA, they are often located inside the workplace, and some OSHA regulations could apply. Finally, these controls must be designed for multiple application to control releases into the air, water and soil.

As time passes, it will be interesting to see if this provision of the law leads to increased funding for the development of such capabilities. Recent hazardous chemical releases, such as the release of more than 1 million gallons of diesel fuel into the Monongahela and Ohio rivers at Pittsburgh, Pennsylvania, illustrate that current technology for handling hazardous wastes is still below the standard of technological development that exists in other fields. Control and prevention technologies are an area of growing interest.

Subsection 3.3.6. Summary, Subtitle A, EPCRA

The description and explanation of Subtitle A is now complete. To summarize, this section covers the release of extremely hazardous chemicals as defined under the law. Any facility or firm that manufactures, handles, processes or stores chemicals that meet the TRQ specifications under the extremely hazardous substances list of EPCRA or the hazardous substances list of CERCLA is required to report at the local, state and federal levels if a reportable quantity is emitted beyond the confines of the facility. The law now moves on to more general reporting requirements for a more inclusive list of chemicals utilized in industry in the United States. Note that we move to Section 311; there are no Sections 306 to 310. This gap is provided so that if Congress wants to add these sections later, it may do so.

SECTION 3.4. EPCRA SUBTITLE B: REPORTING REQUIREMENTS

Subsection 3.4.1. Introduction

While Subtitle A emphasizes the emergency response aspects of the EPCRA, Subtitle B focuses on Community Right-to-Know. This section expands the reporting requirements to include firms and facilities beyond those that handle what EPCRA considers extremely hazardous chemicals or CERCLA considers hazardous chemicals. In this section, facility activity is keyed to the applicability of the OSHA Hazard Communication Standard, 29 CFR 1910.1200. This regulation was promulgated under the Occupational Health and Safety Act of 1970 and specifies how firms are to educate employees regarding the use of hazardous chemicals in the workplace. Since the EPCRA Subtitle B reporting requirement is closely tied to the OSHA Hazard Communication Standard, it is important that the reader understand the provisions of this standard.

The OSHA standard went into effect for manufacturers under Standard Industrial Codes (SIC) 20 through 39 on May 25, 1986. As of May 25, 1988, it was extended to cover all firms regulated by OSHA. This standard differentiates between manufacturers of chemicals and users, storers and processors of chemicals. It is the responsibility of the producer to develop a Material Safety Data Sheet for each chemical produced. This is a technical document that specifies the hazards associated with various chemicals; the proper handling, disposal and cleanup (if spillage or release occurs) for each chemical; and the appropriate methods for protecting people exposed to these chemicals on the job. There is a more complete discussion of the Material Safety Data Sheet in Appendix D.

The OSHA standard defines a chemical as hazardous if it meets certain criteria. It is important to understand that the OSHA definition of "hazardous" is quite broad and includes the vast majority of chemicals used in industry today. Chemicals, including those routinely used in homes, or by consumers or the general public, such as ammonia, acetone, fuel oils and solvents, are regulated as hazards in the workplace and can also be hazardous if used improperly at home. The OSHA standard requires employers to inform employees about the hazards associated with the chemicals they use, as well as the control technologies, such as work practices, engineering controls and personal protective equipment, to be used to minimize these hazards. However, it is the Material Safety Data Sheet that is developed and available under this standard that is the link with Subtitle B.

Subsection 3.4.2. EPCRA Section 311: Material Safety Data Sheets

Section 311 of EPCRA applies to owners or operators of facilities which are required to prepare or have available Material Safety Data Sheets for hazardous chemicals under OSHA. Such a firm or facility must submit either a list of Material Safety Data Sheets or the sheets themselves for each chemical to the following groups:

1. The appropriate LEPC
2. The SERC
3. The fire department or departments with jurisdiction over the facility

EPA has established TPQs for hazardous chemicals below which no facility shall be subject to the provisions of the section. Currently, they do not require the reporting of any chemical that is covered by the OSHA Hazard Communication Standard unless it is present at a facility in amounts equal to or greater than 10,000 lb. For those chemicals that also appear on the Extremely Hazardous Chemicals List established by Section 302 of EPCRA, the minimal TPQ is equal to 500 lbs or the TPQ, whichever is less. This rule holds through October 17, 1989, when the TPQ is reduced to 0 lb for any chemical for which a Material Safety Data Sheet has not been submitted.

This submission is the first of a series of several submissions that are required under Subtitle B. The first of these requirements, discussed above, concerns Material Safety Data Sheets. Another requirement, appearing under Section 312 of EPCRA, mandates the submission of an inventory form that reports the quantity of substances used in the facility. The third section, Section 313, provides a method for tracing the environmental fate of all these chemicals. Sections 312 and 313 will be discussed in greater detail later in this chapter. The details of Section 311, the initial Material Safety Data Sheet reporting requirements, will be explained further.

The law allows the firm to choose whether to submit either the actual Material Safety Data Sheets or a list of them. Some firms may choose to provide the LEPC, the SERC and the fire department with jurisdiction over the facility a complete set of Material Safety Data Sheets. Doing this seems to avoid the list requirements given below; however, the categorization required when a list is submitted must be done in order to fill out Tier I forms, which are discussed later. Therefore, submitting a list may be advisable. Some states are actually requiring a list rather than a complete set of Material Safety Data Sheets.

Each list of chemicals from each facility (if a list is provided) must include the following:

1. The name of the hazardous chemical for which a Material Safety Data Sheet is required under the Occupational Safety and Health Act, according to categories established by the EPA on the Tier I form (see Appendix C)
2. The chemical name or the common name of each chemical, as provided on the Material Safety Data Sheet
3. Any hazardous component of each product, as provided on the Material Safety Data Sheet

This means that all chemicals, whether they exist in mixtures or are identified separately on Material Safety Data Sheets, must appear on the list submitted to the SERC, the LEPC and the fire department.

The OSHA standard does provide for some exceptions, which are extended to EPCRA as well. These need to be considered when compiling the list and include chemicals that fall into the following categories:

1. Any food additive, color additive, drug or cosmetic regulated by the Food and Drug Administration
2. Any substance present as a solid in any manufactured item to the extent that exposure to the substance does not occur under normal conditions of use
3. Any substance to the extent that it is used for personal, family or household purposes or is present in the same form and concentration as a product packaged for distribution and use by the general public

4. Any substance to the extent that it is used in a research laboratory or hospital or other medical facility under the direct supervision of a technically qualified individual
5. Any substance to the extent that it is used in routine agricultural operations or as a fertilizer held for sale by a retailer to the ultimate customer.

If a list is provided, rather than the Material Safety Data Sheets themselves, the hazard category for each chemical must be established. Some chemicals may appear in more than one category. These hazard categories are established by the Tier I and Tier II reporting requirements of Section 312, which will be discussed later. These hazard categories are as follows:

1. Immediate, acute health hazards, including those produced by highly toxic irritants, sensitizers or corrosives as defined under OSHA or any other hazardous chemical that can produce an adverse effect on a target organ that usually occurs rapidly as a result of short-term exposure and is of short duration
2. Delayed, chronic health hazards, including those produced by carcinogens and other hazardous chemicals, that cause an adverse effect on a target organ that generally occur as a result of long-term exposure and are of long duration
3. Fire hazards, including those of flammable, combustible liquids, pyroforics and oxidizers as defined under OSHA
4. Chemicals that may cause a sudden release of pressure, including explosives and compressed gases
5. Reactive chemicals, including unstable, reactive, organic peroxides and water reactive chemicals as defined under OSHA

Any chemical may fall into more than one category. For example, many solvents are both chronic health hazards and flammable. If there are many mixtures at a facility, it is quite possible that chemicals will appear twice. All of these reporting requirements, of course, create serious information problems for those who generate and receive the information. It will certainly take a while for local and state planning agencies, fire departments as well as firms and facilities handling chemicals, to meet the requirements of this act.

If a list of chemicals is submitted instead of the Material Safety Data Sheets, the latter *must* be made available on request in the following ways:

1. To the LEPC: The owner or operator that submits a list must, at the request of the LEPC, submit a Material Safety Data Sheet for any chemical on the list that the committee wishes to examine.

2. To the public: In general, the public has access to this information, and a citizen can request Material Safety Data Sheets for local firms and facilities. However, there are some caveats to be considered. Specific provisions for public access are defined under Section 324 of EPCRA and will be discussed in Subsection 3.5.5. of this chapter.

After the initial submission of the list or a set of the Material Safety Data sheets, if new, significant information is discovered by an owner or operator concerning an aspect of the hazardous chemical for which the Material Safety Data Sheet or the list was previously submitted, a revised sheet must be provided to the appropriate individuals within three months.

In conclusion, Section 311 lays out the first stage of a four-stage reporting process required under Subtitle B of Title III. All firms and facilities with hazardous chemicals, as defined by the OSHA Hazard Communication Standard, 29 CFR 1910.1200, must submit information to the local authorities.

Section 3.4.3. EPCRA Section 312: Emergency and Hazardous Chemical Inventory Forms

Through October 1989, as previously stated, the TRQ for Subtitle B, Section 311, is 10,000 lb unless the chemical appears on the extremely hazardous chemicals list. Then, the action level for reporting is a specific amount listed under the TPQ. However, after that date, these TPQs are reduced to zero. There has been some discussion at EPA about establishing new Chemical Inventory reporting thresholds prior to that date. Therefore, those involved in program implementation should keep abreast of the developments in this area.

The person who is required to submit a hazardous chemical inventory list and/or Material Safety Data Sheets for chemicals at his firm or facility must also submit a Tier One Information Form annually. Tier One reports are, in fact, just the first level of reporting. There are requirements for an additional level of reporting: the Tier Two reports. Copies of Tier One and Tier Two forms appear in Appendix C of this book.

The owner or operator of a facility must submit Tier Two information only on request. However, the Tier Two form can be submitted or used instead of the Tier One form. If this is done, Tier One and Tier Two requirements are also completed. Tier Two information will most likely be needed for reporting under EPCRA Section 313, which is described in Subsection 3.4.4. So, it may be advisable to provide Tier Two forms from the beginning. These forms were developed through the standardized EPA rule-making process and were issued in final form on October 15, 1987. They appear in the regulations at 40 CFR 370 and will likely remain in use for a long time. It is important to note, however, as stated above, that TPQs for these forms will be reduced to zero for all OSHA hazardous chemicals in October 1989 unless this decision is changed by the EPA.

Tier I forms must be submitted annually by March 1 of the new year for the previous year. The following information is required:

1. An estimate, expressed as a range, of the maximum amount of hazardous chemicals in each category present at the facility at any one time during the preceding calendar year
2. An estimate, expressed as a range, of the average daily amount of hazardous chemical in each category present at the facility during the preceding calendar year
3. The general location of hazardous chemicals in each category

The categories used in Tier One and Tier Two reporting appear in Subsection 3.4.2 for submission of Material Safety Data Sheets or lists. As was pointed out there, since Tier One reporting is required, this categorization of all chemicals at the facility, must take place. Here again, as in the previously discussed list required under Section 311, the chemical (especially if it is a mixture) may appear under more than one category. Tier Two information requires the baseline information described above, as well as the chemical name or common name of the chemical, as provided on the Material Safety Data Sheet. In addition, Tier Two forms require the following information:

1. A brief description of the manner of storage of the chemical.
2. The location at the facility of the chemical. (Under Tier One, only the general location is required; under Tier Two the specific location is required.)
3. Whether the owner or operator elects to withhold location information on a specific hazardous chemical from the public under Section 324, which covers trade secrets.

The difference between Tier One and Tier Two information is important to note. Tier Two forms require the disclosure of the chemical names and exact locations of chemicals covered by the law, while Tier One forms only require general information about the chemicals and their locations.

As stated earlier, the entire question of public access to information under this act will be discussed later in this chapter. Suffice it to say here that there are some situations where public access to information may be restricted. However, Section 312 of the law clearly states that a request cannot be refused by the fire department with jurisdiction over the facility to an owner or operator of a facility which files an inventory form under this section. The owner or operator must allow the fire department to conduct an on-site inspection of the facility and must provide specific information on the location of hazardous chemicals. In many communities, this requirement existed prior to EPCRA as a result of local laws.

Tier Two information is required on request by the SEPC, an LEPC or a fire department with jurisdiction over the facility. Also, Tier Two information must be made available to any person or to the public within 45 days of its request. If the information is on hand at the time of the request, it must be made available immediately. However, here again, Section 324 on trade secrets must be considered.

There is another caveat to note regarding the provision of Tier Two information. A person who requests this information must justify the need for it. Once the justification is established, the SERC or LEPC requests the information from the facility owner or operator on behalf of the person making the request. Upon receipt of any such information, the SERC or LEPC makes it available to the person in accordance with the trade secret provisions of Section 324. The point here is that Tier Two information is provided to the public with some limitations that safeguard trade secrets. Therefore, it is necessary that a person requesting this information have a reason for doing so. Requests considered to be reasonable and requests considered to be unreasonable will become more clear over time. However, this does not apply to local fire departments, state planning commissions, or local planning committees, which must have access to the facility to perform an inspection. Finally, the only Tier Two information that can be withheld from an individual is the specific location of a hazardous chemical at the facility.

Subsection 3.4.4. EPCRA Section 313: Toxic Chemical Release Forms

This section of the act defines the last reporting requirement under the law. Section 313, a little-known or -understood provision, is expected to affect approximately 33,000 businesses in the United States and the communities they inhabit. Each of these firms will be expected to submit information, starting July 1, 1988, about chemical usage for the previous calendar year. This report will be required annually.

Section 313 information incorporates the real substance of the Community Right-to-Know aspect of this law. Its purpose is to provide public information on total environmental releases of toxic chemicals by manufacturers. The law defines manufacturers to include all firms and facilities covered by SIC codes 20 through 39. These releases are not emergency releases, but routine, day-to-day releases that are excluded from Subtitle A. They are the result of normal operations. The local smelting facility or plating operation, for example, will have to report about stack emissions, waste water discharges and hazardous waste disposal on an annual basis. It is important to note here that this reporting requirement may overlap with other EPA reporting requirements, such as National Emmissions Standards for Hazardous Air Pollutants (NESHAPS) and National Pollutant Discharge Elimination System (NPDES) permits.

Public access to this information is a key requirement and is clearly written into the legislation. Citizens' groups, individuals, attorneys, sales representatives and competitors will have telecommunications access to the Section 313 data base created by the EPA, which contains information reported by firms. It is the intent of Congress that citizens know about the chemicals being released into their communities, their potential human health effects and their potential for environmental damage.

For the first time, with the gathering of this information, we will have data at the local, state and federal levels that documents the cradle-to-grave fate for a substantial amount of chemical usage in the United States. The extent of this knowledge will far surpass that amassed by any other country in the world, and it is possible only because of the broad-based citizen support for environmental control. Since this information will be provided in raw form for public access, questions of accuracy and interpretation will probably arise. It will be interesting to see how controversies regarding this information will be resolved.

Not all firms covered by EPCRA will be required to report Section 313 information. The reporting requirements under this section go into effect only if a firm meets certain criteria. These include:

1. Employing 10 or more people full time
2. Having business operations included in SICs 20 through 39, the same firms originally covered by the OSHA Hazard Communication Standard
3. Using more than 10,000 lb of a chemical that appears on the Toxic Chemical List

A new list, the Toxic Chemical List, has been introduced in item 3 above. This list contains 329 substances. Though there is some overlap with the Extremely Hazardous Substances List of Section 302, the two are not identical. But once again, commonly used chemicals such as acetone, toluene, methanol and chromium compounds appear on this list. Since a 55-gallon drum of a liquid is estimated to weigh about 500 lb, the reporting requirements are likely to kick in if a firm uses 20 drums of a chemical on the list. Though this is a very crude estimate, it gives an idea of how inclusive this requirement will be.

Manufacturers, processors and importers who are not users are governed by somewhat less stringent thresholds. For example, a nonuser may simply package, warehouse or distribute a chemical. To qualify for reporting, a firm must manufacture or process for each chemical covered in excess of the following amounts for the calendar year:

1987 — 75,000 lb a year
1988 — 50,000 lb a year
1989 — 25,000 lb a year

If the firm uses the chemical as well, it must also report at the 10,000-lb threshold level. So, a firm that uses solvents in paint manufacturing that it also manufactures must report at the 10,000-lb level. If the firm processes solvents for others to use, the higher reporting levels apply.

Whichever reporting threshold applies, a full range of information is required. Each firm subject to these requirements will be expected to provide information on each chemical for the following categories:

1. How the chemical is used
2. The quantity of the chemical that is present at the facility at any time during the calendar year
3. For each waste stream, the waste treatment or disposal methods employed
4. The quantity of the toxic chemical entering the environment by release into the air, ground or water

Some of this information may exist in a facility as a result of the reporting requirements of other EPA and OSHA laws and regulations. The bottom line for this activity is that firms which qualify under these provisions are expected to develop a "mass balance information study" about chemical usage. These studies accumulate information about the quantities of chemicals transported to, produced, consumed, used, accumulated at, released and transported from a facility annually as a waste product, by-product or component of a product or by-product. The purpose of these studies is to identify areas where a chemical may be escaping into the environment.

The EPA has developed a form for this reporting requirement. Whether a firm or facility does or does not use the form is left to its own discretion, but the information provided must be certified by a senior management official. This is a new development, since few environmental laws have so clearly required the identification of a responsible party representing top management.

There is obvious concern about possible problems related to public access to mass balance information. Legal liability is the first thing that comes to mind. Community environmental groups are anxiously awaiting this information in order to scrutinize corporate activity vis-à-vis the environment more carefully. Also, there is concern that the insurance industry will use the information to set premium rates more carefully. Finally, there is concern that this information will not be understood within the appropriate context. As a result, the information may be misused and misinterpreted.

There are also market concerns. Many manufacturers and producers of products containing chemicals on the Toxic Chemical List are worried that their products will be shunned by users. Even though these chemicals are considered hazardous under OSHA, the additional reporting requirements under EPCRA Section 313 are of concern. This may not be a problem, however, because many of the chemicals on the list are widely used, and most acceptable substitutes are also on the list.

Another area of concern for firms required to make these reports is the overlapping and contradictory information that may occur as a result of the reporting requirements of other environmental laws. For example, the Clean Water Act and the Clean Air Act have discharge-permitting requirements for releasing hazardous materials into the air and water. The quantities reported under these laws are often based on judgment calls made by the firms requesting permits for these activities. Without proper coordination, a facility might submit reports under these various laws containing contradictory information. Another concern is that disposal of waste under RCRA also requires reporting and manifesting. This provides another possible opportunity for providing contradictory information under Section 313 reporting and that of other environmental laws.

Section 313 reports are to be provided to the state authority, who then gives them to the federal EPA. Based on these reports, the EPA must establish and maintain a national toxic chemical inventory in a computer data base. The EPA must make these data accessible by computer telecommunications and other means to any person on a cost-reimbursable basis.

Based on this information, the EPA must arrange for a national mass balance study of chemical emissions into the environment. This study is to be carried out by the National Academy of Sciences, using mass balance information collected from the facility mass balance reports under Title 313. This study must be submitted to Congress by October 17, 1991.

Congress made clear the purposes of the study, which are as follows:

1. To assess the value of mass balance analysis methodology in determining the accuracy of information on toxic chemical releases
2. To assess the value of obtaining mass balance information or portions thereof, to determine the waste reduction efficiency of different facilities or categories of facilities, including the effectiveness of toxic chemical regulations promulgated under laws other than EPCRA
3. To determine the utility of such information for evaluating toxic chemical management practices for facilities or categories of the facilities covered by Section 313 of EPCRA

4. To determine the implications of mass balance information collection on a national scale, similar to the mass balance information collection carried out by individual facilities, including implications of the use of such collection as part of a national annual quantity toxic chemical release program

As stated above, this information requirement will greatly expand our understanding of the manufacture, use and environmental state of chemicals in our society. However, it will also be very controversial, since the research methodology used for mass balance studies has not been perfected.

Subsection 3.4.5. Summary of EPCRA Reporting Requirements

In summary, there are five reporting requirements under Subtitles A and B of EPCRA. These include:

1. Initial reporting for firms using extremely hazardous chemicals above the TPQ.
2. The occurrence of a spill or emergency release of chemicals included on the Extremely Hazardous Chemicals List if the spill meets the TRQ. The CERCLA Hazardous Substances List is also applicable to this reporting requirement.
3. A report on Material Safety Data Sheets maintained at facilities that are subject to the OSHA Hazard Communication Standard.
4. Tier One and Tier Two inventory forms for the OSHA Hazardous Communication Standard.
5. Section 313 forms for nonemergency releases of toxic chemicals into the air, water or soil if a firm or facility meets certain thresholds, which are determined by the type of facility and the amounts of chemicals used or stored.

This may all seem rather confusing to the casual observer. It may also pose difficulties for program implementers, whether they are responsible for programs in industry or are state or local official who must set up programs for communities. To understand the process better, Table 3.6 is helpful in identifying these complex requirements.

SECTION 3.5. EPCRA SUBTITLE C: GENERAL PROVISIONS

Subsection 3.5.1. Introduction

Subtitle C, the general provision section of Title III, spells out some basic requirements of the law for various important issues. These include relation-

Table 3.6. Summary of All EPCRA Reporting Requirements

REPORT	PERTINENT SECTION OF THE LAW	CHEMICAL USAGE THAT TRIGGERS A REPORT REQUIREMENT	WHEN A REPORT IS REQUIRED	ORGANIZATION RECEIVING THE REPORT
EPCRA Extremely Hazardous Chemical List	EPCRA Subtitle A, Section 302 40 CFR 300 and 355	Firms or facilities with chemicals on the Extremely Hazardous Chemical List in quantities above the (TPQ)	• One-time reporting requirement • Updates if chemical usage changes	• SERC
EPCRA Extremely Hazardous Chemical release	EPCRA Subtitle A, Section 304	Emergency release above the TRQ for the Extremely Hazardous Chemical List	• By phone when a release occurs with a follow-up written report	• LEPC at the time of the release • Written report to the LEPC and the SERC
CERCLA Hazardous Substances List release	CERCLA (Superfund) 40 CFR 302	CERCLA Hazardous Substances List above the TRQ	When a release occurs	• National Response Center • LEPC • SERC

Report/Document	Regulation	Description	Timing/Requirement	Who Receives
Copies of Material Safety Data Sheets or an annotated list of chemicals	EPCRA Subtitle B, Section 311 OSHA Hazard Communication Standard 29 CFR 1910.1200	Chemicals considered hazardous under the OSHA Hazard Communication Standard	• One-time reporting requirement for each chemical as it reaches the TRQ 0 lb by October 17, 1989	• LEPC • SERC • Local fire departments
Tier One reports	EPCRA Subtitle B, Section 312 40 CFR 370 Also in Appendix A of this book	Same as the Material Safety Data Sheets requirement above	• Annually, by March 1 of the new year for the previous year	• LEPC • SERC • Local fire department
Tier Two reports	Same as Tier I reports	Can be used to replace Tier I	• Required only on request	• LEPC • SERC • Local fire department
Toxic Chemical release forms	EPCRA Subtitle B, Section 313	Firms with SIC codes 20-39 that use chemicals at or above threshold quantities on the EPA EPCRA Toxic Chemical List	• Starting July 1, 1988, for 1987 and annually on July 1 for the previous year's information	• SERC • Federal EPA

ships to other laws, trade secrets, providing information to health professionals, public availability of information, enforcement, exemptions and promulgation of regulations. Each of these sections will be discussed in more detail throughout the rest of this chapter. With the first section of Subtitle C, Section 321, the law has skipped from Section 313 of Subtitle B. leaving room for Congress to add additional provisions.

Subsection 3.5.2. EPCRA Section 321: Relationship to Other Laws

This section clearly states that, in general, nothing in this federal law can take precedence over any state or local law if their provisions are stronger than those of the federal law. This concept, called "pre-emption," is important to understand, as it applies to environmental and occupational health laws. Preemption specifications set forth the circumstances in which federal, state and local laws interact with each other, a basic principle of federalism and part of our constitutional tradition. With regard to EPCRA, the only exception to preemption is that, in those states where Material Safety Data Sheet submissions to local authorities were required under previous laws at the local or state level, these laws must conform to the information requirements under Section 311 of EPCRA. This provision does allow local authorities to increase the quantity of information required from users of chemicals. However, the minimum baseline information required by EPCRA must be included as well.

This provision reflects the current controversy over the issue of preemption. At the time of the writing of this book, the preemption conflict pertaining to the OSHA Hazard Communication Standard and state Worker Right-to-Know laws had been temporarily resolved. The OSHA Hazard Communication Standard is in force in those states that do not have state plans. In states where Worker and Community Right-to-Know requirements were combined, the community portion were upheld by the courts. In fact, since the Supreme Court has not ruled on this issue, there will probably be many more years of legal wrangling before there is a clear-cut decision on whether state laws can preempt the federal law with regard to employee protection under Worker Right-to-Know laws. These issues are particularly important to multistate firms, whose facilities are required to comply with different laws, depending upon their location.

The Congress, however, has made its intentions clear regarding the primary authority of local laws over federal law when it comes to emergency planning and Community Right-to-Know. Under EPCRA, though all states must comply with its minimum requirements, it is the prerogative of the local authority to expand and augment Community Right-to-Know provisions. Some states have, in fact, chosen to do this by expanding the types of industries covered under various provisions of Title III or by requiring that additional information be included in the reports submitted by facilities. This has made it essential that the implementers at state and local levels become aware of any special provisions required in their location.

Subsection 3.5.3. EPCRA Section 322: Trade Secrets

Trade secret protection under EPCRA is limited largely by the results of previous legal decisions surrounding the protection of trade secrets in relation to other environmental matters. The most current experience with trade secrets is associated with the OSHA Hazard Communication Standard. It was during the promulgation and litigation surrounding this standard that the definition of and approach to trade secrets used by the EPA in EPCRA was defined. In the important legal case surrounding this issue, *The United Steel Workers of America* v. *Auchter,* 763 F. 2D 728 (3rd Cir. 1985), OSHA was required by the U.S. Court of Appeals to amend the Hazard Communication Standard to adopt a definition from common law. This definition states that "A trade secret may consist of any formula, pattern, device or compilation of information which is used in one's business and which gives the employer an opportunity to obtain an advantage over competitors who do not know or use it." It was the opinion of the court in the *Auchter* case that the term "trade secret" is *not* intended to provide protection for chemical identities which are readily determinable by reverse engineering. This means that when a chemical's identity can be established using current state-of-the art laboratory techniques, it has been reverse engineered.

The Congressional Conference Report on the Superfund Amendments and Reauthorization Act of 1986 stated that there are four criteria that must be met if the claim that a chemical identity is a trade secret is made. If a manufacturer wants a chemical to have trade secret status, the following conditions must be met:

1. The chemical identity may not be readily discoverable through reverse engineering.
2. Anyone claiming trade secret status for a chemical must show that reasonable measures have been taken to protect the confidentiality of such information and that such measures continue to be used. The information cannot be disclosed to anyone other than a member of the LEPC, an officer or employee of a U.S. agency such as the EPA, or a state or local government, an employee of the firm making the claim or an individual who is bound by an agreement of confidentiality.
3. The information cannot be disclosed to the public under any other federal or state law.

4. The disclosure of the information is likely to cause substantial harm to the competitive position of the person or organization claiming a trade secret.

Under the OSHA Hazard Communication Standard, the burden of proof for trade secrets claims is on the manufacturer. Any Material Safety Data Sheet with the claim of trade secret under the OSHA law is so declared until the claimer is challenged.

The EPA defines a trade secret in the same way that OSHA does. But the provisions of EPCRA grant trade secret status very differently. Under this law, only the EPA has the authority to determine a substance to be a trade secret. An individual or organization claiming a trade secret must provide up-front substantiation to the EPA, while OSHA allows the manufacturer to call a chemical a trade secret without review by the agency.

The rules pertaining to trade secrets under EPCRA appear at 40 CFR.350. There are five separate circumstances under which a claim of trade secrecy may be made. These are:

1. The notification of any changes at the facility which would affect emergency plans under Section 303
2. Answers to questions posed by local emergency planning committees under Section 303
3. Material Safety Data Sheets or Toxic Chemical Lists submitted under Section 311
4. Tier Two emergency and hazardous chemical inventory forms submitted under Section 312
5. The toxic release inventory form submitted under Section 313

There are important things to recognize here. First, Tier I forms do not require specific chemical names, so the concept of trade secrets does not apply. Second, any chemicals used at a facility whose fate is reported under the Clean Air Act, the Clean Water Act or a National Pollutant Discharge Elimination System (NPDES) permit application cannot be claimed as trade secrets.

Another caveat regarding trade secrets that should be carefully noted is that if an emergency release of an extremely hazardous chemical, as defined by Section 302, occurs, there can be no claim of a trade secret. It is the responsibility of the owner/operator to reveal the contents of the release to the best of his knowledge.

When a trade secret claim is made, it is the EPA that determines whether the claim is appropriate. Any firm that is considering making a claim of a trade secret should seek legal advice from an expert in the area of trade secrecy. This book does not attempt to provide information to make a determination as to whether a trade secret claim for a particular chemical is appropriate. It must also be pointed out for those who are community responders, community planners or local authorities that if a firm in your community claims a trade secret, it is important that these persons work very closely with the EPA to determine the procedures and processes necessary to decide whether this claim is substantiated.

There are seven substantiation requirements to claim that a substance is a trade secret. All of the responses themselves can also be considered trade secrets or confidential business information. This notification of confidential business information can be made at the time of the submission of the trade secret form appearing at 40 CFR 350.

1. Describe the specific measures taken to safeguard the confidentiality of the chemical identity claimed as a trade secret.
2. Explain any chemical identity disclosures given to any person who is not an employee of the company or to a local, state or federal government agency that has not signed a confidentiality agreement requiring the agency to refrain from disclosing the chemical identity to others.
3. List all local, state and federal government agencies to which a specific chemical identity has been disclosed. If the government agency denied that claim, this must also be revealed.
4. In order to show the validity of a trade secret claim, the claimer must identify the specific use of the substance claimed as a trade secret and explain why it is a secret of interest to competitors.
5. Indicate the nature of the harm to the competitive position of the firm that might result from disclosure of the specific chemical identity, including an estimate of the potential loss of sales or profitability.
6. Explain to what extent the substance is available to the public or competitors in products, articles or environmental releases.
7. State whether the use of the substance is subject to any U.S. patent.

Based on this submission, the EPA will determine whether the claim provides sufficient information to determine whether trade secrecy is appropriate or if the claim will be disputed. Once a claim has been submitted, the time allowed for determining trade secrecy is fairly rapid, with 10-, 20- and 30-day turnaround times for various phases. The claimer can appeal any decision of the EPA at any point in the process and, in fact, can take a denied claim to court.

It is easy to predict that these trade secret provisions, particularly the follow-up EPA decisions, will most likely be challenged and result in litigation. It is interesting to note that to discourage trade secret claims, the Congress has provided for fines of up to $25,000 for anyone who claims a frivolous trade secret. The intent here is to deter requests of trade secrecy status for chemicals. The EPA has stated in its proposed rules that it intends to prosecute frivolous claims.

As stated before, trade secrecy claims are very complex legal issues. Anyone planning to make such a claim needs the assistance of an attorney who is knowledgeable in this field. This is essential because claiming a trade secret could lead to many years of litigation. It is also important for claimers to understand that they may incur fines because the EPA considers the claim to be frivolous. This is especially true if the claimer first submits a claim and then withdraws it.

Subsection 3.5.4. EPCRA Section 323: Provision of Information to Health Professionals, Doctors and Nurses

Access to information by medical professionals is clearly defined in Section 323 of Title III. Information on specific chemical identities must be provided to health professionals in three particular situations. These situations apply both to chemicals that are claimed as trade secrets and to those which are not. These three circumstances are:

1. For diagnosis and treatment in nonemergency situations
2. For diagnosis and treatment in emergency situations
3. For conducting preventive research studies and providing medical treatment by a health professional who is a local government employee

To fulfill the requirements of this section of the standard, the health professional requesting the information must sign a statement regarding the need to know the chemical identity. He or she must also sign a confidentiality agreement. These statements must be signed prior to disclosure, unless it is an emergency situation. In such cases, these two documents must be delivered later.

It is interesting to note in this section that the term "health professional" is not defined. Under the Hazard Communication Standard, there was substantial controversy regarding the definition of a health professional. Based on experience with OSHA, some of the health professionals that might be included under such a definition would be doctors and nurses. At first, the OSHA standard excluded nurses from the list of professionals able to receive nonemergency trade secret information. This was changed when the standard was expanded to include all employers. In addition, toxicologists, industrial hygienists, safety specialists, and other medical care providers, such as physician's assistants and emergency medical technicians, might be included as well. It is important to note that information requested to treat an emergency medical condition can be requested only by doctors and nurses. The owner/operator can request that a statement of need and a confidentiality agreement be signed after the emergency situation is over.

Subsection 3.5.5.   EPCRA Section 324: Public Availability of Plans, Data Sheets, Forms and Follow-up Notices

In a short, two paragraph section of the law, public availability of information under EPCRA is defined. The broad-based availability of information by individuals and groups in the community described in these paragraphs directly fulfills one of the major goals of this law. It provides for almost complete access to information on hazardous chemicals in the community, plans for preventing contamination of the community by these chemicals, and sets up mechanisms for informing the community about the release of these chemicals in the environment.

Paragraph A of this section delineates the extent to which information must be made available to community residents. The EPCRA documents open to public scrutiny without any restrictions are:

1. The emergency response plan.
2. Material Safety Data Sheets and/or the list of chemicals provided by firms and facilities in lieu of the Material Safety Data Sheets and submitted according to EPCRA Section 311.
3. Inventory forms: Tier One forms are available without restriction. Access to Tier Two forms may be limited, as explained in Subsection 3.4.3 of this chapter.
4. Toxic chemical release forms required by EPCRA Section 313.
5. Follow-up emergency notices also required by EPCRA Section 313.

These documents must be available to the general public during normal working hours at the location or locations designated by the EPA, the SERC or the LEPC.

There are a few exceptions to this open access to information. These exceptions are directly affected by the trade secret provisions of the law. First, for any chemical for which the EPA has granted trade secret status, the chemical identity does not have to be revealed. Instead, sanitized versions of Material Safety Data Sheets can be provided. These sanitized versions must reveal generic chemical categories such as "inorganic acid," but not specific, Chemical Abstract Service (CAS) numbers.

These same trade secret provisions apply to Tier Two reporting forms as well. Firms and facilities do not have to reveal specific chemical identities. In addition, information about the specific location of chemicals at a facility can be withheld from the public. However, community planning agencies must have access to this information if they want it.

As part of the Community Right-to-Know provisions, LEPCs must notify the public of the availability of these documents. A notice must be published in local newspapers that the emergency response plan, Material Safety Data Sheets and inventory forms have been submitted to the LEPC. These notices must be published on an annual basis and must state that follow-up notices may subsequently be issued. The conditions of public access are defined as follows:

1. Public access to information must occur during normal working hours at locations designated by the federal, state and local authorities.

2. If a particular firm or facility in a local emergency planning committee district has not filed a Material Safety Data Sheet on a specific chemical, but instead has submitted a chemical list, the LEPC must request the Material Safety Data Sheet and provide it to the public if requested to do so by a citizen.

3. Anyone requesting Tier II information must request it for a specific facility. In other words, there cannot be a blanket request for all Tier Two information in a local emergency planning district. If the Tier Two information is already on file with the LEPC for the facility, it must be provided on request. If it is not on file, the person making the request must present a statement of general need for the information. If that statement is judged acceptable to the LEPC, the LEPC must request it from the facility and then provide it to the requester.

4. Section 313 information (toxic chemical release forms) must also be made available to requesters. However, this information is gathered at the state level and provided to the EPA by the state. It is the responsibility of the EPA to disseminate this information to the public as computerized data, which must then be made available by telecommunications access. (See Section 3.4.4 of this chapter for a more thorough description of this computerized data base.)

Subsection 3.5.6. EPCRA Section 325: Enforcement

EPCRA contains very strong enforcement provisions. Civil actions may be brought against facilities and facility operators by federal, state or local agencies, as well as by community-based individuals. Failure to comply with any of the reporting requirements of this act provides grounds for such actions. Fines of $25,000 a day can be levied for first offenses. These fines can increase to $75,000 a day for second offenses if a facility fails to comply with the reporting requirements. Frivolous trade secret claims can be penalized up to $25,000 per claim.

In the case of emergency release notification (Section 304), criminal action can also be brought against persons who knowingly and willfully fail to provide notice of emergency releases. The individual can be fined up to, but not more than, $25,000, or imprisoned for not more than two years, or both. Repeat violations carry a maximum $50,000 fine, or five years' imprisonment, or both. The law also provides authority for individuals or groups to bring civil actions, or what are often called "citizens' suits," against firms and facilities for noncompliance. This interesting provision gives citizens the opportunity to play an enforcement role in the implementation of this law. Observers often minimize the importance of environmental laws because of a lack of effective enforcement penalties. State and federal authorities lack the resources to develop strong enforcement programs. With citizen suits as an integral part of this legislation, enforcement becomes much more likely, since any individual or group can sue a firm or facility that does not comply with the reporting requirements. In addition, a citizens' suit can be brought against the EPA and SERCs for not implementing the law.

State and local governments can also sue facility owners and operators for failure to comply. The only limitation on civil action is that citizens' suits may not be brought against the owner/operator of a facility when the EPA has commenced and is diligently pursuing an administrative order or civil action to enforce the requirements of the act against this firm.

SECTION 3.6. SARA SECTION 126: PROTECTION OF EMERGENCY RESPONSE PERSONNEL

Section 126 of Title I of SARA, though separate from EPCRA, affects it because it requires that members of hazardous materials incidents response teams, as well as others involved in hazardous waste site work, be protected while on the job by OSHA standards. OSHA has issued these standards as 29 CFR 1910.120 to meet the requirements specified in SARA.

It is interesting to note that a special provision was written into this section of SARA that mandates coverage of state and local government employees engaged in hazard response operations by the standard. This is important to note since, in some states, government employees are not covered by the OSHA act.

Based on the SARA legislation, OSHA has issued a regulation pertaining to hazardous waste site workers and emergency response personnel. These regulations and their specific requirements are discussed in Chapter 7, Subsection 7.2.2.

The rules and regulations issued by OSHA are extensive. Anyone responsible for supervising personnel involved in hazardous waste and emergency response work should become very familiar with these worker protection requirements.

Chapter 4
OTHER LAWS AND REGULATIONS
RELATED TO ENVIRONMENTAL CONTROL

SECTION 4.1. INTRODUCTION

Besides Title III, EPCRA and the OSHA regulations (29 CFR 1910.120), which set forth worker protection requirements for emergency response and hazardous materials personnel, there are multiple statutes at the federal, state and local levels pertaining to environmental control. In this chapter, many of these laws will be described and discussed. This review is intended to provide some basic knowledge that may be helpful in understanding how to develop an appropriate environmental management program in the facility or community. Its purpose is not to give a detailed description of the requirements of these laws but to provide a framework in which to place EPCRA program planning.

There are, in fact, multiple environmental laws governing various facilities, institutions and situations in this country. These laws have developed in a haphazard and piecemeal way, making an understanding of their applicability difficult. To confuse matters further, these laws are often implemented by different agencies, and authority over certain situations may overlap.

Complicating this problem even more is the constitutional concept of federalism. This issue has been discussed in Chapter 3. However, it is only with a full understanding of the scope of the various laws governing the environment that we can understand how difficult federalism makes the management of environmental regulation. Not only do we have laws at the federal level that may overlap with or confuse the regulatory process, we have this problem at the state and local levels as well. With all the environmental laws, communities at the state, county or municipal level have the prerogative to strengthen the requirements of the laws passed by the Congress. This is allowable as long as the baseline requirements established at the federal level are incorporated into local laws and the local requirements do not contradict the federal requirements. The concept, called "preemption," is something that lawyers, legal scholars, political scientists and governmental implementers have debated since the writing of the Constitution. Because the issue of preemption affects the way laws are implemented at the local level, the possible expansion of requirements makes it difficult for federal and multistate facility planners to develop programs. Many argue that nationally consistent laws would make protecting the environment easier. However, others counter that local initiative protects the diversity that makes our nation strong. The debate regarding issues of federalism directly affects environmental regulation.

SECTION 4.2 NUCLEAR MATERIALS

Radioactive materials are in wide use throughout the United States. These materials are used in military applications such as creating atomic bombs and powering submarines. Also well known to the public is the use of nuclear fuel for powering nuclear energy plants. However, many people are unaware of the multiple other uses for nuclear materials. In any given local community, nuclear materials may be transported on highways and byways, used in research facilities for research applications, used in hospitals for medical treatment as well as diagnostic work, and finally, used in various industrial applications. It is estimated that in the nuclear power area and at atom bomb production facilities, at least 70,000 subcontractors and lower-tier suppliers provide services to 50 prime contractors. And this represents just one aspect of the use of nuclear materials in our society.

There are consumer products as well that contain nuclear materials. For example, many brands of smoke detectors contain small amounts of radioactive isotopes which are used to monitor the presence of smoke. Cathode ray tubes also emit low levels of radiation as components of the television sets in our homes. Radon gas is another source of radiation for many. This naturally occurring source of radioactive material has received attention recently because of its prevalence in the soil and water of many residential areas.

The regulation of the use of nuclear materials is divided among multiple agencies with responsibilities for control and monitoring. These agencies and their responsibilities are as follows:

1. The Mine Safety and Health Administration (MSHA)—This agency is responsible for the protection of uranium miners.
2. The Nuclear Regulatory Commission (NRC)—This agency is responsible for licensing users of radioactive materials. This authority can also be delegated to the states that choose to accept it. There are approximately 20,000 such facilities in the United States.
3. The Department of Energy (DOE)—This agency is responsible for regulating nuclear power plants and atomic bomb fuel production facilities. It is also responsible for regulating seven national laboratories, such as the Argonne National Laboratory in Illinois and the Lawrence Livermore Laboratory in California. The DOE has almost complete authority over these facilities. In fact, this has resulted in some con-

troversy, since employees at these facilities are not covered by the OSHA act.

4. The Department of Defense (DOD)—This agency is responsible for regulating the use of nuclear materials in military application. DOD facilities are exempt from the OSHA act, and employees at these facilities are protected by OSHA programs within the military itself.

5. The Department of Transportation (DOT) — This agency is responsible for regulating radioactive materials when they are shipped from place to place. These shipping activities may also be subject to local ordinances. Individual communities, as well as states, have passed laws pertaining to shipping routes and procedures.

6. The Occupational Safety and Health Administration (OSHA) — This agency is responsible for regulating worker exposure to nuclear materials when they are used in industry. There are specific regulations under OSHA for both ionizing and nonionizing radiation. Radioactive materials have multiple applications in industry, including x-rays used to examine welds on oil pipelines and high pressure vessels.

7. The Environmental Protection Agency (EPA) — The agency is responsible for a broad range of legal protections against environmental contamination from nuclear radiation. The Clean Water Act and the Clean Air Act (both are discussed later in this chapter) grant the EPA authority to become involved in protecting air and water against contamination from radiation emanating from point sources. The EPA also has authority to regulate the disposal of nuclear materials.

Another concern regarding radioactive contamination that should be noted here relates to the natural occurrence of radiation hazards in the environment. We have recently become aware of the problem of radon in the soil, which may result in the contamination of homes and communities. Another community-based exposure to radiation can result from radium-226 (radon) in drinking water. Radon contamination is covered by the SARA act, of which EPCRA is a part. This act, in Title IV, entitles radon gas and indoor air quality research and mandates the EPA to develop a research program to define the extent of the radon problem in the United States and to assess appropriate federal government actions to mitigate the environmental and health risks associated with indoor air quality problems.

SECTION 4.3. GARBAGE DISPOSAL, SOLID WASTE, AND HAZARDOUS WASTE

The reader may remember reading about the barge filled with garbage floating along the East Coast of the United States into the Gulf of Mexico for several months, looking for a place to dispose of the materials piled on it. The prolonged search for a place to dump this garbage and the interagency wrangling between local, state and federal authorities regarding the dumping are indicative of the confusion associated with garbage disposal in the United States. The growing concern about the environment at the local level, which is indicated by the passage of the Emergency Planning and Community Right-to-Know Act, also extends to an interest in waste disposal programs.

The authority for the regulation of waste disposal belongs primarily with the EPA. For EPA purposes, a description of "waste" is divided into two categories. The first, "solid waste," is the refuse generated in our homes and workplaces that does not include specifically regulated quantities of hazardous materials. The second, "hazardous waste," consists of materials containing hazardous chemicals that require special handling so that they cannot contaminate the environment. Though solid waste must also be handled appropriately, hazardous waste generally is regulated by stricter standards because of its increased possibility to cause damage. The EPA has the authority to regulate waste disposal under a variety of laws. This authority can be delegated to the state and local levels.

1. The Solid Waste Disposal Act—This law, first passed in 1965, regulated the dumping of waste. One of its primary features was to stop the open dumping of garbage at the municipal level. The sites established under this act, however, often contained a combination of solid household and industrial chemical wastes. The problems associated with this mixing of hazardous and nonhazardous wastes were not addressed again until 1976.

2. Resource Conservation Recovery Act (RCRA)—This law was passed in 1976 to control the dumping of hazardous materials as a result of our increased understanding of the problems associated with the disposal of these wastes. This law governs the disposal of hazardous materials within the community. It also contains provisions for protecting employees who work at these facilities. At the local level, problems with RCRA-type waste disposal are becoming more and more severe. The appropriateness of underground burial is being questioned. Incineration capacity is limited and also has hazards associated with it. It is the purpose of RCRA to develop a system that established procedures for monitoring hazardous material wastes in a cradle-to-grave manner. As a result, RCRA requirements include rules for testing, identifying, storing, labeling, manifesting, transporting and disposing of hazardous waste. Also included in RCRA rules and regulations are the standards that cover solid waste or what is more commonly known as "garbage."

3. Superfund — In 1980, the Congress passed the Comprehensive Environmental Response Compensation and Liability Act (CERCLA). This act, reauthorized in 1986 as the Superfund Amendments and Reauthorization Act (SARA), contains the Emergency Response Community Right-to-Know Act. This law was enacted in response to the concern about the cleanup of what had become multiple, uncontrolled hazardous waste sites such as Love Canal, New York. It allowed taxes to be levied against chemical products manufacturers. In the 1986 reauthorization, this taxing power was further expanded to include all manufacturers. At the local level, the importance of this law cannot be underestimated. It specifies procedures for cleaning up hazardous waste sites and may also provide the funds for carrying out these activities. Several states have also established state-based Superfund-like programs to help fund cleanup efforts.

When considering the problem of waste disposal, one gets an interesting view of the interaction between industrial progress and environmental control. The laws in place in the 1950's and 1960's concerning waste reflected the understanding at that time of the appropriate measures needed to control environmental contamination. It is only in retrospect that we understand that these laws were inadequate to meet the goals they set. Our scientific knowledge and control technology has lagged behind our concern for environmental protection.

SECTION 4.4. TOXIC CHEMICAL REGISTRATION

The Toxic Substance Control Act, also passed in 1976, requires that all new chemicals produced and sold in the United States must be tested and registered. Premanufacturing notices are the documents that are filed with the EPA by the manufacturer and that report test results. These documents include scientific data provided by the manufacturer about the possible health hazards associated with the chemical and are meant to alert the EPA to specific problems that may develop as a result of the use of these chemicals. The EPA has the option to refuse to register a chemical. If this occurs, the chemical cannot be sold. If an existing registered chemical is put to some new use, the EPA can also issue a significant new use rule. These regulations specify any environmental restrictions on the new applications for these chemicals.

SECTION 4.5. PESTICIDES

Pesticides are used throughout our country. Farmers and the farmworkers they employ use them to control unwanted insects, weeds and rodents.

Pesticides are used in communities to control similar problems in parks, in public spaces and on private property. The use of these chemicals to accomplish these tasks is regulated by the EPA through authority granted by the Federal Insecticide, Fungicide, and Rodenticide Act (FIFRA). Part of the authority of this act is to regulate the production, distribution and sale, including labeling requirements, for all pesticides used in the United States. Parts of this federal authority are delegated to the states, where FIFRA programs are often implemented through Departments of Agriculture. Separate regulations exist for farm use and application of chemicals and for structural pesticides used in buildings.

Ground water contamination resulting from the use of chemicals on farms and in food handling and storage operations has been of growing concern in many communities. However, the EPCRA regulations do not address this aspect of potential environmental contamination. In fact, chemicals regulated under FIFRA are exempt from EPCRA. Farm chemical runoff is considered a nonpoint source contaminant. There is growing evidence, however, that there may be environmental damage as a result of the use of these chemicals. There are currently no laws that address this particular problem.

SECTION 4.6. UNDERGROUND STORAGE TANKS

Here again is a potential environmental hazard that must conform to special regulations. Underground storage tanks are governed by the Solid Waste Disposal Act. Funding for this program has been authorized under SARA. New proposed regulations issued in 1987 mandate increased control of these underground containers. These regulations require that all underground storage tanks be registered with state authorities. New tanks must reflect certain anticorrosion measures that are mandated by the law. Tank construction standards have also been developed. The object of these regulations is to protect the ground water from contamination. Since the EPA estimates that 50% of Americans get their drinking water from ground water wells, these regulations are meant to control the safety of this resource.

SECTION 4.7. TRANSPORTATION OF HAZARDOUS CHEMICALS

The transportation of hazardous materials is regulated by the DOT under the Hazardous Materials Transportation Act. "Transportation" is defined to include the shipment of chemicals by land, air, water or pipeline. The rules and regulations that are authorized by this act specify strict labeling and placarding requirements for containers and vehicles transporting hazardous materials. The labels appear on the containers of products being shipped. The placards appear on vehicles carrying the shipments. Someone who understands the placarding language can generally identify the contents of any vehicle without actually seeing manifests. These placards are the diamond-shaped signs containing numbers that appear on many trucks and railroad cars. This law also mandates the manifesting of all chemicals transported within and imported into the United States.

SECTION 4.8. POINT SOURCE ENVIRONMENTAL CONTAMINATION

A "point source contamination" is defined as a contamination of the environment from a known single source. In other words, if a facility puts an overflow or effluent pipe into a river, this is considered a point source of contamination. Another example is a stack used by a facility to discharge materials into the air. These types of environmental releases are regulated by the Clean Water Act (CWA) and the Clean Air Act (CAA), respectively. Both of these laws are implemented by the EPA. Firms and facilities are granted permits to carry out activities covered by these laws. A substantial amount of the enforcement of these laws has been delegated to the local level. State and community environmental control programs often set standards that go beyond the requirements at the federal level for clean air and water.

There may be some important overlap between the EPCRA and these laws. Reporting requirements under Section 313 contain information that may already exist because of permitting requirements under the CWA and the CAA.

SECTION 4.9. RETAIL PRODUCTS

The safety of consumer products and any environmental hazards that may be associated with them are regulated in a variety of ways. First, the Consumer Product Safety Commission has a responsibility in this area. Second, the Food and Drug Administration regulates additives in foods and the licensing of prescription drugs to be used in the health care industry. Finally, the FIFRA, mentioned earlier, regulates herbicides and pesticides for consumer use. The provisions of this act have resulted in the restriction of certain FIFRA chemicals for use in the home, even though these chemicals may be available to licensed operators for use on a farm or in a building.

A recent new development in the area of consumer protection legislation is Proposition 65, passed in California. This law requires the labeling of any consumer product containing a carcinogen or reproductive hazard. Its implementation has caused much controversy in California.

SECTION 4.10. STATE AND LOCAL LAWS

Recently there has been a trend toward state and local laws that control the use of chemicals. Like locally passed worker and community Right-to-Know requirements, these state and local laws are often precursors of federal action. In this regard, there are two important developments in state laws. The first one is Proposition 65, enacted in California and described in Section 4.9.

The second set of laws to consider are the growing number of land transfer acts. These laws reflect current concern regarding the assumption of liability for contamination of property by previous owners. The New Jersey law, for example, requires that before commercial or industrial property is transferred from one owner to another, an environmental audit and environmental certification must be completed. As the number of states with land transfer laws increase, such a law may be passed at the federal level.

Chapter 5
PROGRAM PLANNING REQUIREMENTS FOR THE EMERGENCY PLANNING AND THE COMMUNITY RIGHT-TO-KNOW ACT

SECTION 5.1. INTRODUCTION

In Chapter 3 of this book, the details of the EPCRA were discussed in detail. Understanding the requirements of this law is certainly the first step in planning a program. However, creating the structure and organization to implement EPCRA programs, identifying staffing needs and coordinating between various program elements form the heart of the matter. In most communities, some of the program elements were in place prior to the passage of EPCRA. For example, many localities have existing emergency response planning agencies, and firms or facilities have gathered and disseminated information in response to Worker Right-to-Know laws. However, there is less guidance and less previous program experience to help us with regard to the Community Right-to-Know aspects of the law.

Although programs for emergency planning and Community Right-to-Know have gained general acceptance among citizens and are gaining increasing acceptance among firms, it is important to note that there are also disincentives to implement the EPCRA. The strongest disincentive to consider is the cost involved. Small firms, in particular, find the burdens of this environmental regulation especially heavy. Often they do not have experienced staff to handle the requirements of the laws or the resources to hire consultants to provide the services required. Additionally, firms often feel that revealing information about current or previous chemical usage can increase their liability. This concern results in the fear that employees or neighbors might bring suit for real or imagined damages incurred as a result of chemical exposures.

Another disincentive considered important by federal, state and local governments relates to the cost of developing response programs. Though Congress authorized funds for incident response through the Superfund taxing structure, enabling local communities to receive reimbursement for the costs incurred when responding to emergencies, very little money has been authorized for implementing the preventive planning and information programs established by EPCRA. This creates resource shortages for program implementation at the local level. Where there is strong demand at the local level for these programs, funds will be allocated, counteracting the cost disincentives. In communities where there is less public pressure, these programs will likely be underfunded. It will be interesting to see how funding mechanisms influence the implementation of these programs at the local, state and federal levels.

The objective of this chapter is to provide program planners and implementers with useful approaches to the program planning process. However, there are some important caveats that must be mentioned. Local conditions vary dramatically from state to state and from county to county. Some communities have developed emergency response programs based on years of experience in responding to emergency hazardous materials incidents. These programs have often been developed with the support of the Chemical Transportation Emergency Center (CHEMTREC) and the Chemical Awareness and Emergency Response (CAER) programs developed by the Chemical Manufacturers Association (CMA). The CMA has pioneered in the effort to make the program planning process for EPCRA a cooperative effort among all parties involved. They have helped set the tone for the implementation process that has begun since the passage of the EPCRA. Resources are available through the CMA, as well as from other industry organizations and from the federal government. These are described in more detail in Chapter 8, which discusses available program support resources.

This chapter is organized to help the reader understand the interrelationship between the various program planning target groups: the federal government, firms and facilities, state governments and local authorities. The program planning needs for all four of these entities are described in detail. An effort is made to categorize the program planning needs for each of these groups according to the same four types of information. The tables in this chapter will allow readers to understand the interrelationship among the various governmental levels and organizational authorities required for the implementation of this program.

The program planning matrix in Table 5.1 identifies 16 cells of a program planning matrix. Hopefully, this systematic approach to the program development process will be useful to the reader. Throughout this chapter, information is discussed that provides guidance for filling out these cells in any situation. For each program planning unit, the four program planning elements listed above will be described.

The chapters that follow provide information concerning certain topics that need extra attention. The considerations associated with emergency preparedness is discussed in Chapter 6. Worker protection programs and training for employees of firms and facilities, as well as emergency responders, is the focus of Chapter 7. Finally, Chapter 8 contains information on resources available to implementers. Though these program components are mentioned,

Table 5.1 Program Planning Matrix

	PROGRAM PLANNING UNITS			
PROGRAM PLANNING ELEMENTS	Federal Government	Firms and Facilities	State Government (SERCs)	Local Authorities (LEPCs)
Purpose and authority				
Goals and objectives				
Program plans				
Program evaluation				

when appropriate, with regard to the program planning matrix, the special considerations surrounding these issues requires the more detailed discussion given them in the separate chapters.

SECTION 5.2. DEFINING PROGRAM PLANNING ELEMENTS

Table 5.1 identifies four program planning target groups and four program planning categories. This section of the chapter explains and defines these entities. Each program planning category for each program planning target group will be discussed. First, however, it is important to understand the interrelationship among these program planning categories.

Subsection 5.2.1. The Federal Government

The federal government is the first program planning unit to be considered. Three federal agencies—the EPA, OSHA, and FEMA—provide leadership at this level for government implementation of the EPCRA. Additionally, the DOT is secondarily involved in EPCRA compliance. All these agencies receive guidance regarding their role in the EPCRA program planning process directly from the Congress. The Congress wrote the EPCRA with a mandate for these agencies to implement it through the use of the regulatory process.

Subsection 5.2.2. Firms and Facilities

Firms and facilities that manufacture, use and/or store materials considered hazardous under EPCRA are an important planning target group because it is their activities and use of chemicals that trigger and motivate the response of all the government agencies involved in implementation. They receive guidance for their activities from the law itself, as well as from the federal agencies mentioned above. The regulations promulgated by these agencies define program planning targets for firms and facilities. However, guidance for program planning at the firm or facility level can also be influenced by additional factors. First, corporate or organizational policy can influence how firms and facilities respond to EPCRA requirements. Another important influence is the role that trade associations, interest groups and customary practice play in guiding the response of firms and facilities to the EPCRA. Yet another influence on firms and facilities is the legal cases that will become precedents guiding implementation of the law. Finally, fines and other sanctions imposed on firms and facilities by federal, state and local level authorities will also play an important role in shaping compliance strategies.

Subsection 5.2.3. State Governments

State governments are the third program planning target group considered in Table 5.1. Because of the provision for state and local preemption under EPCRA, state implementation procedures will vary. Their first guidance comes from the federal law itself, which creates baseline implementation requirements. Under the law, each state governor is mandated to appoint a SERC. This state commission starts the program planning process, based on federal law.

In many states, laws and legislative mandates are required to establish these programs. This provides a ready opportunity for making additions and changes to the basic EPCRA requirements. Since a state must at least meet EPCRA standards, changes at the state level will generally result in more stringent requirements such as increasing the number of chemicals on the Extremely Hazardous Substances List or the Toxic Chemical List. Another possible change might be to include more firms and facilities mandated to comply with various aspects of the law. It is also at the state level that funding mechanisms may be created.

State-level program planners and SERCs are also influenced by the needs and requests of local planning bodies. Local conditions will play a role in influencing how SERCs develop regulatory and reporting requirements at the state level. For example, states are responsible for establishing rules and procedures for public access to information collected under EPCRA. Pressure from local communities can play a role here.

Subsection 5.2.4. Local Authorities

Finally, SERCs organize local authorities into LEPCs for program planning purposes. These committees are made up of local representatives; however, they are appointed by the governor or the SERC. The geographic areas covered by these LEPCs influence, to some extent, their role and program planning responsibility. Here their guidance is derived from the federal and state laws. But they must also respond to local needs. It is at the local level that implementation of EPCRA will be most varied, depending on the needs of communities. The variation in the program planning process at the local level will be influenced by the hazard assessment determinations, the membership of LEPCs and the community response to the program planning process. Where there is a history of cooperation among various groups, the process will be much smoother than where there has been contentious interaction among firms and facilities and community residents.

Subsection 5.2.5. Purpose and Authority

Each of the four program planning target units—the federal government, firms and facilities, SERCs and LEPCs—are required to develop response programs for EPCRA. They need to respond to four program planning elements as part of the program planning process. These are the entries on the left-hand side of the program planning matrix of Table 5.1 and include:

1. The purpose of and authority for the programs
2. Program goals and objectives
3. Program elements
4. Program evaluation

Though all planning target groups may not explicitly implement each program planning element, any complete program planning process must, indirectly at least, address these issues.

The first program element is the establishment of an overall purpose and authority for the programs. This process helps set the mood for the program planning process to take place. This statement of purpose and authority that implementation bodies develop for their EPCRA programs defines the scope and importance of these programs in relation to those of other programs established by their organizations. Organization theory teaches us that even if there is no formal statement of purpose for a program, an informal sense of purpose and authority does exist in every setting. Though there are certainly exceptions, in most cases the less formal the articulation of program purpose and authority, the less focused the program itself will be. Looking at this in another way, a statement of program purpose and authority can provide the broad stroke that creates the overall picture of an EPCRA program.

Subsection 5.2.6. Goals and Objectives

Whereas statements about program purpose and authority give a sense of the big picture, goals and objectives identify the program and procedural standards used to establish specific program elements. Besides providing programmatic guidance, specific goals and objectives establish baseline measures for judging the success or failure of these programs during the evaluation process.

There are various categories of goals and objectives to consider. Table 5.2 provides them in outline form. The first and most obvious objective is to fulfill legislative and regulatory mandates. However, to understand program planning objectives as just a straightforward response to regulations is to misunderstand the intent of Congress and to misjudge public attitudes and concerns about environmental protection. Regulatory compliance alone is not enough. Other objectives must be considered as well. Even though these additional objectives are also determined by the legislative mandate, it is helpful for program implementers to identify objectives beyond those specifically mentioned in the laws and regulations.

Three additional objectives to be considered here are:

1. Information and knowledge of objectives
2. Behavioral objectives
3. Attitude objectives

Looking at program planning as a response to this hierarchy of objectives rather than just establishing a list of "to do" items creates a logical, step-by-step approach rather than a piecemeal response to program planning.

First of all, what information and knowledge objectives are required to implement this law? All the reporting requirements mandated by EPCRA can be categorized as the obvious first goal of information and knowledge program planning. However, there are other important goals to consider as well. Another typical information goal specifies how information gathered under this law is to be organized and disseminated. Some considerations in this regard would be whether to computerize information, where to maintain information to allow public access, and how to notify the public about this information. A relevant question to ask might be whether public notification as required by law is sufficient, or whether additional information goals that create increased community awareness and understanding are appropriate for program planning.

It is important to remember that with all program planning associated with this law, many of the goals and objectives are mandated by the federal law itself. However, local communities, as well as state legislatures, can and will make decisions to augment the basic information requirements that firms and facilities must provide to comply with the law.

Another program goal to consider is behavioral goals and objectives. These can be understood as tasks and procedures that program participants are expected to perform. Behavioral objectives for program implementation represent the cornerstone of the program planning process and are important because they define the expectations of individuals and groups associated with program implementation. Defining specific expectations of program planning units through the use of behavioral objectives can help avoid mismatched expectations. If the individuals, organizations, and firms and facilities participating in the program implementation process are clearly aware of and agree about what is expected of them, they are much more likely to respond to these expectations at a level of performance that is acceptable to all.

Specifying behavioral objectives also plays an important role in the program evaluation process, because these objectives provide a basis for judging the success or failure of the program. Reviewing program implementation against a preestablished set of expected behaviors makes it easier to identify program strengths and weaknesses. There are many behavioral goals that can apply across program planning units. At the level of the individual, behavioral goals might specify the skills required for a person to participate in emergency response actions. The ability to operate certain equipment, such as supplied air breathing apparatus, is an example of an individual behavioral objective. For firms and facilities, installing, operating and maintaining hazard warning alarm systems illustrate organizational objectives. Such organizational objectives can also be reduced to the individual level by specifying the activities of each person involved in this process.

The final program goals and objectives to consider are attitude objectives. Program planning units must understand that the attitudes of citizens, as well as those of the participants in this process, are of paramount importance. Since our attitudes about safety on the job or in the community are shaped by our confidence in those who are communicating information about possible risks to our safety and health, understanding and establishing the objectives for attitude and confidence building are essential for successful implementation of the Community Right-to-Know program process. Building the community's confidence about the emergency response capability could be considered an essential attitude objective. Developing this confidence through effective communication provides another example.

Table 5.2 Establishing EPCRA Program Goals and Objectives

1. Information and knowledge goals and objectives
   a. EPCRA reporting requirements
   b. Additional state and local information requirements
   c. Methods for organizing the information
   d. Approaches to information dissemination
2. Behavioral objectives
   a. Individual behavioral objectives
   b. Organizational behavioral objectives
3. Attitude objectives
   a. Building confidence
   b. Achieving effective communication

Subsection 5.2.7. Program Plans

The third program planning category to consider is the development of the program plan itself. Even though program plans will differ for each of the four program planning target groups, there are commonalities among them. By viewing the similarities in program plans for the various program units of EPCRA, one can begin to identify areas of overlap. This can initiate the first step in developing cooperative approaches to compliance that will eliminate duplication and conserve expensive resources. Table 5.3 provides this information in outline form.

Staffing EPCRA programs and identifying the individuals responsible for program implementation is the first step in the program planning process. In some cases, these staff needs can be fulfilled by reassigning existing staff; however, in other cases, this will not be adequate. New staffing patterns must be established, and individuals to fill these positions may need to be recruited.

A hazard assessment is the next logical step. In this process, questions about the number and quantity of chemicals that exist at the state level, in each local community and at individual firms or facilities are answered. This assessment also fulfills a necessary information goal and provides the knowledge necessary to meet the behavioral goals of EPCRA.

The next two program planning elements make up the core of an EPCRA program. The first is prevention planning. This may include programs for education and training, chemical storage, and monitoring of chemical handling. The next task in the process is to plan for emergency response activities. This includes developing emergency plans and evacuation programs that coordinate these efforts among the various response units, such as fire departments, hospitals and police. Also to be considered here are the ways firms and facilities will cooperate with and participate in response teams.

The next program element to consider is the identification of reporting

Table 5.3 Elements of a Program Plan

1. Identify and fulfill staffing needs
2. Perform a hazard assessment
3. Do prevention planning
4. Do emergency response planning
5. Keep records and gather information
6. Establish reporting procedures
7. Enforce regulations
8. Establish relations with the community

requirement target dates by establishing the programs and designing the systems required to meet these targets. Regardless of whether one is a generator of information, a recipient of it, or both, establishing appropriate reporting procedures is essential for effective program plans. Prerequisite program elements to consider in this regard are the recordkeeping and information gathering and generating procedures to be used to meet the reporting requirements and target dates.

Programs must be specific with regard to enforcement efforts and abatement, and must establish sanctions for noncompliance. This has applications at both the government and private sector levels. For example, governmental authorities, both SERCs and LEPCs, need to consider methods for levying fines against firms and facilities that do not comply. With regard to such compliance, methods that encourage implementation of prevention plans are essential. Often it is the case that unless there is some internal sanction for disregarding safety procedures, managers and supervisors may make choices that favor increased production over prevention. Though this may appear efficient at the time, it may reflect a misunderstanding of long-term organizational goals. Rewards for appropriate behavior can also provide reinforcement for implementation.

Finally, the last program planning step to consider is community relations needs. This is an essential element, since the overall goal of EPCRA is to provide information to various constituencies. Without specific plans for information dissemination, this program will *not* be successful.

Subsection 5.2.8. Program Evaluation

The last program planning category to consider is program evaluation. The planners must judge how well the program, as implemented, has fulfilled its goals and objectives and, more generally, the overall purpose of the program. Without a formally established evaluation plan, there is no methodical way to find out how programs should be improved.

The evaluation process can be, and often is, very complex. However, this is not always necessary. Evaluation can take place on a small scale and can be built in as a program planning element. For example, analyzing the results of emergency simulation drills prior to the occurrence of an incident can strengthen a community's ability to respond to an emergency situation. Another type of evaluation that can be built into program planning is the gathering of statistics about levels of compliance. For example, an LEPC can create a computer data base that lists all target firms and facilities that must comply with the EPCRA. Monthly and quarterly review of levels of compliance can identify noncompliers and can initiate program activities designed to contact such firms. This provides ongoing evaluation of compliance and acts as the mechanism for more thorough achievement of program goals.

SECTION 5.3. FEDERAL GOVERNMENT PROGRAM PLANNING MATRIX

The first sections of this chapter described an approach to EPCRA implementation that is based on a program planning matrix. The next four sections put specific information into each of the matrix cells. The first program planning unit to be considered is the federal government, followed by firms and facilities. Finally, state and local government programs will be covered.

Subsection 5.3.1. Purpose and Authority of Federal Programs under EPCRA

The EPA is the federal government agency that has been designated as the primary implementer of the multiple requirements of EPCRA. The authority for this responsibility flows directly from the law itself. It is Congress that delegates authority for EPCRA to the EPA. The EPA does not have the status of a cabinet-level organization such as the Department of Defense or the Department of Labor. Instead, it is set up as an independent executive agency reporting directly to the President. This agency, created by the Congress in the early 1970's, was authorized to respond to the legislators' understanding that public interest and sentiment favored the protection of the environment from hazardous chemicals and other pollutants. Though the EPCRA is very broad in scope and, as a result, leaves many implementation decisions to the EPA, the Congress included specific goals, lines of authority, chains of command, target dates and reporting requirements for the federal, state, and local governments, as well as the firms and facilities subject to the law.

In the past, some have criticized Congress for being negligent in the policymaking process. Of particular interest is the critique of political scientist Theodore Lowi in his book *The End of Liberalism*,[1] where he

---

[1]Theodore J. Lowi, *The End of Liberalism,* 2nd ed., New York, W.W. Norton & Company, 1979.

castigates legislative policymakers as delegating too much authority to the bureaucratic agencies. Title III indicates that legislators have taken this critique seriously. Responsibility and authority are clearly specified in this law, with precise requirements described in detail.

At the federal level, this law has a twofold purpose. First, it is intended to strengthen the response to chemical emergency incidents. Second, it is meant to increase public knowledge of and access to information about the presence of hazardous chemicals in the community and about routine releases of these chemicals into the environment. How the Congress expects the EPA to achieve these general purposes, can be seen in the specific goals established in the law.

Subsection 5.3.2. Goals and Objectives of Federal Programs under EPCRA

In order to ensure the EPA's compliance with the EPCRA, the Congress described specific tasks for the agency with identified deadlines. As you review the actual law, which appears in Appendix A, you will note alternative requirements when and if EPA misses the established deadlines. Congress included these target dates to ensure that the EPA would respond to this new initiative. Their efforts seem to have been successful because EPA met every deadline in 1987. This has not always been the case in the past.

There are four specific goals delineated in the EPCRA that the federal government was expected to accomplish:

1. A national response team was to be created. It represents a cooperative effort among 14 federal agencies with emergency response responsibility. This national response team was required to and did publish guidelines on emergency response planning. This work, entitled *Hazardous Materials Emergency Planning Guide,* is discussed in more detail in Chapter 6, which is devoted to emergency response planning. It is based on the EPA's chemical emergency preparedness program developed on an advisory basis after the Bhopal incident.
2. The second goal was to establish two lists of chemicals to be used in the implementation process. The first of these is the list of extremely hazardous substances and their threshold planning and reporting quantities, which is known as the "Section 303 Chemical List." The second one is the list of toxic chemicals for which routine release reporting requirements are established under Section 313 of the law.
3. The third goal was to establish the reporting requirements, and the forms associated with these requirements, based on the two lists mentioned above. Also included are the Community Right-to-Know reporting requirements. These are triggered by OSHA Hazard Communication Standard applicability and by the chemical storage threshold quantities

established by the EPA. As a result of this procedure, the EPA has developed Tier One and Tier Two reporting forms, which appear in Appendix C. How they are to be filled out and used will be discussed further as we describe the rest of the program planning units.

4. The fourth goal was the creation of a trade secret program for certifying chemicals as trade secrets.

The Congress also mandated the EPA to perform two evaluation studies regarding emergency preparedness and Community Right-to-Know. One of these studies, required by Section 305 of the law, reviews emergency systems for monitoring, detecting and preventing releases of extremely hazardous substances at representative facilities that produce, use or store these substances. This report is due to the Congress 18 months after the passage of EPCRA or by April 1988. At the time this book was written, the report had not yet been issued by the EPA.

The second required evaluation study is the mass balance study described in Subsection 3.4.4. Its main purpose is to assess the value of chemical mass balance information in order to determine the accuracy of information on routine toxic chemical releases. Another goal of the study is to assess the value of using the information for determining waste reduction efficiency and for evaluating toxic chemical management practices of firms and facilities using chemicals on the Toxic Chemical List. This study is also meant to evaluate the implications of mass balance information collected on a national scale through Section 313 of EPCRA. The intent here is to determine the usefulness of this information as part of a national annual quantitative toxic chemical release program.

This review of EPA requirements shows that the overall purpose of the agency's programs for EPCRA is to set the parameters by which state and local authorities can implement Community Right-to-Know and emergency planning programs. The Congress clearly saw that actual, day-to-day program implementation would occur at the state and local levels. EPA's role, as defined by the Congress, was to set the standards for local and state program implementation.

Subsection 5.3.3. Plans for Federal Programs under EPCRA

The EPA's primary program mandate is to establish procedures for firm and facility reporting requirements. The agency has divided this task into four major areas of responsibility:

1. Sections 301, 302, 303 and 304—Emergency Planning and Emergency Notification. This program is organized under the Office of Solid Waste and Emergency Response. The mailing address for the Preparedness

Staff is WH-562A, USEPA, 401 M Street S.W., Washington, D.C. 20460. The EPA has also set up a Chemical Emergency Preparedness Hotline at 1-800-535-0202. It was the responsibility of this group at the EPA to establish the list of extremely hazardous substances and their TPQ and TPR values. The final rule, published in the Federal Register on April 22, 1987, includes requirements for emergency planning and release notification. These reporting rules are discussed in Section 3.3 of this book.

2. Sections 311 and 312—Community Right-to-Know Reporting Requirements. The Office of Solid Waste and Emergency Response also developed the hazardous chemical inventory forms, with specific reporting requirements. These are known as "Tier One" and "Tier Two" forms and are reproduced, with the EPA's instructions, in Appendix C. This reporting requirement for a firm or facility begins when OSHA-defined hazardous chemicals are used in an appropriate quantity.

3. Section 313—Toxic Chemical Release Reporting and Emissions Inventory. The Office of Toxic Substance of the EPA is responsible for this aspect of EPCRA. Their address is TSCA Assistance Office (TS-799), Office of Toxic Substances, USEPA, Room E-543, 401 M Street S.W., Washington, D.C. 20460. They can be reached by phone at 202-554-1411. The final rules and forms associated with the toxic chemical emissions inventory were issued on February 8, 1988. The form, called "EPA Form R," must be submitted annually on or before July 1 for the previous calendar year.

4. Sections 322 and 323—Trade Secret Provisions. The responsibility for this EPCRA requirement is carried out by the Office of General Council, Contracts and Information Law Branch, LE-132G, USEPA, 401 M Street S.W., Washington, D.C. 20460. They can be reached at 202-382-5460. The proposed rules were published in the Federal Register on October 15, 1987. These rules also contained a proposed form. It is likely that modifications will be made in the trade secret requirements as a result of public hearings and legal actions. Until these rules are finalized, the proposed rules provide guidance for implementers.

To avoid delay on the part of the EPA, as explained earlier, the Congress specified particular dates by which all of these planning elements were to be completed. If EPA failed to meet these deadlines, default requirements, generally more strenuous than those originally specified, were provided. To avoid triggering these default requirements, EPA sometimes had to work feverishly to meet the target dates. For example, for the trade secrets requirement, the proposed rule was published in the Federal Register on October 15, 1987, the specific target date written into the law.

Besides the obligation to create lists and develop forms that reflect the reporting requirements of Title III, EPA was required to develop a few independent program elements. Program development was placed at the state and local levels. One program area particularly designated for the EPA, however, was the development of the guidelines for emergency preparedness mentioned in Subsection 5.3.2.

In addition, the EPA must implement under EPCRA to develop the mass balance study for toxic chemical usage in the manufacturing sector. This can be considered a recordkeeping and data analysis requirement. The law clearly specifies that EPA must computerize the information received on EPA Form R and make it available to the public.

The final program responsibility of the EPA is enforcement. However, this responsibility is shared with state and local officials. The EPA has been mute on this issue. Only time will tell how the agency will carry out this responsibility.

Subsection 5.3.4. Evaluation of Federal Programs under EPCRA

Evaluating the strength and weaknesses of the EPA programs is clearly the responsibility of the Congress. This is carried out through the federal government's oversight authority. The Congress has built into the EPCRA a review of certain aspects of program implementation in the years following 1991.

The Congress mandated the EPA to provide information to be used by the Congress to evaluate the EPCRA program. These reports, due June 30 and October 17, 1991, require the Comptroller General to report to Congress on toxic chemical release information collection, use and availability, and the EPA to report to Congress on the mass balance study (Section 313 of the law).

There is a built-in incentive for the EPA to make these reports in a timely fashion and to provide the information in a way that will enhance the EPA's ability to achieve its own organizational goals. These goals are strongly influenced by the various interest groups that are concerned with EPA policy implementation. It is anticipated that prior to the due date of these evaluation studies, interest groups such as the National Resources Defense Council, the Wildlife Federation, the Chemical Manufacturers Association, and other trade associations will issue reports of their own, reflecting the point of view of these groups. These documents will evaluate the EPCRA programs established by the EPA. They will have an impact on the type of report issued to Congress by the EPA.

Congressional evaluation can also be based on information gathered by the Congress itself or by other agencies such as the General Accounting Office or the Congressional Budget Office. These agencies are authorized by the Congress to make independent evaluations of government programs. By the early 1990's, we can expect to see studies by these agencies regarding EPCRA implementation as well.

As the implementation of the EPCRA programs develops, political input will directly affect the outcome of the evaluation process. Recognizing the political nature of the evaluation process is important. The point of view of the evaluator plays a vital role in shaping the end product. To make evaluations more objective, it is important to establish clear program goals at the beginning. But goals change, and the overall result of these evaluations will also be influenced by public attitudes toward environmental protection at the time the reports are issued. Ideally, the evaluation process will result in alterations in program plans that will strengthen the purpose and authority of the law and shape the continued implementation according to reassessed goals and objectives.

SECTION 5.4. PROGRAM PLANNING FOR FIRMS AND FACILITIES

In the first section of this chapter, the generic elements of the program planning process were described. Next, program planning at the federal level was discussed. It is now time to apply this perspective to the particular situations firms and facilities may face in implementing an EPCRA program. Obviously, the first step is to determine if the firm or facility is subject to the law. It is important to understand here that a firm's or facility's status and its relationship to this law are very much dependent upon whether it must implement the OSHA Hazard Communication Standard. Until May 1988, only firms in SIC Codes 20-39 are included. After May 23, the law is extended to all firms with chemicals defined by OSHA as hazardous.

Any firm that is currently subject to the OSHA Hazard Communication Standard that stores chemicals in excess of 10,000 gallons at one time is automatically subject to the requirements of EPCRA. In addition, any firm that does not handle such chemicals at the 10,000-gallon level, but does store or use other extremely hazardous chemicals in excess of the TPQ, is subject to the law. Any firm or facility TPQ for such substances as chlorine, at 100 lb, and ammonia, at 500 lb, stored at any one time during the year, triggers reporting under the Extremely Hazardous Substances List. So, for many firms, even though they may not store chemicals in large quantities at the 10,000-lb level, for extremely hazardous substances the EPCRA trigger level is reduced.

Also, for the OSHA chemicals, the current 10,000-lb threshold level will be reduced to zero in 1989. Therefore, reports made in 1990 that reflect the January–December 1989 chemical storage period will be requested for any firm or facility that is covered by the Hazard Communication Standard.

Because of these requirements, it is likely that most firms and facilities that use chemicals in their operations will have to fulfill the reporting requirements of the law. Once it is established that a firm or facility does come under the law, the program planning process should be initiated.

Subsection 5.4.1. Purpose and Authority of Firms and Facilities under EPCRA

For firms and facilities, this program in many ways is an extension of programs in place for the OSHA Hazard Communication standard, as well as for other regulatory requirements related to chemicals such as Hazardous Materials Transportation and clean air and water rules. The organizational purpose and authority provided for the existing programs will therefore extend and overlap with the EPCRA program. It will be necessary for organizations to coordinate the purpose and authority that has been created for other chemical-handling programs.

Two differing approaches create a continuum that reflect the range of possible responses to Right-to-Know laws. This continuum begins with a strongly prevention-oriented program at one end and moves to a response-oriented approach at the other end. Obviously, the overall goal of this law is to encourage the preventive approach. There is much debate as to whether firms and facilities have begun to or are motivated to establish a prevention-oriented approach to environmental protection.

Variables influencing the firm's decision on this issue include the following:

1. Fear of future liability.
2. Pressure from insurance carriers or, in the case of self-insured firms, risk management concerns that influence prevention strategies and the prevention orientation.
3. Concern for employees' health and well-being, as well as a commitment to strong community relations. These factors are often influenced by a firm's or facility's concept of its long-term versus short-term goals. If the firm or facility plans to remain in the community for the long term, the development of good community relations helps to fulfill long-term goals. If chemical hazards are an issue in the community, prevention activity becomes important.
4. Particular past experience of individual firms or facilities with hazardous materials. Firms or facilities that have in the past, had difficulty from a legal or a regulatory standpoint regarding environmental matters, may choose to try to break a pattern of non-compliance. EPCRA response may provide the vehicle for the effort.

It is important to acknowledge that the overall climate in which an environmental protection program functions has a lot to do with the effectiveness of its outcome. Scholars such as Zofar,[2] in his pioneering work on safety climate, have clearly stated that the context in which programs function is an important influence on their success or failure. This concept of the safety climate is reflected in the level of corporate or institutional leadership that authorizes these compliance programs and determines how much corporate or institutional responsibility and authority is given to the implementers.

For example, in a firm or facility where the chief executive officer provides visible support for program implementation and delegates authority for decision making as well as resources to program planners, it is more likely that there will be compliance with the program throughout the organization. In the alternative situation, where program planning and implementation are delegated with minimum authority to staff without traditional organizational clout, this program will probably not be taken seriously by those involved. As a result, implementation will be sketchy or spotty at best.

Regardless of the individual's relationship to a firm or facility required to implement EPCRA, the authority and sense of purpose given to the program will send a very clear message regarding intent. This is true whether the individual is an internal staff member or an external observer or regulator such as a state or local government authority or a member of the community. It will also influence every stage in the program planning process, as well as the effectiveness of the implementation program and the regulators' and community residents' judgment of the results.

SUBSECTION 5.4.2. PROGRAM PLANNING GOALS AND OBJECTIVES FOR FIRMS AND FACILITIES UNDER EPCRA

As was stated earlier in the discussion of program goals and objectives, the first goal to consider is regulatory compliance. The EPCRA and the accompanying regulations clearly state two regulatory goals. The first regulatory goal for firms and facilities is emergency planning as a method of preventing environmental and human health hazards. This goal is implemented through the identification of extremely hazardous chemicals and the reporting requirements of the act. The second regulatory goal is driven by the Right-to-Know aspects of EPCRA. It requires firms and facilities to provide a broad range of information to multiple recipients.

If a firm or facility chooses regulatory compliance as its only goal, per-

---

[2]D. Zofar, D. Safety Climate in Industrial Organizations: Theoretical and Applied Implication, *Journal of Applied Psychology*, 1980, Volume 65, No. 1, 96-102.

functorily proceeding through the program planning steps described below will explain exactly what is required by EPCRA.

From the point of view of firms and facilities, establishing goals and objectives has been an issue directly related to regulatory activity, particularly in regard to compliance with OSHA. There is a clear-cut overlap between OSHA compliance and environmental protection compliance under EPCRA. For years, firms have argued that performance-oriented standards rather than specific standards are appropriate for employers.

A performance standard, such as the Hazard Communication Standard, sets overall program goals but allows each implementing firm or facility to reach those goals through procedures that they themselves develop in relation to their own situation. More specific standards, such as those developed by EPA for the CWA or pesticide labeling, require clearly spelled out activities and provide, through the regulatory process, step-by-step compliance requirements for firms or facilities. To understand the difference between the two approaches to regulatory goals and objectives, we can look at labeling requirements under the OSHA Hazard Communication Standard and the standards of the DOT and the EPA under the FIFRA.

The Hazard Communication Standard requires only that labels on chemical containers give the chemical's name and the specific effects on target organs or, more broadly, appropriate hazard warnings. The FIFRA, as well as DOT labeling, specify requirements including such items as the size and color of labels, the exact wording of labels and how labels are to be displayed.

Program planning goals for firms and facilities under EPCRA are clearly performance oriented. While the reporting requirements are specific and are based on lists established by the EPA, the methods used to implement these goals and objectives are left to the discretion of the firm or facility itself. This has both advantages and disadvantages. Though it allows much flexibility in implementation, the firms and facilities themselves must identify the appropriate goals and the steps needed to implement them.

Though industry has clearly favored the development of laws and regulations with a performance orientation, the actual implementation of such laws can result in an added burden to these facilities. First of all, this performance approach necessitates that firms seriously consider implementation goals that are broader than proforma, step-by-step compliance with regulatory requirements. Once these goals have been established, program evaluation is judged against them. Future review and scrutiny by superiors, regulators and the legal profession in cases of litigation create a record of commitment to policies and procedures that the firm may or may not have met. Since these goals and objectives are internally generated, it looks particularly bad if a firm or facility must defend its actions if they are not implemented.

However, many firms and facilities expand the goals beyond simple regulatory requirements and establish organizational objectives that direct their activities more clearly. This may not be done at the highest level of authority in the organization, but the staff assigned to implement EPCRA should seriously consider this approach. Goals and objectives can be created in the three areas discussed in Subsection 5.2.6 of this chapter. These areas are information and knowledge, behavior and attitude objectives.

The information objectives of EPCRA closely coincide with the information requirements of the OSHA Hazard Communication Standard. The clearest example is collecting and updating Material Safety Data Sheets for chemicals in use. Additional information goals to consider include acquiring and maintaining information, with regularly scheduled updates, about methods and techniques used to prevent environmental and occupational contamination by hazardous chemicals. To implement this information goal, resources must be allocated to send staff members to conferences, subscribe to appropriate magazines, and communicate with suppliers of chemicals. Through this process, staff members can establish and maintain a level of information flow that will assure that appropriate information is gathered. Many firms and facilities find it appropriate to meet the current standard of practice for chemical safety in industry. Knowledge of this standard is also necessary to attain behavioral and attitudinal goals. Firms and facilities that are serious about implementing EPCRA programs must therefore formulate and implement information objectives that are reasonable and feasible, given the resources available.

Behavioral objectives are the next level of goals to consider in the program planning process. These goals must be stated in terms that reflect quantifiable actions on the part of employees. A firm or facility might establish behavioral objectives such as: "All employees handling hazardous chemicals will be trained to carry out procedures that prevent the risk of environmental contamination through proper containerization of chemicals, proper storage and proper handling procedures."

Another example of a behavioral goal relates to emergency preparedness. A behavioral goal for an emergency response might be to train and test employees regarding their ability to respond to emergency spills or leaks. Such goals might specify behaviors regarding various types of immediate remedial action, such as spill control procedures using absorbent materials. In larger facilities, behavioral goals might include procedures to be used by established emergency incident response teams who are called to the scene to handle chemical accidents.

Establishing behavioral goals for individual prevention must also be considered here. Such goals would include establishing rules such as no smoking, eating or drinking in the presence of hazardous chemicals or requirements for personal protective equipment to be used while handling chemicals.

Behavioral goals must be coordinated with OSHA Hazard Communication Standard objectives as well. Consistent policies across program areas will have a positive effect on program implementation and will influence attitudes about safety procedures.

Other behavioral goals to consider are those associated with the public information aspects of this program. The Chemical Manufacturers Association, as well as other groups, encourages companies to participate actively in the community affairs aspects of EPCRA. For example, a local firm or facility might consider the behavioral objective of staff participation in LEPCs. Similar participation in SERCs could be another behavioral objective. For the small-scale operation, this volunteerism may seem expensive and may in fact be impossible. However, it is important to recognize that this expenditure of human resources may minimize the expense of other goals, particularly in the area of information. Direct involvement in community planning for hazardous material emergency responses provides easy access to meaningful knowledge about program implementation. It may also provide information about hazards, as well as guidance on program planning procedures. Knowing how other firms respond to EPCRA requirements can reveal valuable information about the acceptable level of compliance for firms similar to your own.

Attitude objectives at the firm or facility level are much more difficult to quantify than either regulatory or behavioral objectives. Attitude objectives are concerned with how to influence people's perceptions, fears and attitudes about handling chemicals and the risks associated with chemical exposure. These attitudes can vary dramatically from individual to individual and depend, to some extent, on experience and previous behavior. They range from the standard cavalier attitude of some persons to the chemophobic concerns of others.

Attitude objectives for the firm or facility need to be considered first in regard to managers and supervisors because they clearly influence the safety climate of the organization. A typical attitude objective might be to increase the awareness of chemical risks because of excess exposure to toxins. The individual who thinks that using benzene or asbestos without protection is safe because, after 30 years of use, he has still not become sick may be difficult to influence.

Since attitudes in general are shaped by the behavior of peers, standard practice and information, safety attitudes will be influenced by the total message communicated by the firm's or facility's program for handling chemicals. Because EPCRA is meant to focus on prevention programs, attitudes can play an important role with regard to the effectiveness of this type of program. The safety climate is directly related to the safety attitude. Shaping attitudes about chemical-handling practices has been receiving increasing attention in the last few years. A new discipline, known as "risk communication," has emerged as an area of great concern among regulators at the EPA, as well as among groups such as the Chemical Manufacturers Association. The issues associated with risk communication are discussed more fully in Chapter 6. This is an area to watch as EPCRA implementation proceeds, since any Right-to-Know program has an occasional hidden risk communication component.

In closing, a fair amount of time has been spent discussing goals and objectives. This emphasis is appropriately placed here because it is through goals and objectives that the program planning process takes shape. Attempting to plan programs without clearly stated goals and objectives, regardless of the organization or facility concerned, will lead to inappropriate and inadequate program planning.

Subsection 5.4.3. Program Plans for Firm and Facility Implementation of EPCRA

For the purpose of this book, the program planning process has been divided into eight steps. These steps were first identified in Table 5.3 and discussed in a generic fashion in Subsection 5.2.7. However, it is obvious that this division is somewhat arbitrary. Several of these steps could be combined. Alternatively, several of them could be subdivided to create even more steps. In this section, each of these steps will be discussed from the point of view of firms and facilities. It is also important to note that though this information is presented in a step-by-step format, in reality many of these activities can and will be carried out simultaneously. In fact, coordination between the various aspects of an implementation program is key to its success.

Step 1: Identify and Fulfill Staffing Needs. Those responsible for implementing environmental and occupational health programs often complain that staffing needs are not adequately met. This is the case in many situations, in firms as well as in government agencies. However, the strength of any program depends to a large extent on the skills and energy of the persons who work on it.

The law clearly states that each firm covered by EPCRA must appoint a facility planning coordinator. This individual is responsible for coordinating firm or facility activities with the LEPC. In small organizations, it is logical to consider this person as the firm or facility program coordinator responsible for implementing the program as well. If the program in the firm or facility is large enough to support a larger staff, a staff structure is required so that various responsibilities can be divided among the staff members.

When identifying staff needs for this program, one thing to consider is that it may only be possible to maintain a limited full-time staff, if such a staff is available at all. However, staff support for this program can be identified and provided on an as-needed basis. For example, few facilities care or want to support full-time emergency response teams. Instead, these teams are often staffed by individuals who have other primary responsibilities. Identifying appropriate staff members who want to do the work will also help improve program implementation. When establishing an emergency response team at your facility, recruit among all employees. Often people already working there have outside interests that will help them develop appropriate skills. Examples include people with first-aid and emergency response capabilities such as those who serve as volunteer firefighters. Security personnel at your facility may be off-duty police officers with some knowledge of emergency response procedures. People such as these can fit into the program with various levels of commitment.

But creating an emergency response team and appointing the facility planning coordinator are just two of the various compliance components of EPCRA. Staffing needs include people who can fill out the reporting forms required by the law. This may require someone with engineering or other technical skills. Developing the mass balance information study under Section 313 requires sophisticated technical skills. In large-scale operations, individuals with the required skills most likely have already been assigned responsibilities in the environmental engineering or employee health and safety area. In smaller operations, people involved in environmental and occupational safety compliance may have other duties as well.

The number of people involved in EPCRA program implementation will vary depending upon the size of the firm or facility, the nature of the chemicals involved, and the importance that top management gives these programs. Regardless of these factors, the leadership capability of the person in charge of the program will directly influence the program's success. Placing someone who has energy and commitment to this program in the leadership position will strengthen it. He or she will be able to get the best results, in spite of the constraints placed on program implementation.

Since the staff dedicated to these programs may be limited, it is often necessary to look elsewhere for program support. As a result, gathering additional resources for program implementation is an essential step in developing program plans. Corporate environmental compliance managers, who often work with small budgets for big programs, say things such as "I look for all the help I can find." This search for support and resources can play an important role in the success or failure of the program. Once staff leadership and dedicated program personnel are assigned, it is important to identify additional sources of support.

The first to consider are the internal resources that already exist in the firm or facility. To be considered here is support from technical departments. In multifacility firms, access to corporate resources can lighten the burden of individuals called on to respond to these laws at the local level. For example, working with the purchasing department may make completing a hazard assessment inventory much easier. Another internal resource that can be utilized is the training and human resources development departments at the local or corporate level to help design educational programs for the staff involved in hazardous materials handling.

In larger multiorganizational, multistate firms, corporate headquarters may have programs in place or available to local facilities for their use. Identifying resources and communicating needs to other internal organizational departments may reveal resources that were previously unknown. In fact, in many organizations, resources are duplicated by various departments because of lack of communication and coordinator among them. The insurance department, the safety department and the medical department may all have resources that can help to implement EPCRA programs. Soliciting support from these sources and developing a cooperative response effort will help minimize the difficulties created by the lack of dedicated program staff.

External resources also provide a system of support that should not be overlooked. Trade associations often provide services for members that may make the EPCRA program much easier to handle. Any firm or facility covered by this act should contact its trade association as a first step in identifying external resources.

Additional external resources are the federal, state and local governmental authorities involved in implementation. These organizations are often quite willing to give advice, over the phone or in writing, regarding implementation.

Another local institution to contact for resources is the local chamber of commerce or manufacturing association. Often these groups have programs that can assist in EPCRA implementation, as well as other environmental programs. Using local business associations as a resource may put the organization in touch with other firm or facility program managers. Creating a network of others doing similar work can provide invaluable information.

Step 2: Perform a Hazard Assessment.   Now that the staff has been identified and possible resources have been evaluated, it is time to discuss program planning in order to explain hazard assessment. The concept of a hazard assessment can have various meanings, depending upon the extent of the hazards and the purpose of the evaluation. From the point of view of a firm or facility, the primary purpose of an initial hazard assessment related to EPCRA is to determine which aspects of the law affects the organization. Additionally, the results of this assessment will provide information required under the reporting provisions of this law. The hazard assessment can also provide information that will help the organization evaluate whether its response programs are adequate given a known level of hazard.

If the firm or facility is subject to the OSHA Hazard Communication Standard, it is more than likely to be subject to EPCRA. The only circumstance in which EPCRA might not apply at the present time is if the quantity of OSHA Hazard Communication Standard chemicals used and stored at one time does not meet the minimum 10,000-lb requirement of EPCRA. The final rule for reporting requirements, which appears in 40 CFR Part 370, provides for this quantity to decrease to zero by March 1, 1990. Remember also that if the company stores or uses a chemical on the EPCRA Extremely Hazardous Chemical List, there is a TPQ that triggers EPCRA applicability. Though it is possible that these reporting requirements will change, from a practical standpoint, linking the hazard assessment procedures for EPCRA to the OSHA Hazard Communication Standard is appropriate for firms and facilities.

OSHA Hazard Communication Standard compliance also requires information gathering as part of its hazard assessment process. For firms and facilities using chemicals, this is usually accomplished by assembling and reviewing the Material Safety Data Sheets provided by the chemical suppliers. If the firm or facility is a chemical manufacturer or formulator, the OSHA Communication Standard requires it to develop Material Safety Data Sheets. In these cases, information requirements including data on toxicology, epidemiology, and clinical case studies of the human and environmental health hazards associated with these chemicals are part of the assessment.

Once the firm or facility knows that the OSHA Hazard Communication Standard triggers EPCRA compliance, a more thorough analysis is required. By matching the chemical names or Chemical Abstract Service (CAS) numbers that appear on the Material Safety Data Sheets with the two EPCRA chemical lists, the company can identify another situation where its chemical usage may overlap with EPCRA rules. These two lists are:

1. The Extremely Hazardous Chemical List (Section 302 list)
2. The Toxic Chemical List (Section 313 list)

Additionally, the remaining Material Safety Data Sheets provide the information needed for Section 311 and 312 reporting.

Another hazard assessment requirement is to consider the possibility of environmental or human contamination from the unplanned release of hazardous chemicals. Where and how chemicals are stored, how access to these chemicals is controlled, and what levels of expertise are required for handling these chemicals must all be part of a hazard assessment.

Executives in firms and facilities often lack a thorough understanding of the extent to which hazardous chemicals are used and handled there. Knowing about every chemical in your facility, where and how they are stored, and who controls them is a central part of the hazard assessment process. Since, for many facilities, reporting this information is a requirement of EPCRA, beginning the hazard assessment with a complete chemical inventory will clearly strengthen the program.

Creating a chemical inventory is a useful approach to satisfying these information needs. Under the OSHA Hazard Communication Standard, as well as under EPCRA, the firm or facility is probably responsible for maintaining a complete inventory of all hazardous chemicals stored or used there. The Company must use a chemical identity that is referenced on the appropriate Material Safety Data Sheet. For its own protection, the company should list all chemicals in the inventory, including those not covered by EPCRA rules. For both safety and potential liability reasons, the firm or facility should know about all the substances on its premises.

To maintain an updated chemical inventory, it is necessary to establish a company policy on proper procedures for new chemicals entering the facility. This inventory might contain the following information for each chemical used in the facility:

1. The name of the chemical, including its trade name, chemical name and CAS number.
2. The name and location of everyone in the facility who uses the chemical. This list will help determine who needs to be trained in appropriate handling.
3. The amounts and location of the chemical kept in the facility.
4. The information on the label affixed to the container by the manufacturer.

This inventory, combined with the Material Safety Data Sheets provided by the supplier or developed by the firm or facility, will give a complete record of every substance used in the workplace.

To turn this chemical inventory into a hazard assessment, it is necessary to cross-reference chemical usage information with the various laws that govern chemicals. A computerized data base would be most helpful in this regard. By using a computerized system, one can keep an accurate record regarding the various laws that govern the use of chemicals in this country, and internationally if the firm is an international supplier of chemicals. Each chemical could be listed in the data base by chemical name, common or trade name, CAS number and additional inventory information such as the quantity stored and the name of the supplier. Then each chemical could be assessed according to the requirements of various laws. Besides EPCRA Section 302 (Extremely Hazardous Chemicals) and Section 313 (Toxic Chemicals), reporting requirements exist for CERCLA (Superfund), and RCRA. If the company is a shipper of chemicals, state laws and even laws of the European Economic Community may also apply.

The final task in the hazard assessment process is to identify the potential hazards associated with each chemical. This information should appear on the Material Safety Data Sheet for each chemical, though not necessarily according to EPCRA categories. For EPCRA purposes, using hazard categories created for Tier One and Tier Two forms seems most appropriate. These categories appear in Table 5.4. The chemical inventory can be modified to include hazard categories for each chemical. Don't forget, however, that some chemicals may fall into more than one category; make sure that you account for this possibility when designing your system.

Appropriate hazard assessment procedures are the cornerstone of EPCRA program planning. The information that must be gathered from the hazard assessment data base includes the names of extremely hazardous chemicals and toxic chemicals that are used in the facility. This also provides a general overview of chemical usage at the firm or facility. Careful analysis of the data may help identify ways to reduce the risk of chemical accidents in the workplace.

Steps 3 and 4: Do Emergency Response and Prevention Program Planning. We have finally reached the heart of the matter: the program planning process. Program planning can be divided into two parts. The first, is emergency response; the other is prevention planning. Emergency response planning is described more completely in Chapter 6. Some of the issues to be considered are as follows: First of all, a facility planning coordinator must be appointed. Evacuation and emergency plans must be drawn up. These plans require coordination with hospitals, firefighters and police, as well as the LEPC.

Table 5.4. EPCRA Hazard Categories

PHYSICAL HAZARDS	HEALTH HAZARDS
1. Fire	1. Immediate (acute)
2. Sudden release of pressure	
3. Reactivity	2. Delayed (chronic)

Note: See the Tier One and Tier Two forms in Appendix C, where these categories are used.

Hazardous materials incident teams must be created. Finally, evaluation mechanisms for reviewing and testing these programs need to be established.

Prevention will be discussed here in some detail, however. It is important to remember that prevention of chemical accidents that can affect communities and the environment is one of the major concerns of this legislation. Prevention planning is most clearly linked with the behavior and attitude objectives discussed above. Since preventive behavior is not often rewarded organizationally or monetarily, creative methods for encouraging prevention activities are needed.

The first consideration in prevention planning is the issue of facility siting. For existing facilities, this is to some extent a moot point; however, when expansion plans and growth are anticipated, facility siting may become a major consideration. Planning and zoning bodies have increasingly scrutinized the placement of facilities handling chemicals in residential and commercial areas. As we become more conscious of our concern for environmental quality, the issue of facility siting will become more and more important. Some municipalities have already developed strict zoning requirements and permitting procedures. You should be aware of these in your local areas, if they exist. By doing this, you may avoid expensive mistakes. If your facility already exists in a mixed-use zoning area, it is necessary to be sensitive to the concerns of your nonindustrial neighbors.

An essential element of prevention planning is to establish rules and procedures for proper handling of chemicals. The safety programs that already exist at the facility or firm should, in fact, serve this purpose. Safety programs may include policies for handling chemicals, use of personal protective equipment, and preventive maintenance for engineering controls, as well as other methods of accident and illness prevention. Reviewing these programs for their relevance to EPCRA compliance is an important step in the planning process. If a safety program does not exist in your firm or facility, it is essential that you establish one.

The next most important part of prevention planning for chemical hazards is the development of procedures for monitoring the use of chemicals. In the firm or facility, monitoring systems including warning bells signaling increased emissions are often part of engineering controls. In fact, preventive engineering is growing in importance as a method of controlling hazardous releases. However, these programs often require sophisticated monitoring apparatus. For example, carbon monoxide and ozone monitors can be placed in stationary locations. In situations where highly flammable or combustible materials are used, explosion level meters may also be used as stationary instruments. This type of equipment requires constant checking to ensure proper calibration and maintenance. However, since it is not fail-safe, total reliance on instrumentation is inappropriate.

Industrial hygienists may also monitor the workplace environment on a regular, nonstationary basis to determine whether preventive engineering has appropriately protected the facility from fugitive emissions. Prevention monitoring can take many forms. Industrial hygienists, safety specialists and engineers should be consulted when establishing prevention monitoring programs.

Another aspect of the prevention planning process is the education and training programs established by the facility. Education and training programs for employees involved in handling hazardous chemicals provide a forum for communicating behavioral goals and objectives. These programs also provide employees with the training needed to meet these objectives. We have seen a vast increase in the use of education and training programs in industry. They have become a vital part of the prevention process. Chapter 7 describes specific training requirements associated with the relevant laws and regulations.

In conclusion, program plans will vary depending upon the requirements of the firm or facility and the particular situations and chemicals used on site. The key to successful program planning is to ensure a high level of coordination and cooperation among the various groups involved in this process. This cooperation is to a large extent dependent upon how clearly the firm's or facility's executives communicate their commitment to this program. Program planning becomes very difficult if the cooperation of program staff is minimal.

Step 5: Keeping Records and Gathering Information. Documentation of activities under EPCRA is an essential aspect of implementation. The recordkeeping process actually began in step 2, hazard assessment. Systems and electronic data bases established for this purpose can be very useful as recordkeeping tools. However, documenting policies and procedures in a manual for EPCRA compliance may also be very useful. Such a manual should describe all aspects of the EPCRA program.

Another form of recordkeeping that can make filling out of reporting forms easier in subsequent years is to keep well-documented copies of all forms submitted and procedures used for compiling information used on the forms. This procedure may seem obvious; often, however, this type of documentation is not done. Even if the information required under EPCRA has been computerized, hard copy documentation can provide essential backup. For the small company, electronic data management may not be appropriate or feasible. In these cases, hard copy data management becomes essential.

Step 6: Reporting Procedures. There are a variety of reporting requirements specified under EPCRA. Reporting requirements are summarized in Table 3.5 of this book.

The first reporting requirement is to notify the state of your existence as an EPCRA facility. Next, on an annual basis every March 1, inventory reporting (tier I) forms are required for all firms subject to this law. On October 17, 1987, firms and facilities were also required to submit a list of the chemicals there for which Material Safety Data Sheets were available or, in lieu of the list, the Material Safety Data Sheets themselves. Updates must be provided on a regular basis. The minimum threshold levels for this type of reporting decrease over the years, and updates may become important.

Since applicability to the firm or facility may change over time, identifying target dates and reporting requirements should be closely linked to hazard assessment. Creating a systematic approach for meeting these targets is important for proper program planning. Depending upon the quantity of chemicals on hand, varying lead times will be required to complete the data required on these forms. A tickler system or a program planning chart can help provide adequate time to gather the material needed to complete these forms.

Since this is a basic aspect of the public information responsibility of firms and facilities, its importance must be emphasized. During the startup years for EPCRA, state, local and federal agencies may give some leeway to firms and facilities that do not meet the target dates. However, as implementation of the law proceeds, these grace periods will probably no longer be acceptable. The observance of precise reporting target dates will strengthen the program and result in less scrutiny of the firm or facility by public or government agencies. It is likely that, as LEPCs identify firms covered by the law, the LEPCs will create their own tickler systems to ensure that firms comply appropriately.

Another important reporting requirement under this law covers Section 313 reporting, which has been described in detail in Chapter 3. This report necessitates an account of all fugitive emissions of hazardous chemicals listed on the Section 313 Toxic Chemical List and requires careful planning to prepare. As stated earlier, this is an often poorly understood and underestimated requirement of EPCRA. Resource personnel such as engineers, chemists and operations control staff will need to participate in this process. Program planners must ensure adequate time for preparing the information required in this report.

Step 7: Establishing Sanctions and Enforcement Procedures for Noncompliance.   If the firm or facility has established behavior objectives as part of its goal-setting process, procedures that establish sanctions for noncompliant behavior can become very important in maintaining the program. If employees are expected to behave in certain ways when handling hazardous chemicals, based on an existing safety program, monitoring this behavior and creating sanctions for noncompliance provides one method for enforcement. An alternative to negative reinforcement is positive reinforcement. Rewards and incentives for using appropriate safety practices can also play an important role in encouraging appropriate behavior when handling hazardous materials.

It may seem unnecessary to monitor program implementation. However, since EPCRA provides stiff fines for noncompliance, any compliance program worthy of mention will have compliance monitoring built in. This can help avoid government sanctions that may result from non-compliance. When evaluating management-level activity, achieving compliance goals can be included as part of performance appraisal mechanisms or salary reviews.

When judging the achievement of safety behavior goals by hourly employees, sanction mechanisms must be designed to meet fair employment practices standards. The approach to sanctions for noncompliance should be realistic in relation to other such sanctions established by the firm or facility. The establishment of such standards necessitates coordination with other human resources management procedures established by the firm or facility. For example, three-stage warning systems leading to dismissal may already exist. Understanding previous practice here is essential to avoid legal complications resulting in sanctions against employees. Any employee sanction system should be developed with assistance of the corporate legal council.

Step 8: Establishing External Relations.   Since one of the legislative goals of EPCRA is to provide public information regarding hazardous chemicals used in firms and facilities, a public relations and risk communication program is an essential step in the program planning process. Chapter 2 is dedicated to this phase of program development. There are multiple psychological and attitudinal considerations when planning for external communications. Risk communication has become a sophisticated information science with growing importance. It provides the public face for an EPCRA program and directly affects credibility with product users (if the firm is a manufacturer), as well as with the neighbors in the community. How extensive the information program will become depends on its objectives and goals. This decision is also affected by the view of the role of the firm or facility in the community.

Public information programs include such direct methods as plant tours for community members in which procedures and methods for chemical containment are explained. Other techniques for disseminating information include press releases about program planning processes published by the firm and public speaking programs to describe these policies to community groups and local residents.

Section 5.4.4. Program Evaluation for Firm and Facility Implementation of EPCRA

Program evaluation provides the last step in the program planning process. Evaluation in this context should consist of the methods used to determine the success or failure of various elements or of the program as a whole. Success and failure are subjective concepts whose meaning changes depending upon the criteria established to make these judgments. The most logical evaluation criteria are based on the goals and objectives that the firm or facility chooses to establish in the program planning phase described in Subsection 5.4.2.

When program goals and objectives are established, it is very important that the evaluation criteria be considered as part of the process. When evaluation is considered as an afterthought, the ability of the program planners to evaluate the effectiveness of their programs will be hindered. Any evaluation process that does not review programs in light of established goals and objectives will lead to difficulties in making changes to correct deficiencies revealed in the evaluation process. This can be clearly understood when considering a program planning and evaluation technique commonly used in industry and government.

Management by objectives, a widely known administrative practice, is the most common evaluation method used. Measurable and quantifiable objectives are identified so that at various points in the program planning process, data collected regarding these objectives can be measured against the objectives themselves.

Evaluation using management by objectives can be based on a variety of measurable phenomena. The most commonly used entities are behavioral objectives. Evaluating these measures is most appropriate when trying to determine the efficacy or efficiency of individual behaviors. For example, if a firm's or facility's Hazard Communication Standard or EPCRA program requires employees to be capable of performing a particular behavior, such as maintaining and wearing respiratory protection under certain circumstances, various techniques can be used to evaluate this behavior.

There are multiple measures that can be used to directly evaluate the behavior of individuals. Observation is one such technique. The staff involved in program implementation, such as safety and health personnel or line supervisors, can make spot checks and record the level of employee compliance with appropriate procedures. Emergency drills, for example, can be used to evaluate whether employees still use proper respiratory protection. These drills can occur some time after the initial training or last use.

Direct observation as an evaluation technique can have its drawbacks, however. If spot checks are not appropriately presented, employees may view them as a punitive measure rather than as part of a positive planning process. Another drawback is that employees may comply or perform appropriately only when they know they are being observed. At other times when they are not observed, they may revert to inappropriate or incorrect behavioral patterns established many years previously. By not making these changes in behavior permanent, employees may actually reflect the company's policy not to take Hazard Communication Standard and Community Right-to-Know program implementation seriously.

Alternatively, lack of compliance with stated behavioral goals and objectives may reflect an incorrect understanding of the importance of the program. Problems may exist in the objectives themselves or in their implementation. Revamping training programs may be one corrective measure. Developing stronger programs to influence attitudes and communicate corporate goals may be another solution.

Another evaluation technique that judges the specific behavioral objectives established for the program is to institute pre- and posttraining testing for employees. Employee testing regarding procedures associated with safety and health practices has been growing in popularity since the institution of the OSHA Hazard Communication Standard. The tests are administered before and after training for particular behaviors or information. Results of the tests are designed to measure how well the employees understand the material presented. Before the employees are trained, a pretest to measure their understanding of the required behavior is given. After the training is complete, a posttest is given to determine if their understanding of the behavior has increased.

This pre- and posttest methodology has three drawbacks. First, it measures only the quantity of learning, not the actual performance. For example, although the test might indicate that the employee knows that he or she should use a respirator and knows how to use one in specific conditions, this evaluation method does not reveal whether or not the employee will actually use it. Second, the written record established as a result of the test, must be maintained for legal purposes. Third, determining a passing grade on such a test may pose some difficulties. It is important to consider what would happen to an employee who does not pass.

To avoid the pitfalls of direct observation and of pre- and posttest evaluation techniques, indirect measures of employee behavior may allow one to identify activities that represent changes in employee behavior. For example, one could measure the use of personal protective equipment by counting the disposable items used before and after employees participate in a training program designed to implement new goals and objectives. If an operation requires respirators that use disposable filters, one can compare the number of filters used before and after training. If an operation requires disposable ear plugs, increased use of the ear plugs after training could indicate increased compliance.

Another indirect measure of compliance with goals and objectives is related to physical measurements. A review of incident reports regarding unplanned spills and releases over time is an indirect evaluation technique.

For example, charting the number of hazardous spill incidents per month, or the number of medical incidents related to hazardous chemicals, can provide an indirect measure of the effectiveness of programs that are established based on specific goals and objectives.

Evaluaters look very favorably upon behavioral objectives as the cornerstone of an evaluation program. However, establishing emergency planning and Community Right-to-Know programs requires goals and objectives that are not necessarily behaviorally oriented. Though many social scientists believe that all goals and objectives can be reduced to behavioral concepts, there are some goals and objectives that necessitate a broader view than is provided by behavior measurement at the individual level.

Another debate among social and management scientists relates to the difference between quantitative and qualitative evaluation. Though there has recently, been some blurring of the differences between these two methodologies, it is important to recognize the difference. While quantitative evaluation focuses on measurable behaviors of the individual or the group, qualitative evaluation deals with the overall mood, attitude and culture of the organizational environment. Gathering data to make such a qualitative evaluation can be difficult. A commonly employed technique is the use of the anonymous survey. Surveying target populations, such as mid-level managers and supervisors, or even hourly employees, regarding their attitudes toward the environment and the firm's or facility's program implementation may provide such a qualitative view. Using the pre- and postprogram survey format for program implementation could also help to quantify these measures. Pre- and postsurvey formats, in fact, blend qualitative and quantitative measurement techniques.

Another form of qualitative evaluation involves monitoring the media reports on the program. Clearly, a media campaign resulting in complimentary articles regarding programs established at a firm or facility is a good judge of the success of such an effort. In an actual emergency, an evaluation of press reports of the firm's or facility's response can provide another kind of qualitative assessment.

For example, the press, in general, judged the Johnson & Johnson Company positively in its handling of the cyanide/Tylenol poisoning incidents. That situation clearly demonstrates that the program goal of Johnson & Johnson to maintain its credibility and reliability in this emergency situation, was achieved. While the sales figures for Johnson & Johnson provided quantitative data on the success of their response, those sales figures and the behavior of the individuals who continued to purchase Johnson & Johnson products were very much influenced by the attitudes conveyed in the press. Therefore, evaluating the public relations aspects of the program through an analysis of the press response to the company's actions, though not always definable in hard numbers, can be very useful in determining how the program needs to be strengthened.

Another evaluation technique is to review the budget process. Using budgeting figures as the basis of evaluating programs has become an absolute necessity in our market-based economic system. Getting the biggest bang for the buck is any modern manager's goal. Given the limited resources for program implementation, evaluating the budget process and comparing the dollar costs of objectives reached is extremely useful. If data management, for example, is a very expensive part of the program planning budget, it may make sense to evaluate whether computerizing data (if not already accomplished) will reduce the cost of data management.

It may also be useful to determine whether using inside resources is more or less expensive than buying services on the outside. Once again, using the data management example, the added flexibility that might be obtained by designing your own computer-based data management system may not be worth the additional cost when a turnkey off-the-shelf program is available. The difference in cost may be great enough that the added advantages of a customized data base management system may not be justifiable.

The final area to consider is the evaluation of regulatory compliance. In some ways, this should be the most simple criterion to evaluate. However, the complexities of the EPCRA requirements program may make it difficult to match regulatory requirements with program elements. In fact, because of the various interpretations of the different aspects of this law, evaluating regulatory compliance can be very complex.

There are several techniques for regulatory compliance evaluation. The most obvious one is to seek confirmation from government authorities at the local, state or federal level that activities related to this law, particularly in regard to reporting requirements, have been performed by the firm or facility. Government agencies, however, are reluctant to give any kind of certification that regulatory requirements have been fulfilled. Many firms and facilities feel that it is better to minimize contact with regulators because this will limit the level of scrutiny. Though this may be true in certain situations, it is a technique worth considering. Developing close working relationships with local, state and federal regulatory bodies to demonstrate the intent to comply provides the basis for judging whether the program does, in fact, meet the requirements of the law. The cooperative effort represented by this kind of feedback and information flow can give the firm or facility the sense that law has been addressed appropriately.

Another evaluation technique to determine if the objective of regulatory compliance has been met is to perform a regulatory audit. In this context, such an audit is done by an expert who has had experience implementing this law. He or she reviews the program documents, interviews individuals and observes procedures to determine that the objectives of the law have been met. In many large corporations, such an auditor might be supplied to the local facility by headquarters. This individual may be from the corporate environmental department, law department, public relations or human resources department. This individual, or a team of individuals, evaluates the program based on the law itself and on corporate policy regarding the law.

A regulatory audit may also be performed by an external consultant. Using an external consultant to evaluate how well the firm or facility has complied with the law may provide an easy way to assess the program with fewer resources. However, you must remember that you hire consultants at your own risk. In general, the adage that "You get what you pay for" applies most appropriately to the consulting field. Receiving competitive bids, checking references and interviewing consultants will help guarantee that you understand what you are buying. In fact, many large firms hire consultants to audit environmental health programs as a check against their own internal complacency regarding environmental matters.

Since environmental monitoring is a cost activity rather than a revenue-generating activity, the tendency in firms is to minimize expenditures in this area. However, as the environmental awareness and concern of the public grows, the long-term impact may be negative to the firm. Therefore, it becomes important to maintain a very strong evaluation program to ensure that environmental programs are accomplishing the goals and objectives established for them.

Finally, EPCRA itself provides some evaluation mechanisms that need to be considered. In particular, the reporting requirements for Section 313 of the law provide a built-in chemical use evaluation for the manufacturing industries in the United States. Mass balance studies at the firm level, as well as the aggregation of these data in the national data base created by EPA, will result in the ability of the government, citizens in general and firms in particular to evaluate the cradle-to-grave use and disposal of chemicals. These mass balance studies will lead to the evaluation of the goals and objective of the EPCRA program as a whole. Based on these studies, legislators at the federal, state and local levels, will probably augment or change the legislation in the future.

In summary, evaluation is a very important element of the program planning process. One important implication of evaluation must be considered before we close this discussion. Documented evaluation results that are not implemented, or that do not result in changes in program processes, can increase the liability of the firm or facility. If an external auditor identifies deficiencies in the program planning process for emergency response, and if an emergency occurs and these program deficiencies result in additional environmental or human health damage, the firm or facility is assuming additional liability. Therefore, evaluation results that are not implemented provide important evidence if litigation occurs. Firms or facilities trying to limit their liability might therefore conclude that evaluation should not be included in their program because of the potential of creating a record of malfeasance. This belief is in fact naive and inappropriate, since ignorance is no defense against illegal or inappropriate practices.

SECTION 5.5. STATE GOVERNMENT PROGRAM PLANNING FOR EPCRA

Subsection 5.5.1. Purpose and Authority of State Programs for EPCRA Planning

It is at the state government level that the public sector authority for the EPCRA program planning process is initiated and the programs begin to be implemented. The purpose of these programs as defined by the act is to develop state and local government emergency preparedness capabilities, as well as to establish Community Right-to-Know information access procedures. The law requires substantial exchange and cooperation between state and local authorities, as well as between these government bodies and the firms and facilities covered by the EPCRA.

The federal law delegates overall responsibility to the states to create two program planning units, the SERC and the LEPC. The law also specifies some basic goals that these groups are required to accomplish. However, the law also provides for the state and local governments to expand on the programs they mandate as long as they meet the minimum standards spelled out in the legislation.

Although this broad authority has been delegated to states and localities, the Congress as well as the EPA have made virtually no effort to provide funding for these programs. The scope of state and local implementation programs depends to a large extent, upon the funding allocated for them. Therefore, in any given state or locality, the amount of money authorized in relation to the number of facilities covered under the EPCRA will influence the scope of implementation. Since implementation of this legislation occurs primarily at the local level, the Congress probably rationalized its lack of financial support as a test of the local commitment to environmental protection programs. To a great extent, the level of local funding will directly reflect public sentiment for environmental programs in any given state. But funding for state-level programs is influenced by more than public sentiment. Many factors, including the availability of funding, the political clout of special interest groups and the competing interests of other public service programs such as education and health care services for the medically indigent, will influence funding for state and local EPCRA programs. As these programs develop, it will be interesting to track the ratio of firms and facilities covered by the law to state and local budgetary allocations. This comparison may provide an index of the commitment to EPCRA.

Subsection 5.5.2. Goals and Objectives of State EPCRA Programs

The primary goal of state EPCRA programs is to establish the organizational structure for program implementation. The governor of the state appoints the SERC, which is then responsible for setting up local emergency planning districts and appointing members to the LEPCs for each district. It is the overall goal of the SERCs to ensure program implementation at the local level by establishing rules and regulations for these programs. Under the legal requirements of EPCRA, these standards must include methods and conditions of public access to information and criteria for LEPCs when establishing emergency response capabilities.

Another objective of SERCs is to develop enabling legislation at the state government level that authorizes the implementation of EPCRA programs. This can become a very important aspect of state-level activity, particularly in those states where there is an expansion of requirements for firms and facilities beyond the baseline established by EPCRA. These legislative authorization procedures can become very complicated and politically charged, depending on the political situation in any locality.

Some SERC have gone beyond pro forma implementation of EPCRA requirements and have tried to influence the context in which the law is implemented. Writing mission statements or statements of goals can create such an atmosphere, especially when these statements include goals that encourage broad-based participation in support for the emergency planning process. They may also reflect efforts to coordinate the activities of various state agencies involved in emergency planning and community preparedness. Since jurisdictional disputes among state agencies can lead to program design conflicts, efforts to negotiate divisions of responsibility can contribute greatly to program implementation efforts. If mission statements or program goals are not specified at the state level, the activities of the SERC may lead to a confusing situation. The clarity of program goals will reflect how seriously any particular state takes its EPCRA programs.

Subsection 5.5.3. Plans for State Programs of EPCRA

Those involved in and experienced with the program planning process understand that any program planning group such as a SERC needs to develop a mission statement or a set of organizational goals. This document provides a framework for establishing specific program elements. In the case of the EPCRA, these planning elements are specified by the federal legislation. They are described below.

Step 1: Designate Local Planning Districts.   Under the law, it is the state's responsibility to define the local planning group by specifying the geographic area covered by the local planning districts. The federal law does not define how these geographic decisions are to be made; it leaves this issue up to each state. Many states have assumed that the county-by-county planning district designation is appropriate. However, there are many exceptions to that approach. In some states, county-by-county designations were made, with the exception that large municipalities would be designated as separate emergency planning districts. For example, in the State of Illinois, though the emergency planning districts are organized on a county-by-county basis, the City of Chicago exists as a separate emergency planning district. Therefore, in Cook County, there is a countywide emergency planning district which excludes the City of Chicago, because the city constitutes an emergency planning district of its own. In this situation, where for practical purposes there is overlapping jurisdiction, coordinated program planning becomes essential.

In other states, some counties have been combined to constitute unified emergency planning districts. The justification for this organizational scheme is that on a county-by-county basis there may be inadequate resources or a minimum of covered facilities. This may make county-by-county organization, particularly in rural areas, impractical and unnecessary.

Finally, in some states where there is a minimum amount of industry, the state as a whole has been designated as the local emergency planning district. This means that all program implementation is carried out at the state level.

Step 2: Appoint Members of LEPCs.   The individuals designated to be member of LEPCs are specified under the law. They include representatives from civil defense, fire departments, law enforcement agencies; members of the media; hospital and health department personnel; representatives of transportation authorities; owners of toxic or hazardous waste disposal sites and facilities handling hazardous materials; and community representatives. Elected local officials must also be represented.

Recruiting these personnel for LEPCs, which is often a volunteer activity, has been difficult in some localities. Manufacturing associations have encouraged their members to volunteer for such committees, though in some places, finding industry representatives has been difficult. In other situations, industry representatives have dominated LEPCs and there has been less community participation. SERCs have also considered existing emergency preparedness groups as another source of members for these committees. Emergency planning agencies have existed for many years to combat the consequences of natural disasters such as floods and earthquakes. They have also been established to handle civil defense preparedness. However, these groups often lack the complete spectrum of membership required under the law.

Some states have taken a public approach to recruiting members of LEPCs. The SERCs have used the media to publicize and to recruit members for the local committees. For example, the State of Michigan sent press releases to local newspapers asking for volunteers to nominate themselves for the state's LEPCs. Since the intent of this law is to make the emergency planning and Community Right-to-Know process an open public issue, this kind of public relations and publicity can be considered appropriate.

Step 3: Promulgating Rules Regarding the Extremely Hazardous Chemicals List. Some states have chosen to accept the Extremely Hazardous Chemicals List as promulgated by the EPA. However, under EPCRA, state authorities have two methods for expanding the number of facilities covered by this list. First, the SERC can expand the number of chemicals on the list. Second, the governor or the SERC can reduce the TPQ required to trigger the law. The SERC can do this if public notice is given and an opportunity for comment is provided.

It is the responsibility of a firm or facility to notify the state of the existence of these chemicals in the workplace. Once the state receives this information, it must be provided to the EPA and the LEPC.

Step 4: Develop Rules for Community Access to Information. It is the responsibility of the SERC to establish policies and procedures regarding community access to information, particularly Tier One and Tier Two information (see Appendix C). Since Community Right-to-Know is a very important aspect of this legislation, and probably one of its more controversial aspects, setting up rules for access to information may cause differences to develop among the various groups represented on the SERC.

Another important consideration regarding access to information is that this information is expected to be available at the local emergency planning district level. Yet it is at the state level that the rules for access are made. Conflicts may develop due to differences in attitudes that may exist between citizens at the local level and those making rules and regulations at the state level. Here again, political pressures will play a role in resolving any conflicts of this nature.

The variables to consider when developing plans for access to information include:

1. The time and place where access is made available.
2. The cost of providing information: Will a charge be levied for copying forms? How will these costs be determined? Under what circumstances will these costs be waived?

The special case of Tier Two information must also be considered. These forms provide specific information about the quantities and location of chemicals at facilities. Under the law, these forms are available only on request. If a firm or facility chooses to submit Tier Two information, the problem is lessened because the information is on hand. When a firm or facility submits only Tier One forms, a mechanism must be created for responding to requests for Tier Two information. The SERC must establish rules and procedures for soliciting the information from the firm or facility. The law states that requesters of this information can be required to provide justification for their need to know. However, if the justification is acceptable according to the state's established rules, the firm or facility must provide Tier Two forms.

Though the SERC is charged with the responsibility for establishing a mechanism for community access to information, this commission may create a baseline access policy and leave expansion of that policy to the discretion of the LEPC. This mechanism of baseline policy setting at the state level, with the possibility of expansion at the local level, is consistent with the other provisions for program implementation of this law. But the more fragmented the compliance rules become, the more expensive and time-consuming program implementation is. Issues related to access to information may become a source of conflict in those localities where community activists on environmental issues feel that industry is not responsive to the requirements of this law. However, it is too early in the implementation process to identify trends regarding these matters.

Step 5: Collect Section 313 Information.   Under EPCRA, mass balance information regarding the use of chemicals on the Section 313 List of Toxic Substances is provided by firms to the SERC, not to the LEPC. Once it is received, the state is responsible for transferring this information to the EPA. Identifying firms that come under Section 313 requirements and assuring that these reports are submitted on an annual basis are two of the program planning responsibilities of the SERC.

Step 6: Enforcing the Law at the State Level.   Though the enforcement responsibilities of federal, state and local authorities are generally specified in the law itself, it is in the SERCs that state enforcement policies and procedures will be established. An example of a program enforcement policy that needs to be considered is how aggressive the state and local law enforcers should be regarding noncompliance. Should they, for example, seek out all firms to determine their applicability to this law or should they rely on self-reporting by firms? Another issue is how severe penalties for late reporting should be. That is, how aggressive should state law enforcement officials be regarding firms that provide information, but not on a timely basis?

How enforcement will be carried out at the state level depends in many ways upon the political climate that surrounds the implementation of the EPCRA. Often local prosecutors like to use enforcement actions against recalcitrant firms or facilities to attain compliance among all firms. Clearly, enforcement is a very expensive process, and the level of funding for this activity will determine how it is implemented. Enforcement actions are also time-consuming. Nevertheless, many state and local attorneys general use enforcement actions to gain publicity to further their political careers.

Subsection 5.5.4. Evaluation of State Programs under EPCRA

At the state level, the law requires few evaluation procedures. However, there are some. One such requirement is that public notice must be given and public comment solicited before any state regulation can be promulgated. This allows public participation in the program planning process and provides the possibility of external evaluation by interested parties affected by these regulations.

Another evaluation mechanism built into the state authority is its responsibility to review local emergency plans. The frequency of this activity is not defined as specifically as it is at the local level, where it must be performed on an annual basis. However, through the evaluation of various emergency plans, SERCs can, get a better understanding of the level of preparedness of LEPCs. This can result in formal or informal standard setting to improve the compliance of less prepared local groups.

State legislature provide another evaluation mechanism. Since the state legislature is involved in allocating funds for many of these programs, the authorization process provides an evaluative component. Other evaluation mechanisms, such as public hearings or funded evaluation studies, can also be established through the state legislative process.

Internal program evaluation for SERCs can be handled similarly to the evaluation procedures described for firms and facilities in Subsection 5.4.4 of this book. It is common knowledge that the evaluation process is expensive and time-consuming. Also, establishing outcome measures of success can be difficult. For these reasons, evaluation studies are not often carried out.

Finally, the bottom line in evaluation for SERCs is how well plans are implemented when an emergency response is necessary. But there is an important issue to consider here. Experience can help us do a better job, but the irony here is that these plans are meant to prevent the necessity of implementing them. This is not to say that evaluation is not useful. It is meant to suggest, however, that evaluation may be more effective when it focuses on prevention techniques as well as response actions.

SECTION 5.6. PROGRAM PLANNING FOR LEPCs UNDER EPCRA

Subsection 5.6.1. Purpose and Authority for LEPCs under the EPCRA

The LEPCs form the base of the implementation pyramid for the EPCRA. It is essential to understand the role of the LEPCs. They are responsible for carrying out programs as authorized by the Congress and passed through the federal government bureaucracy to the state government and finally to the local level. Though the authority for LEPCs emanates originally from the federal law itself, local communities are also given the power to expand coverage for firms and facilities under this law by augmenting already authorized programs.

The overriding purpose of the LEPC is to implement systems designed to prevent or limit emergency incidents. This is difficult to do unless a co-operative effort is made by all groups concerned. This includes local responders such as fire departments, police, ambulance services and hospitals, as well as the firms and facilities whose chemical usage may result in an emergency situation.

The funding mechanism for this law provides an interesting commentary on the authority provided to the LEPC. At the county or community planning district level, the adequacy of the funds provided will directly affect the strength of the implementation program. Since funding for the local program will be generated predominantly at the local level, the amount of funding provided will serve as a direct measure of the importance given to this program by locally elected officials as they reflect the concerns of the electorate.

Subsection 5.6.2. Goals and Objectives of LEPCs under EPCRA

The primary goal and objective of the LEPC is to establish policies and procedures that are designed to prevent the necessity for an emergency response as a result of spills or accidents involving hazardous chemicals. Secondly, if such events do occur, the goal of the LEPC is to develop response plans that lead to the most speedy and efficient method of providing of emergency response services. As a result of these overriding goals, a clearly identifiable objective is to establish cooperative and coordinated relationships between various members of the emergency response community.

As is true at the state level, the development of a mission statement or a statement of program planning goals is appropriate here. Without such a formal statement, authority and responsibility may become confused. A document such as a mission statement is not meant to substitute for the development of the emergency response plan. Instead, it supplements and precedes the plan itself, and provides the authority and mechanisms for developing the plan.

Subsection 5.6.3. Program Plans for LEPCs

Program planning at the local level requires an effort commensurate with the risk level likely for emergency incidents. Quantifying this risk must be part of the local planning effort itself. Risk analysis is discussed in full in Chapter 2 and therefore will be covered only briefly here. However, the issues related to risk analysis and communication are essential for program planning at the local level. As a result, all pragmatic decisions must be made in this context. These decisions are also influenced by the other members who make up the planning units identified in the program planning matrix in Table 5.1. These include the federal and state governments, as well as firms and facilities.

While the discussion presented in this chapter is limited, this book in its entirety reflects the total understanding needed to implement this program at the local level. Becoming aware of the responsibilities of firms and facilities under EPCRA, as well as state implementation requirements, makes the local planners' job easier. Without this understanding, local plans may be developed in a vacuum.

Section 301(c) of the EPCRA states exactly what EPCRA expects the LEPC to do. As with the SERC, there are six basic steps required for local program implementation. They are described below.

Step 1: Establishing the LEPC. This process is fully described under the discussion of state-level programs, because it is actually the responsibility of the SERC to appoint the LEPC. However, SERCs may appoint LEPC members only as a formality. It may be the responsibility of the LEPC chairman to recruit volunteers to serve on the committee. In order to be in compliance with the law, each LEPC, at a minimum, must include delegates from the following groups:

1. Elected state and local officials
2. Law enforcement, civil defense, firefighting, first aid, health, local environmental, hospital and transportation personnel
3. Broadcast and print media
4. Community groups
5. Owners and operators of facilities subject to the law's requirement

While the committee itself is expected to appoint the chairman, there may be situations where the committee chairman selects the committee.

Step 2: Develop a Mission Statement.   Though not required by the law, this statement has been justified in Subsection 5.5.2. It is meant to provide the framework and the approach to be taken in carrying out the remaining program planning elements. Given the diversity of the membership on the LEPC, writing such a statement may require some negotiation among the members of the committee. How smoothly this task goes will indicate whether the committee can anticipate a cooperative effort with regard to LEPC responsibilities.

Step 3: Creating Rules Under Which the LEPC Will Function.   The law clearly specifies that the LEPC must create a set of rules under which it will function. These rules concern items such as public notification of committee activities, public meetings to discuss the emergency plans and requests for public comments. Rules specifying the methods the LEPC will use to respond to public input, as well as the methods for distributing the emergency plan, are also required.

Note here how prominent public participation in the LEPC process needs to be. Since public access to information is a major motivating factor behind the legislation, this should not be surprising.

Step 4: Develop an Emergency Response Plan.   Developing an emergency plan is the primary responsibility of the LEPC. In many localities, such plans already exist. They may be based on EPA guidances under Chemical Emergency Preparedness Program guidance or on previously developed programs at the state level. The specific requirements of an emergency response plan, as developed and recommended by the EPA and others in the national response team, are discussed in Chapter 6, which is dedicated to this subject.

Step 5: Receiving and Handling Information.   The bulk of the paperwork generated by EPCRA is to be organized and stored by the LEPC. It is at the local level that requests for information are received and fulfilled. Section 301(c) of the law also specifies that a member of the LEPC must be designated as an Information Coordinator. This individual, under the direction of the LEPC, is responsible for responding to requests for this information. It is important to review the volume of information that the LEPC will handle. First, there will be Material Safety Data Sheets or lists of these sheets for every firm or facility subject to the OSHA Hazard Communication Standard. Since most firms in the manufacturing sector have a minimum of 100 such sheets, and some firms several thousand, depending on the size of the industrial base in the community, this may result in a massive amount of paper. Additionally, there will be tier I and possibly tier II forms for each firm or facility. Beyond this, there will be emergency release incident reports and reports on the existence of chemicals on the Extremely Hazardous Chemicals List. Therefore, it is essential that LEPCs consider and develop programs regarding these information storage and dissemination procedures.

The first decision to make concerns the storage of this information. Fire departments are identified as one place where information can be located, particularly information related to extremely hazardous chemicals described in Sections 301, 302, and 303 of the EPCRA. The law also states that fire departments must have access to tier I information. In many locations, fire departments may coordinate emergency response programs. If this is the case, the fire department becomes the logical place for Material Safety Data Sheets or for lists and information about how and where extremely hazardous chemicals are stored.

However, using fire departments may be deceptively simple because there is likely to be more than one fire department in each local planning district. The question then arises of whether to subdivide the storage of information according to the boundaries developed for local fire districts. Maintaining records and assuring public access might grow to nightmarish proportions if the information is not stored in a centralized location. The extent of the information management problem should begin to become clear to the reader.

Another consideration here is the methods used to keep track of the information. Computerization of records seems to be a logical solution. However, this can be very expensive and time-consuming. Also, personnel, hardware and software that are appropriate for the task may not be available.

It is likely that solutions to these problems will vary from LEPC to LEPC. Information sharing between the many local planning units in the state may provide help in answering the information management questions. The SERC may provide some guidance as well.

When considering how this information should be stored, it is also important to remember that public access to this information is guaranteed under the EPCRA. How accessible community residents feel the information is to them will determine whether the community considers the program successful. Making access difficult in communities where environmental concerns are greatest provides a strong disincentive for a cooperative effort and hinders the process of developing trust. The more accessible information is, the more likely community representatives will feel that the law is being implemented appropriately. Establishing community access to information is an essential part of this process. No LEPC chairman will want to see a headline in the local newspaper that broadcasts the difficulty local environmental groups had in gaining access to information required under the law.

Step 6: Enforcement. LEPC members must be directly concerned with enforcement because emergency preparedness depends on the participation of those likely to generate an emergency incident. However, enforcement capabilities at the local level may, in fact, be severely limited. This is another reason why every effort must be made to encourage the cooperation of all members involved.

When cooperation strategies are unsuccessful, enforcement programs play a more important role. When singling out noncompliant firms for sanctions, it is necessary to praise the majority of firms who participate appropriately. The first task of any enforcement effort is to identify all firms and facilities subject to the compliance effort. This can be done using telephone directories, business directories and lists from the tax roles. Environmental agencies may already have lists of companies that are subject to other environmental laws. Using surveys mailed to the firms and facilities, identifying and tabulating results against document submissions will provide a method of identifying noncompliant firms and facilities. The LEPC may want to establish follow-up procedures before enforcement action is taken. This will allow firms a chance to comply.

SERCs are a source of information for LEPCs regarding noncompliance. A statewide coordination effort regarding enforcement has certain advantages. If a firm in one local emergency planning district is fined for noncompliance and a firm in another district is not, there may be many years of litigation involved in resolving the differences. However, over the long term, fines may provide a revenue source that can be tapped. Therefore, strict enforcement of recalcitrant firms may become a public policy choice.

Subsection 5.6.4. Program Evaluation at the Local Level under EPCRA

At the local level, the only evaluation requirement that is discussed in the EPCRA is that LEPCs must review, on an annual basis, the emergency response plans developed for their district. However, many communities may want to expand the evaluation aspects of their program. One area to consider is the use of public hearings and notifications to allow community representatives and citizens to participate in the evaluation process. This type of evaluation can be useful in fostering cooperative efforts.

Local legislative bodies can also provide an evaluation mechanism through funding authorization processes as well as oversight hearings. However, this is not always possible, since local legislative bodies often lack the resources to do this kind of evaluation. Methods of evaluating the program, including outside audits and others mentioned earlier, should be considered by LEPCs.

But the ultimate evaluation of these programs will come when the emergency response plan must be implemented for an actual emergency. If evaluation of preparedness program waits until an emergency event, the program will probably fall short. Therefore, it is advisable to build evaluation mechanisms into the program planning process.

Chapter 6
EMERGENCY RESPONSE PREPAREDNESS

SECTION 6.1. INTRODUCTION

Emergency response preparedness at the local level is one of the primary goals of the EPCRA. The law delineates very specific requirements for these plans. The overall plan is to be developed by the LEPC and reviewed by the SERC. The LEPC must review and revise the plan annually. The public must be invited to participate in this process through open meetings and public hearings.

The EPCRA outlines a set of requirements that provide baseline procedures that must be included in an emergency response plan. However, to implement these procedures appropriately, it is important to understand the context and the community orientation that these plans require for success. This chapter provides information on and explains the various considerations that go into this planning process.

First of all, what is emergency preparedness? It is the set of plans and procedures developed to respond to transportation or fixed facility releases of hazardous chemicals. Under the EPCRA, the target for emergency preparedness at the local level is the approximately 400 chemicals on the Extremely Hazardous Substances List developed under Section 303 of the law. However, this list only provides a baseline. Communities may and have included other chemicals, such as natural gas and motor fuels (which are exempt under EPCRA), as part of the emergency preparedness planning process. Natural disasters can also be considered part of the emergency preparedness response capability. Such events as floods, earthquakes, tornadoes and hurricanes require many of the same response actions, i.e., evacuation, temporary housing, and medical treatment for accident or injury victims, as well as possible food and water distribution programs. Since many of the first responders to these incidences are the same, whether they are chemical-related or natural disasters, the planning processes for both types of events should be well coordinated.

An important difference between chemical or man-made disasters and natural disasters must be noted. In the case of a chemical emergency, the need for immediate access to information about the potential hazards related to the chemicals involved is essential. While the natural disaster may create great devastation, it is the chemical disaster that requires the expertise of a wide variety of specialists in order to limit the damage. While floods recede and hurricanes and tornadoes leave an area when the weather systems pass, chemical disasters, if not cared for appropriately, can continue to harm a community for a long time. Therefore, preemergency planning for remedial action can often play an important role in limiting the damage that results from a chemical emergency incident.

SECTION 6.2. PROACTIVE VERSUS REACTIVE PLANNING

There are two aspects to consider when embarking on emergency planning. Of the utmost importance is the necessity to consider the ways in which emergency incidents can be prevented. In fact, prevention should be the first goal of any chemical emergency preparedness plan. The next aspect of the planning process to consider is response planning. Even with the most complete prevention provisions in place, a program must also exist for responding to emergency situations when the prevention methods fail.

Another way of looking at this difference is to understand that the prevention process is proactive, while the response action is reactive. It is logical to assume that the more resources are placed in a proactive program, the less likely will be the necessity to react to an emergency event. A proactive or prevention plan focuses on the activities carried out at the firm or facility level. Engineering controls, warning systems, organizational communication structures and spill or release containment procedures are all part of such a plan. However, when considering the cost of program design and implementation, given the limited resources available for this kind of activity, it is understandable that many communities, firms and facilities choose to focus on response programs rather than prevention programs.

Traditionally, business and industry have favored the reactive approach because prevention planning is often very expensive. However, with the increase in liability costs and the lack of availability of insurance under many circumstances where hazardous chemicals are concerned, business, industry and communities have begun to reevaluate the proactive approach as more appropriate. In fact, organizations such as the Chemical Manufacturers Association have developed programs and policies for their members that encourage a prevention orientation.

The EPCRA has, in fact, codified the shift from a reactive to a proactive response. This emphasis on prevention has gained favor as the public awareness of emergency response needs has become greater. The gas release in Bhopal, India, and the fuel spill into the Monongahela River outside Pittsburgh, Pennsylvania, are just two events that have had an influence on public sentiment in this area.

SECTION 6.3. EMERGENCY PLANNING AT THE FEDERAL LEVEL

Local government emergency response planning has been going on for many years. However, only since the 1980's have strong legislative mandates to implement this process existed. At the federal level, the first of these legislative efforts was associated with the Superfund law. Section 105 of CERCLA requires that a national contingency plan be developed for environmentally related chemical emergencies. Federal authority was established to initiate this program. It requires that chemical accidents or incidents be reported to the National Response Center, which is under the authority of the U.S. Coast Guard. The national response effort is directed by the National Response Team, also mandated under CERCLA.

This legislative mandate provides the framework for the creation of regional response teams. These teams are organized on the basis of the ten EPA regional districts. Each team includes representatives from federal agencies at the regional level, as well as state representatives. The National Contingency Plan itself requires that several federal agencies participate in this planning process. These agencies include the EPA, Coast Guard, Department of Commerce, Department of the Interior, Department of Defense, Department of State, Department of Justice, Department of Transportation, Department of Health and Human Services, Federal Emergency Management Agency, Department of Energy and Department of Labor. Table 6.1 provides a list of the states included in each regional response planning district.

SECTION 6.4. EMERGENCY PLANNING AT THE LOCAL LEVEL

Local response planning was not part of the original National Contingency Plan. Though CERCLA required that state representatives participate in planning at the regional level, it was not until the passage of the SARA, Title III, EPCRA, that local planning requirements were specified. This new law requires the states to establish SERCs, which are responsible for designating local emergency planning districts and LEPCs to function as emergency preparedness planning agencies at the community level. By extending the requirement for emergency planning to the local level, the Congress initiated a planning process that requires the cooperation of local firms and facilities, government service organizations such as police, fire, and health service agencies, and community representatives.

EPCRA, it must be noted, also allows local laws and regulations to be established. These laws and regulations may go beyond the federal requirements and, in many localities, may have been enacted *prior* to the enactment

Table 6.1 Regional Response Districts and EPA Regional Offices

Region I

(Connecticut, Maine, Massachusetts,
New Hampshire, Rhode Island, Vermont)

John F. Kennedy Building, Room 2203
Boston, MA 02203
(617) 565-3715
RPC: (617) 861-6700

Region II

(New Jersey, New York, Puerto Rico,
Virgin Islands)

26 Federal Plaza, Room 900
New York, NY 10278
(212) 264-2525
RPC: (201) 321-6657

Region III

(Delaware, Washington DC, Maryland,
Pennsylvania, Virginia, West Virginia)

841 Chestnut Street
Philadelphia, PA 19107
(215) 597-9800
RPC: (215) 587-8907

Region IV

(Alabama, Florida, Georgia, Kentucky,
Mississippi, North Carolina,
South Carolina, Tennessee)

345 Courtland, Street, N.E.
Atlanta, GA 30365
(404) 347-4727
RPC: (404) 347-3931

Region V

(Illinois, Indiana, Michigan,
Minnesota, Ohio, Wisconsin)

230 S. Dearborn Street
Chicago, IL 60604
(312) 353-2000
RPC: (312) 886-1964

Region VI

(Arkansas, Louisiana, New Mexico,
Oklahoma, Texas)

1445 Rose Avenue, 12th Floor
Dallas, TX 75202-2733
(214) 655-6444
RPC: (214) 655-2270

Region VII

(Iowa, Kansas, Missouri, Nebraska)

726 Minnesota Avenue
Kansas City, KS 66101
(913) 236-2800
RPC: (913) 236-2808

Region VIII

(Colorado, Montana, North Dakota,
South Dakota, Utah, Wyoming)

One Denver Place
999 18th Street, Suite 1300
(303) 293-1603
RPC: (303) 293-1723

Region IX

(Arizona, California, Hawaii,
American Samoa, Guam)

215 Fremont Street
San Francisco, CA 94105
(415) 974-8071
RPC: (415) 974-7460

Region X

(Alaska, Idaho, Oregon,
Washington)

1200 6th Avenue
Seattle, WA 98101
(206) 442-5810
RPC: (206) 442-1263

Note: Write directly to the EPA Regional Preparedness Coordinator (RPC) of the appropriate
EPA regional office.

of Title III. Since these laws can expand federal requirements, it is important to be aware of them.

Another situation must also be considered. Several states, such as Pennsylvania, New Jersey, and Illinois, had passed state emergency planning laws before the passage of Title III. Some of the local or state laws have contradictory or repetitive procedure and program requirements. In Illinois, for example, a local chemical emergency planning law was passed in September 1985. This law, entitled "The Illinois Chemical Safety Act" (P.A. 84-852), established reporting and planning requirements. However, EPCRA and the Illinois law use two different lists of hazardous chemicals, each containing several hundred chemicals for which emergency planning is required. These two lists overlap for only approximately 10 chemicals. The two laws also have different requirements for reporting and planning. This is the case in other localities as well. It is the responsibility of state legislatures to make sure that these conflicts are resolved.

As a result of this duplication and overlap in some localities, there has been much confusion regarding implementation of emergency planning requirements. It is hoped that as local communities, states and the federal government gain experience, these problems will be worked out. Though many people involved in implementing these programs bemoan the fact that there are complex, overlapping laws and regulations, our federal system of government clearly establishes the right of local communities to develop their own standards for emergency planning.

As part of the EPCRA legislation, the National Response Team was given the responsibility to create a document to be used by local communities to assist in the emergency planning process. This document, entitled, the *Hazardous Materials Emergency Planning Guide,* was published by the National Response Team in March 1987. It is available from the National Oil and Hazardous Substance Contingency Plan, G-WER/12, 2100 Second Street, S.W., Washington, D.C. 20593. It provides excellent guidance on the preparation and implementation of hazardous substance emergency plans. Anyone involved in this process needs to obtain a copy of this document. It reflects the program planning and response experience of the multiple agencies making up the National Response Team and provides invaluable support for planners at the local level.

There are several important ways in which communities can influence the success of responses to incidents. The first step in this process is to make a thorough assessment of the level of potential hazard that exists in the community. This assessment process, discussed in Chapter 2, provides the information base necessary to develop an effective emergency response plan. The EPCRA requires that firms and facilities in local communities report the necessary information to the LEPC. Since complete information is necessary for an effective program, the LEPC may have to investigate to make sure that all firms and facilities have in fact complied with the law. An incomplete assessment of the level of potential hazard in the community will result in an incomplete plan.

Using local business directories provides a way to identify nonrespondents among firms and facilities. Though this process may be time-consuming and require computer-based data management, a thorough approach to emergency preparedness cannot occur without it. A resource that local communities can call on for assistance is the SERC. It is also the responsibility of this commission to collect data from firms that must respond to this law. The SERC may also be involved in creating an identification system which can be shared, targeting firms and facilities subject to the compliance requirements of EPCRA.

At the local level, prevention planning can provide another method of reducing potential damage from emergency incidents. This requires that the LEPC identify and improve warning systems for such emergencies. Many firms and facilities, particularly in the chemical industries, have such warning systems in place. Identifying them, evaluating their effectiveness and encouraging the improvement of these warning systems constitute an overall policy program goal that local communities can adopt to improve their emergency planning capabilities. Besides firm- and facility-based warning systems, civil defense and fire warning systems exist in most communities. Testing of these systems may already occur on a regular basis. However, notification and warning systems designed to inform those involved in responding to chemical emergencies may not be tested regularly. These special warning provisions need to be established and tested as part of the emergency planning process.

The Congress felt that this area of prevention was quite important and as a result, required the EPA to develop a national study that would assess the technology and existence of emergency warning systems. The requirements, specifications and timetable for this study were described in Subsection 5.3.4 of this book.

Initial training and repeat training of industry and local response personnel can also play an important role in preventing and quickly responding to emergency situations. In the last decade, training has gained increased favor as a method of increasing the safety of individuals in the presence of chemical exposures. A more detailed discussion of the training process is presented in Chapter 7. It is important to note here that because emergency planning and Community Right-to-Know are designed to prevent as well as react to emergency incidents, the fewer the incidents, the more important training becomes. Actually responding to chemical emergencies in the community provides the best training environment from the point of view of an educator. Learning by experience is an essential part of any training process.

EPCRA is designed to prevent incidents from occurring; therefore, learning through experience, a standard educational technique, is in fact not always possible or appropriate. Creating emergency incidents in order to train personnel is unethical and would not be recommended by anyone. Thus, training in the classroom and through simulation takes on special importance.

Cooperation and team building are other methods that communities can use to influence the response to incidents. As the various participants in the program planning process work together at the local level, these cooperative efforts will lead to working response teams that can effectively plan and respond to emergency incidents. The various aspects of team building to be considered are discussed in the next section of this chapter.

Finally, it is important to recognize that planning alone is not enough. For a plan to be effective, it must be tested and evaluated. Finally, based on these tests and evaluations, it must be revised. Any document developed as part of the local emergency planning committee's activity must be understood to be a working document, i.e., one that can and will be updated and revised based on experience. If testing, evaluation and revision are not an active part of the process, these plans will not provide the guidance required to accomplish the goals of Title III. In fact, this part of the process is deemed so crucial that Congress wrote into the law the requirement that LEPCs review their plans on an annual basis. Responding to this requirement in a perfunctory manner, without evaluating and reassessing the effectiveness of the plan, will only lead to a weakened response capability at the local level.

SECTION 6.5. THE TEAM APPROACH TO EMERGENCY PREPAREDNESS

The EPCRA codifies the requirement for a team approach to the emergency planning process. The law as explained earlier, requires that LEPCs include representatives from a variety of community institutions, including the following:

1. Elected officials
2. Law enforcement, civil defense, firefighting, health, local environmental, hospital and transportation personnel
3. Broadcast and print media
4. Community groups
5. Owners and operators of firms and facilities subject to the requirements of Title III of SARA

This requirement guarantees that all groups involved in and responsible for various aspects of the EPCRA will be represented at the LEPC to develop the emergency plan.

For the process to work, it is necessary that a cooperative and coordinated approach to the planning process become one of the primary goals of the local response initiative. This approach is clearly justified because of the multidisciplinary needs of the response plan. It is clear that no individual can be an expert in all aspects of emergency response programs. Without the support and participation of a variety of groups, these plans will not succeed.

Team building for crisis intervention activities can be a slow, arduous process and can require time and experience to implement. For the team to be effective, it is necessary that a growing level of trust develop among team members and that the process of team building result in increased understanding and developing expertise through sharing among all team members. As the committee develops and the team gains experience and modifies its procedures based on these experiences, the credibility of the team will increase.

There are several factors that can facilitate the team-building process. First, a strong and authoritative leader is essential. Such a leader is not someone who is bossy. Since much of the work will be done on a voluntary basis, the chairman must be able to create a positive environment that encourages, rather than discourages, participation. Though the chairman of the LEPC is not likely to be the highest elected official in the community planning district, the person who does provide team leadership must have the support of this official.

Another important element in team building is to choose members for the LEPC with broad experience in the emergency response process. This seems patently obvious; however, in many cases, experienced individuals may not present themselves as volunteers to the committee. They must be sought out by those in leadership roles. The broader the expertise available to the committee, the more effective the team will be in developing and implementing emergency plans.

Not only the experience but also the consistency of participation by the team members must be considered. Imagine a situation where a local citizen with great expertise is recruited to participate in the emergency planning process. This person would appear to be a great asset to the committee. However, if this individual regards his or her role as that of a figurehead or legitimator rather than that of a participant, and does not consistently participate, he or she could have a demoralizing effect on the team building process. Therefore, when choosing team members, it might be advisable to consider a less skilled but more dedicated individual who is willing to learn and participate with others in the planning process.

Another important aspect of team building is open communication among team members and the establishment of mutually agreed upon goals and expectations. A variety of approaches to goal setting have been discussed throughout this book. Whatever method is agreed upon, the goals become the ground rules for the team building effort. Organizational goals certainly need attention, but so do the goals and expectations for individual team members. Here the leadership capability of the LEPC chairman is important. It is the chairman's responsibility to make sure that the responsibilities placed on individual team members are realistic. Having team members review and evaluate plans on a continuing basis, and, based on these shared experiences, exchange expertise and receive additional training, will strengthen the team building process. It is when the team works together on a consistent basis and establishes mechanisms for evaluating whether the goals have been met that the working relationships of the team and its plans will solidify.

Finally, one of the more important aspects of team building is to have the resources available to implement the team's developed plans. Realistically, the planning process must consider what resources are available so that the plan reflects the resource limits of the community. In an era of shrinking government resources, it is easy to understand that demoralization and dissatisfaction will set in if the resources available are not appropriately assessed. The point here is to make sure that expectations are not raised beyond what is possible.

The National Response Team's *Hazardous Materials Emergency Planning Guide* comments that the team building process can create an environment in which a balance is struck between the various economic, political and social interests involved in the EPCRA process. To state this more directly, the emergency planning process is a political one in which trade-offs will occur and bargains will be struck. This is exactly the process the Congress anticipated when it identified the requirements for LEPC membership.

Individuals from such disparate groups as private sector firms, community environmental groups, government social service agencies such as police officers and firefighters, and health providers such as hospitals need to develop working relationships to make the LEPC achieve its goals. Disincentives to this process certainly exist. Among the public agencies themselves, jurisdictional concerns and old rivalries existing between various response agencies in various townships may hinder the development of good working relationships. Industry interests may find the cooperative process to be new and uncharted territory that does not reflect previous experience emphasizing the primacy of proprietorial and trade secret concerns. Finally, community groups may be suspicious of information provided or promises made by both elected officials and industry representatives as a result of past confrontations or negative experiences.

All of these economic, political and social concerns must be considered as part of the team building process. Minimizing their importance will only hinder the team building effort. Directly addressing these historic differences and various interests through strong leadership and the development of mutually agreed upon goals will, in fact, strengthen the team building program that is required to implement the EPCRA appropriately.

Local communities will experience various levels of difficulty in establishing LEPCs. In some places, there will be a paucity of input from the various groups required by law to participate. Of particular concern here are unorganized interest groups such as community residents who do not have an identified voice in the community. In these instances, organizations such as church groups, American Heart Association or American Lung Association chapters and other health-oriented community organizations can be seen as fulfilling the requirement for community participation, especially when no organized environmental group exists.

Another problem hindering team building in a local community might be the lack of community expertise in the area of emergency response. In this situation, local university personnel, as well as consulting organizations, may provide the needed expertise. The use of such resources may be costly. However, these costs may be considered part of the proactive process and may save money in the long run if appropriate plans are developed and emergencies are avoided.

In other locations, there may be an abundance of input. Although it is hard to think of many places where this might occur, participation in the emergency planning process may become attractive, from a public relations standpoint, for a variety of institutions in the community. Representatives from firms and facilities, local health care providers and various environmental groups may want to participate actively in this process in order to build credibility, gain visibility and achieve a good public relations effect. In these cases, where there is an overabundance of participators, it is essential that volunteers not be turned away. However, committees that become unwieldy because of the vast number of people who want to participate can also be detrimental to the planning and team building process. In these cases, it is important for the chairman to develop a mechanism for handling this abundance of resources. One possible solution to this interesting dilemma is the creation of advisory groups to review plans publicly. This is, in fact, a requirement of the law itself. The development of task forces or subcommittees to provide a framework for greater participation and to create an environment for compromise among disparate groups may provide another solution.

Successful team building and cooperation among the various interests represented on the LEPC takes time. Patience should be the byword. If expectations are too high, implementation will be difficult. It is important to view the team building process in the context of long-term goals, as well as in terms of the immediate requirement of the law for developing an emergency plan.

SECTION 6.6. DEVELOPING THE EMERGENCY RESPONSE PLAN

Every local emergency plan will be different, since the possible risks involved, the local geography and the response capabilities will vary from location to location. Also, the SERCs in some states may propose and implement special requirements for emergency plans. Given these factors, the rest of this chapter will discuss the process of creating such a plan. Table 6.2 provides a schematic that is helpful in understanding the process. Table 6.3 provides a general outline that may also be helpful in thinking about emergency plans. Once again, the *Hazardous Materials Emergency Planning Guide* mentioned earlier is a very useful document in this process.

Several factors must be considered when developing this plan. First, the plan must be written to include understandable explanations of programs already in place. This is necessary so that the plan can provide guidance and clear instructions for new participants in the response process. Next, the plan must clearly identify step-by-step actions to take when responding to emergency incidents. Finally, the plan must contain provisions for personnel training and for evaluation and revision of the plan itself.

Development of the plan can be divided into a five-step process. These steps are necessary components for completing a plan. They can be subdivided further into more discrete tasks. However, a review of these five basic steps provides an overview of the total process.

The first step is to review any emergency plans that already exist. In many instances, local authorities have already established emergency response plans that can be expanded by the LEPC. These plans may have been developed by various organizations but never codified into a comprehensive document. Hospitals often develop emergency plans for handling multiple accident victims. Fire departments, in cooperation with local firms and facilities, may have also established emergency plans as a result of previous incidents or as part of prevention planning programs.

The second step is to identify chemicals in the community and, based on this assessment, to perform a hazard analysis. Hazard analysis will require individual expertise that the LEPC team members may have. If not, resources outside the LEPC will have to be found.

The third step is very important. It is essential that an assessment of current preparedness, prevention and response capabilities in the community be made. For example, does appropriate hazardous materials response equipment, including personal protective devices for first responders, exist?

Table 6.2 Overview of the Planning Process

```
  ┌──────┐      ┌─────────────────────┐
  │ Start│─────▶│ Determine that a    │
  └──────┘      │ Plan is Needed      │
                └─────────────────────┘
                          │
                ┌─────────────────────┐
                │ Select Planning Team│
                │ Members and Team    │
                │ Leader              │
                └─────────────────────┘
                          │
                ┌─────────────────────┐
       ┌───────▶│ Begin to Plan       │◀───────┐
       │        └─────────────────────┘        │
       │             │       │       │         │
┌──────────────┐ ┌──────────────┐ ┌──────────────────┐
│Review and    │ │Assess        │ │Conduct Hazards   │
│Coordinate    │ │Response      │ │Identification    │
│with Existing │ │Capabilities  │ │and Analysis      │
│Plans         │ └──────────────┘ └──────────────────┘
└──────────────┘   │        │
          ┌────────────────┐  ┌────────────────┐
          │Assess Industry │  │Assess Community│
          │Response        │  │Response        │
          │Capabilities    │  │Capabilities    │
          └────────────────┘  └────────────────┘
                      │
              ┌─────────────────┐
              │   Write Plan    │
              └─────────────────┘
    ┌──────────────────┐  or  ┌──────────────────┐
    │Develop or Revise │◀───▶ │Develop or Revise │
    │Multi-Hazard      │      │Hazardous         │
    │Emergency         │      │Materials         │
    │Operations Plan   │      │Emergency Plan    │
    └──────────────────┘      └──────────────────┘
              ┌─────────────────┐
              │Seek Plan Approval│
              └─────────────────┘
              ┌─────────────────┐
              │Revise, Test, and│
              │Maintain Plan    │
              └─────────────────┘
```

Source: Adapted from National Response Team, *Hazardous Materials Emergency Planning Guide,* Washington, D.C., 1987, p. 3.

Table 6.3 Hazardous Materials Emergency Response Plan Outline

A. LEPC Mission Statement
  1. Purpose and Authority
  2. Goals and Objectives
B. Legal Authority and Responsible Parties
C. Relationship to other Emergency Plans
D. Instructions for using the Hazardous Material Plan
E. Telephone Contacts for Emergency Assistance
F. Response Procedures
  1. Initial Notification
  2. Incident Command System, Direction, Control and Authority
  3. Lines of Communication Among Responders
  4. Warning Procedures and Emergency Public Notification
  5. Community and Public Information Program
  6. Citizen Protection
    a. Indoor Protection
    b. Evacuation Procedures
    c. Alternative Public Protection Strategies
      (1) Public Water Source Protection
      (2) Fire and Rescue
  7. Health Care Services
  8. Response Worker Protection Program
G. Containment and Cleanup
H. Follow-up Investigation and Documentation
I. Procedures for Testing and Updating the Plan
  Appendix 1: Abbreviation and Glossary
  Appendix 2: Record of the Initial Adoption of the Plan
        and Its Amendments
  Appendix 3: Hazard Analysis
  Appendix 4: Resources
    1. Laboratory, Consultants, Technical Support Services
    2. Library Services
    3. Emergency Telephone Numbers

Are there enough fire protection personnel in the community, and are they appropriately trained? If professional personnel are not currently available in existing government response agencies, are there volunteers who can implement the plan?

The fourth step is to complete the hazardous materials emergency response plan. This plan will be based on the information gathered in the preceding three steps. A sample outline plan has been included in Table 6.3.

The fifth step is to make sure that the plan works. This requires an ongoing plan for program review. This review process should be as open as possible and should encourage participation. Document review by both LEPC members and external experts, as well as citizens, will lend credibility to the planning process. Since experts are not always trusted by community members, it is important that community members be convinced, through participation and review, that the plan is adequate.

Besides the document review, the plan must be actually tested. Simulated implementation of the plan should involve all plan participants. Though these tests may at first involve only those responsible for implementation, there is great value in a publicly announced response simulation. This can include press coverage and community volunteers. Once this plan has been publicly tested, it is important to provide follow-up information on how the plan worked and what the LEPC is doing to correct its weaknesses.

As the plan is updated, it is important that all those who have responsibilities related to implementation of the plan, even if they are not part of the LEPC, be informed of these updates. It would be quite confusing if methods and routes of transportation for emergency response were changed and the participants were uninformed.

Finally, one of the most important evaluative procedures that should be instituted is a postincident review. When considering such a review, it is important that both the positive and negative aspects of the plan be considered. Positive as well as negative feedback will build the morale of the team and improve the plan. Of special concern in a postincident review is the effectiveness of communication among team members and responders. This will allow evaluation of the communication procedures. Since communication is an essential element of the planning process, breakdowns in communication should be identified and corrected.

SECTION 6.7. PROTECTION OF EMERGENCY RESPONSE PERSONNEL

There has been growing interest in ensuring that emergency response personnel are protected while responding to emergency situations. Regulations for a hazardous materials worker protection standard were mandated by the original SARA. This standard, issued by OSHA as 29 CFR 1910.120, is discussed in detail in Chapter 7.

Chapter 7
TRAINING, PERSONAL PROTECTIVE EQUIPMENT AND MEDICAL SURVEILLANCE

SECTION 7.1. INTRODUCTION

Training of employees has become an implementation focus of Right-to-Know and hazard communication rules and regulations. These requirements combine concepts of risk communication and behavioral goals. The underlying principle is that individuals cannot be expected to perform tasks in a safe manner unless they are taught how to do so. Training requirements for the early efforts at environmental regulation were limited and not very specific. As the legislation became more complex and inclusive, these training requirements grew in scope as well.

In addition to an increased emphasis on training, SARA has codified medical surveillance requirements for those involved in a wide range of activities related to hazardous materials. Of particular importance here are the medical surveillance requirements for emergency response personnel. The rules also cover individuals involved in RCRA (controlled hazardous waste site operations) and those involved in Superfund (uncontrolled hazardous waste site) activity. Since this requirement covers a much broader range of employees, it was not made a part of Title III. Instead, it appears in Section 126 of SARA. It required that OSHA develop a standard concerning health and safety conditions of employment as well as medical surveillance.

It is interesting to note that the law specifically mandates that the training, medical surveillance and worker protection provisions apply to state and local employees because some state governments do not have programs in place to protect state and local employees under OSHA provisions. Since OSHA traditionally has not covered state employees unless the states themselves expand that coverage, the intent of Congress here is clear. Congress wanted to make sure that all state and local government employers were required to protect employees from health hazards on the job at a level of safety equal to or greater than that required by private firms already covered by the OSHA standard.

In the rest of this chapter, training requirements, training programs, worker protection and medical surveillance will be discussed. The purpose is to provide information for implementing worker protection compliance programs.

It is important to recognize that these standards and requirements can change over time. At the time of the writing of this book, interim standards for medical surveillance and training have been established. Final standards will probably be issued by early 1989. Until that time, the interim standards must be implemented. The approach to training and medical surveillance codified in the interim standards has been developed over several years of OSHA activity. The interim standards, as they have been published, reflect this understanding. It is unlikely that major changes in these standards will occur though the requirements will probably become more specific. Anyone who has responsibility for implementing these programs, particularly in the areas of training and worker protection, should request a copy of these standards from OSHA or the EPA and read them carefully. This standard appears at 29 CFR 1910.120. It should *not* be confused with the Hazard Communication Standard, which appears at 29 CFR 1900.1200.

SECTION 7.2. TRAINING REQUIREMENTS

Subsection 7.2.1. Training Overview

The increased importance placed on training indicates an underlying assumption that knowing about hazards and how to protect onself from undue exposure to these hazards will lead to behavioral changes, so that work on the job will become safer. Though this link between knowing and doing is not always as definite as one would like (for example, many people know of the hazards associated with smoking, but still, through habit and addiction, continue to smoke), it is clear that without knowing, it is impossible to act appropriately when facing hazards.

There is growing evidence in the professional literature that behavioral changes regarding chemicals can result from training. We also know through anecdotal experience that there is an increased awareness of the hazards associated with chemicals. For example, one sometimes still hears people say, "I've worked with this chemical for thirty years, and it hasn't hurt me yet. Why do I have to do anything now?" Prior to Worker Right-to-Know efforts, this was a common occurrence. Now a more common statement by employees is, "If you knew this chemical caused cancer, why did you wait so long to tell me about it?"

In fact, general awareness of the potential hazards of chemicals has increased. Firefighters, often the lead group in emergency response situations, have over time changed their approaches to hazardous materials incidents. In earlier days, emergency response personnel actively fought chemical fires, patrolled burning tank trucks, and traversed a highway where such trucks had caught fire. Today the more common practice of first responders is to allow these fires to continue to burn until all combustion has ceased.

Over time, through training and experience, firefighters have begun to learn that the risk associated with possible explosion or spreading of the fire is greater than the risk of delaying rush hour traffic.

When implementing training programs, it is recommended that a formal hazard communication plan be written. With this step, one can be assured that, if the training program is implemented as intended and described in the plan, the program will be in compliance with current laws and regulations. Thorough documentation of training program activities is essential.

Subsection 7.2.2. Specific Training Requirements of 29 CFR 1910.120

Section (l)(3) of 29 CFR 1910.120 specifically describes the training requirements for employees responding to emergency incidents. Employees involved in emergency response organizations and teams such as fire brigades, fire departments, firm or facility emergency organizations, hazardous materials teams, spill response teams or any other group responsible for emergency response must be trained appropriately.

The law requires that a training program be specific in length, depending upon the type of work that the individual does. In some cases, particularly with regard to firefighters and police officers, specific training requirements may exist at state and local levels as well.

These individuals must be trained to a level of competence that will enable them to protect themselves and other employees in the recognition of health and safety hazards. Specific curriculum items specified by the standard include:

1. Methods to minimize the risk from safety and health hazards
2. Safe use of control equipment
3. Selection and use of appropriate personal protective equipment
4. Safe operating procedures to be used at the scene of the incident
5. Coordination techniques to use with others in order to minimize risks
6. Appropriate response to overexposure to health hazards or to injury to oneself and other employees
7. Recognition of subsequent symptoms which may result from overexposure

The standard recognizes that everyone who may be involved in responding to hazardous materials incidents does not need to receive the total curriculum. This would be unrealistic, since all police officers who are the first to respond to an accidental release would have to have such training. Instead, the standard prescribes a more reasonable approach. This alternative approach requires that persons who are the first to arrive at an emergency incident must be given awareness training. This training is intended to provide information on recognizing that an emergency response situation exists.

Without complete training, these persons must be instructed not to attempt to control the hazard themselves. Instead, they should be instructed to summon a response team that is fully trained.

These incident response groups, called "HAZMAT teams" are expected to be able to perform at a high level of competence. Training is used to achieve this performance level. The interum standard requires HAZMAT team members to receive a minimum of 24 hours of training annually, with training sessions provided on a monthly basis. This minimum may increase over time, as these standards are revised and finalized.

Subsection 7.2.3. Setting up a Training Program

The procedures and processes used to set up a health and safety training program for emergency response personnel or employees who handle hazardous materials are similar to those used to set up the EPCRA program itself. Instead of focusing on the overall program, they focus on specific training requirements.

Training, to be effective, should not be seen as a one-time effort, but rather as a continuing process. Learning by doing is considered one of the most effective methods of training. Actual experience in carrying out emergency response programs cannot replace classroom learning. It is essential to understand that the training process is ongoing and continuous. Though the law requires specific classroom time allocations, for some persons a well-thought-out training program will include refresher and reinforcement opportunities. For emergency responders, such activities as emergency drills, simulations and inspections of equipment and certification of their readiness, can all be part of a training program.

The 29CFR 1910.120 interum regulation recognizes this concept when it allows employees to certify their competence rather than providing specific classroom training requirements. Research literature, as well as common sense, tells us that if skills are learned in a classroom and are not tested in practice, the further in time one gets from the actual training process, the less likely one will remember how to perform them. Therefore, training in the use of respiratory protection equipment, for example, needs to be reinforced routinely if the equipment is not used regularly.

Developing training programs can be expensive and time-consuming. Often, using existing institutions such as universities or private consulting firms that have appropriate training programs may be more cost effective than developing an entirely new program. However, since classroom instruction is only one part of the training process, it will be necessary to consider the broader training context, including ongoing reinforcement through the simulation and testing of systems in place for community response.

The need for such an approach points out a very important aspect of the training process. Everyone understands that training communicates information and develops skills for people involved in the training activities. However, the training program itself cannot establish policy. It is the role of training to communicate policies and procedures, not to create them. As a result, the training program must reflect the actual response program that has been developed. A training program can never accomplish its goals unless the response program it is based on is itself strong. Communication of information will only be as good as the information itself. The weakness in a community response plan will become obvious when trying to explain it during a training program.

Developing a training program can be divided into 10 steps:

1. Training needs assessment
2. Develop training goals and objectives
3. Determine a target audience for training
4. Based on the above criteria, determine the contents of a training program
5. Plan the training program presentation
6. Make the presentation itself
7. Evaluate the program
8. Document the program
9. Determine the need for ongoing training activities
10. Implement ongoing training activities

The steps required to implement these procedures parallel those required for the overall EPCRA program. A fair amount of information has been developed to assist firms, facilities and institutions in developing appropriate training programs. One such document is the OSHA voluntary guidelines on the development of training programs. This document is available from OSHA. It was originally published in the Federal Register on July 27, 1984. In addition, several books and magazines are devoted to this subject. Information about them appears in Chapter 8. Persons responsible for developing safety training programs should read this literature and become familiar with the procedures.

Pedagogical techniques for training about environmental health and safety activities can be debated. Approaches vary from firm to firm or community to community, but there are certain things that should be integrated into a training program.

First of all, the program must recognize that as one's responsibility and authority increase, one's understanding must also increase. Therefore, continuing education for all people involved is a necessity. Also, the scientific knowledge about the hazards associated with chemicals continues to increase, as does our understanding of the techniques used to prevent exposure. Because of this, there is a need to continue to upgrade our level of performance and understanding of these issues. Finally, lectures and book learning are fine and are required to understand an environmental safety and emergency response plan. However, since this program is so directly dependent on the activities of the participants, actual hands-on experience with equipment is an essential and necessary component of health and safety training.

In closing, identifying lively and knowledgeable instructors is central to a successful training program. Many believe that teaching is an art and that some people are especially good educational artists. A program can be improved as a result of strong instructional leadership.

SECTION 7.3. A PERSONAL PROTECTIVE EQUIPMENT PROGRAM

Two OSHA standards govern the use of personal protective equipment (PPE) when responding to hazardous materials incidents. The most recently issued standard is 29 CFR 1910.120, the hazardous waste site worker standard. The other standard, 29 CFR 1910.134, is the OSHA respirator standard. The PPE that is subject to these requirements includes the various types of breathing apparatus and the protective clothing such as totally encapsulating chemical protective suits.

Emergency response personnel, when responding to emergency releases, are required by 1910.120 (l)(3)(ii)(D) to wear positive-pressure–self-contained breathing apparatus. This rule is in force until the person in charge determines, through the use of air monitoring, that a decreased level of respiratory protection will not result in hazardous exposure to the employees responding to the incident.

It is necessary to develop a written program for the use of PPE, especially when apparatus to protect employees from breathing contaminated air is used. Both standards require such a written program. It is also logical that such a document be developed and implemented.

Employees using this equipment must also receive training in its use and limitations. This training must include hands-on experience with the equipment. When training programs are designed to fulfill requirements of the various laws and standards, instruction and practice with PPE becomes a major component of the curriculum. Community-based firefighters and facility-based fire brigades should spend a significant amount of time working with PPE, practicing with it, maintaining it and updating it.

Respirator specifications are established and tested by the National Institute of Occupational Health (NIOSH). This organization, established by the OSHA act and part of the Department of Health and Human Services, is

Table 7.1 Elements of a PPE Program

1. Possible site hazards (based on a community hazard analysis)
2. Employee medical fitness for wearing respiratory PPE
3. Conditions of use for PPE
4. Specifics related to the work mission, its duration and the medical support available on site
5. Selection of PPE
6. Maintenance and storage of PPE
7. Decontamination procedures
8. Fitting for appropriate PPE
9. Donning and doffing PPE
10. PPE inspection schedule and procedure
11. Monitoring PPE while in use
12. Limitations of PPE at extreme temperatures

headquartered in Cincinnati. At its laboratory in Morgantown, West Virginia, the PPE is tested. Each approved respirator is issued a NIOSH certification number, which must appear on the device itself.

The use of PPE requires preplacement medical exams. The purpose of this exam is to evaluate the physical capability of an individual to use such equipment. Since breathing apparatus can create additional stress on the lungs, breathing capacity plays an important role in the ability to use the equipment safely.

The elements of a PPE program appear in Table 7.1. This program is expected to be summarized in written document that is available to and can be copied by employees who are subject to its requirements. It is important to note that this program must be seen as part of the emergency response plan discussed in Chapter 6; as such, it must be available for public scrutiny. As the use of PPE increases, appropriate plans and the testing of these plans will also become more important. Developing such a plan takes special expertise in the selection, use and maintenance of PPE. In many communities, local volunteer fire departments do not have the funds to purchase and maintain this equipment. In these cases, local industry may provide the needed resources to establish such a program.

SECTION 7.4. MEDICAL SURVEILLANCE

Medical examinations for emergency response personnel are necessary and required by various standards. There are three reasons for this activity. The first is to determine an individual's fitness to wear PPE, particularly respiratory PPE, on the job. Another reason has to do with the stress of the work. If the work is particularly heavy or if it needs to be done in hot environments, it is important to know if a person's biological systems can perform under this stress. Finally, the medical exam provides information about the health effects that may result from exposure to hazardous chemicals.

One of the regulatory requirements mandating physical exams for emergency response personnel is the previously discussed OSHA standard, 29 CFR 1910.134. This standard covers respiratory PPE and requires all persons who wear it while performing their job to have a medical examination to determine their fitness for equipment use. The respirators covered by this standard include the half-face piece dust or fume respirators, negative-pressure respirators, supplied-air respirators and air-purifying respirators.

Section 126 of SARA, entitled "Worker Protection Standards," also requires a program of regular medical examinations, monitoring and surveillance of workers engaged in hazardous waste operations which expose them to toxic substances. This requirement also pertains to emergency response personnel who may be exposed to a hazardous substance above established exposure levels. It is codified in Section 1910, 120 (iii)(f), of 29 CFR OSHA.

The standard defers to the medical profession for determining the content of the exam. However, it is clear on a few things. First, the exam must be done by a physician or under a physician's supervision; a physician must give a written opinion concerning the exam; and finally, the employee must have access to the report. The standard also requires that the exam be performed and paid for by the employer, not the employee. An exam must be conducted prior to assignment, then at least once every 12 months, and at termination if the employee has not been examined in the last 6 months.

Employees are often reluctant to undergo medical examinations associated with their work. However, since working with hazardous materials is potentially harmful to one's health, baseline and repeat medical monitoring is advisable. The purpose is to determine the acute results of exposure or the employee's work capabilities. These exams, occurring on an annual basis, are also meant to track the chronic and subacute effects of exposure to hazardous chemicals.

Finding personnel to provide these services at the local level may be difficult. The discipline of occupational and environmental medicine is highly specialized, and fewer than 1,000 physicians in the United States are trained and board certified to practice it. There are several universities with occupational medicine training programs funded by NIOSH. These training programs have generated and increased the number of professionals in this area, but the number still remains small.

Growing numbers of physicians are taking an interest in occupational and environmental medicine. Since this area of expertise is highly technical and specific, it is important to find someone with special experience and training. A good source of such physicians is the American Academy of Occupational Medicine, located at 2340 S. Arlington Heights Road, Arlington Heights, IL 60005. It is important to identify a reliable and experienced source to provide services. It may be necessary to pay additional fees in order to find a credible specialist, but the requirements of the law are so specific that a physician who is unfamiliar with this standard may not be able to provide appropriate services.

Chapter 8
RESOURCES FOR IMPLEMENTATION

SECTION 8.1. INTRODUCTION

Garnering resources to implement EPCRA programs may be difficult, especially during times when the funds for such programs are severely restricted. Firms are also hesitant to authorize expenditures for such support programs. Often it is difficult to justify support for prevention programs—exactly the kinds of programs EPCRA is meant to encourage. It is ironic that while SARA levied a tax on industry to raise funds to clean up existing uncontrolled hazardous waste sites, often called "Superfund sites," and a mechanism for funding emergency spill cleanups, the law provided no money for implementing EPCRA activities at the state and local levels. Given the scarcity of funds, it is important to identify resources that communities can use to help implement this law at the local level.

SECTION 8.2. FUNDING RESOURCES IN THE PUBLIC SECTOR

The most obvious resources to consider for community-based implementation are financial ones. With appropriate financial backing, program implementation will, of course, become a much smoother process. However, the reality is that many state and local governments do not have excess revenues to devote to EPCRA activities. Since many of the responsibilities for these programs overlap among various governmental agencies, it is also possible that jurisdictional disputes regarding allocation of funds may occur.

Various states and localities have chosen different methods to fund EPCRA compliance programs. Among the variations to consider are:

1. Reallocating funds in existing budgets of pertinent agencies or creating new line items in these budgets.
2. Receiving separate budgetary allocations from state or local legislatures. This can be done through the use of special grants-in-aid.
3. Taxing producers of chemicals for their chemical usage. Such taxation can be indirect; for example, some states have used a fee system for firms that file information under EPCRA.

Each of these funding sources has advantages and disadvantages. The first alternative (using existing budgets) may result in shifting funds from a program that has less support or is harder to justify than EPCRA programs. This may result in the demise or deemphasis of some existing programs. However, if EPCRA funding can be made a budgetary line item, it will be easier to obtain funding on an annual basis. It is often easier to receive funds annually for an existing budgetary line item than to seek special grants or allocations for specific programs year after year. By making EPCRA enforcement programs part of the standing operations of the organization, it becomes easier to justify the continued expenditures.

The second option, special grants or allocations for EPCRA programs, can be useful as well. These grants can fund startup costs or special projects and purchases required to maintain an effective EPCRA program. However, they have one serious disadvantage as a long-term funding scheme for EPCRA compliance. Since EPCRA was designed to be an ongoing, consistent process, and since its success depends upon this consistency, returning year after year to funding authorities such as state legislatures and county boards is counterproductive, since it can only deplete resources for implementation. Anyone who has ever been involved in the budget authorization process knows that governmental bodies are often reluctant to allocate funds on a special basis without large amounts of information and justification of need. Providing that kind of input year after year is time-consuming and often demoralizing. Therefore, authorizing funding over a multiyear period is preferred over annual requests.

The third funding source for public agencies is taxation. Here again, there are advantages and disadvantages. Requiring firms to pay filing fees when submitting information to state and local agencies may seem efficient and effective as a new source of revenue. However, charging firms to fulfill requirements may discourage compliance. Some states, such as North Carolina, have chosen this option. It will take a while to see whether this method is effective. An alternative source of funds from chemical users might be fines levied against those firms that do not comply with the law. This mechanism has been written into the law; in fact, the fines authorized by the law may seem high—as much as $25,000 to $75,000 a day. However, the costs and time involved in collecting these fines may be great. It is not realistic to consider fines as a source of day-to-day operating budgets for these programs.

Persons who are seeking public sector funding for their program, regardless of which of the three mechanisms or others is chosen, should be realistic about their expectations. Documenting and justifying the activities and costs, and quantifying as best as possible the benefits of these programs, are essential. If there is one thing that legislators understand, it is public pressure. Therefore, efforts to justify funding based on public sentiment regarding prevention of environmental incidents can be an important strategy.

SECTION 8.3. FUNDING RESOURCES IN THE PRIVATE SECTOR

In the private sector as well, resources for prevention are often scarce. Health and safety professionals in firms complain that their programs are the first to be cut in times of financial scarcity. However, the climate, to some extent, is changing. Because of the intense public concern about environmental safety and the repeated examples of unsafe industrial practices leading to major accidents, firms have become more cognizant of the need for funding, particularly in regard to EPCRA.

The budgeting process in firms varies markedly from place to place. Once again, startup costs as well as operating expenses should be considered when developing budgetary requirements for implementing EPCRA programs.

In the private sector, as in the public sector, corporate decision makers must be made aware of the increased pressure being placed on firms to implement these programs. In many industries, particularly those that use large quantities of chemicals, the attention that top executives pay to the environment has increased rapidly. Since these programs must be funded by increasing the price of products manufactured or services provided, or by reducing the profits distributed to stockholders, justification of program expenditures for EPCRA to some extent depends on the organizational culture, as well as on the willingness and ability of firms to absorb these costs.

In both the public and the private sector, the funding process can take on a political character that may complicate the issues. It is important to be aware of this and to take appropriate action when preparing budget requests. In the public sector, developing the broadest possible coalition to support funding efforts is an appropriate strategy. In the private sector, soliciting and receiving support for EPCRA programs from the highest corporate officials is effective.

Another strategy for increasing the funding in the private sector is to evaluate the various places in the corporate structure where spending for environmental control programs occurs. Often these programs are scattered throughout the organization. If consolidation can reduce program overlap, financial resources may be utilized in a more efficient manner.

SECTION 8.4. OTHER TYPES OF RESOURCES

Funding is not the only resource to consider when implementing EPCRA programs. These programs require the cooperation of both firms and facilities, as well as local, state and federal governments, and resources can be found in the public and/or the private sector. In a cooperative effort, it is possible that there will be cross-fertilization of resources between the public and private sectors. In some places, however, this level of cooperation may not be possible. Even within the public sector itself, there are overlapping jurisdictions and "turf battles" that can affect the way different agencies cooperate.

However, in spite of these potential difficulties, it is important to remember that providing resources can result in public relations benefits. Volunteering nonfinancial support services for EPCRA implementation provides an opportunity for individuals, organizations, firms and facilities to build networks in the community. For example, health care providers and independent consultants, as well as community residents with special expertise, often volunteer resources in order to give themselves exposure and build credibility.

Accepting these kinds of voluntary efforts can be helpful but may also create a new set of problems. Because the services are voluntary, and because the individuals and organizations may not place the highest priority on providing them, there may be a resulting lack of consistency. In spite of this, it is very important that program implementators not neglect opportunities to develop voluntary support network for their programs. And in order to minimize these problems, getting commitments on the part of voluntary providers that are either in writing or publicly stated can help ensure that these resources are provided on a regular and consistent basis.

The types of voluntary resources to consider fall into four categories; personnel, technical support, equipment needs and direct services. Skilled personnel for implementing these programs are often hard to find. Though personnel needs may be limited during program planning and maintenance phases, they may be increased at the time of an emergency. Volunteers who identify themselves at a time of crisis can be helpful but are not adequate for planning purposes. Therefore, identifying individuals who can support programs requires attention and time. The types of volunteers required during an emergency include individuals with transport vehicles such as school buses or trucks to move people and equipment. Staffing schools or other facilities for people who have been evacuated from their homes are also necessary. Personnel needs will vary depending upon the potential hazards and the community risk analysis. Recruiting personnel with varying types and levels of expertise required for the emergency response activities is an essential part of the program planning activities.

Another form of support and a resource to consider are individuals with appropriate technical skills. This area overlaps with personnel resource issues because most technical support is provided by individuals. However, some clear-cut technical needs can be identified, and people with these skills may be available. Computer and data base management skills are growing areas of expertise for many citizens. Planners may find someone in the community who is already employed by a government agency or in the private sector and who can help develop the technical aspects of the program's information management systems. This person might not be appropriate for providing direct emergency response input, but can be very useful in setting up computer systems for implementing such programs. Other people with technical skills to consider are those with expertise in the medical and environmental hazards associated with chemicals. People with skills in public relations and communications may also provide a useful resource.

Emergency response equipment is often expensive to purchase and difficult to maintain. Identifying existing equipment resources and allocating those resources for the emergency planning process can be helpful. Often large private firms have firefighting and emergency response equipment on hand. With proper agreements in place, these resources can be utilized during emergencies. The equipment may also be useful when carrying out drills and tests of emergency response plans.

Volunteer services can also be a resource to consider when designing and implementing EPCRA programs. Local health care facilities may be willing to provide, at a reduced fee or no fee at all, training for cardiopulmonary resuscitation or first aid. Local firms may be willing to volunteer the services of professional staff to help train others for emergency response.

SECTION 8.5. WHERE TO FIND RESOURCES

Whether one is developing private or public sector EPCRA programs, it is often the case that resources available within the organization are ignored. Since cooperation is an assumption of the EPCRA, identifying resources within organizations may, in fact, provide a lot of help that might otherwise go untapped.

In the public sector, the agencies that should be considered for potential resources are fire departments, police departments and emergency management agencies. However, there are other agencies to consider. First of all, health departments often contain staff with expertise in a variety of appropriate disciplines. Toxicologists and epidemiologists are the first that come to mind, but soil and water testing personnel may also be available and may provide technical expertise. In addition, the staff at public hospitals and community-based health care facilities may have knowledge and interest in these areas. Though the EPCRA is particularly geared to community concerns, the resources that may exist in state and local departments of labor, particularly those people involved in regulating occupational health, can provide an untapped resource for environmental control.

In the private sector, those responsible for EPCRA planning do not always look to other groups within the organization to support their activities. For local operations, it is important to assess resources that may exist at the corporate level of the firm. Often corporate-level staff is dedicated to the tasks required for EPCRA. The availability of these resources is not always communicated to the firms at the local level. Support from corporate headquarters is an untapped resource to consider.

Another important resource in firms and facilities is the public support of chief executive officers and top plant and facility personnel. Public, verbal and written statements that support the EPCRA effort will make it much easier to get cooperation within the organization for the programs one is responsible for developing.

There are several departments in the firm or facility that may have responsibility for environmental and occupational health control. These include engineering departments, personnel departments, health insurance and risk management departments, and occupational health and safety units. Training departments or human resource departments may also provide a helpful resource. Any of these departments may have the responsibility to lead the EPCRA implementation effort. Whichever group is assigned primary authority, it makes sense to look to other departments for support. In the private sector, using the team approach for EPCRA programs will result in added resources even though the lead group may not directly control these resources. Here again, rivalries can make it more difficult to recruit such support, but it is in the interest of the firm to develop this cooperative effort.

SECTION 8.6. EXTERNAL RESOURCES

Looking within the organization for resources to develop EPCRA programs is certainly useful. But this support is not always available. As a result, those with direct responsibility for EPCRA implementation must often find resources outside of the organization. There are a variety of external resources to consider and a variety of sources for such support.

Subsection 8.6.1. Professional Organizations

Many organizations of safety and health professionals can provide training and information services for implementing EPCRA programs. Among these are the National Safety Council, the Professional Firefighters Association, the American Industrial Hygiene Association, the American Society of Safety Engineers, the American Chemical Society, the American Occupational Medicine Association and the American Occupational Nursing Association. These organizations produce documents and set standards for the implementation and standardization of various aspects of EPCRA programs.

Subsection 8.6.2. Trade Associations

Most industries have established trade associations which provide services to members. The trade association with the most direct involvement in

Community Right-to-Know programs is the Chemical Manufacturers Association. Over the last decade, they have developed a variety of programs such as the Chemical Awareness and Emergency Response (CAERO) program to assist member firms and communities to develop Community Right-to-Know programs. Many other groups have also developed programs that help members implement EPCRA compliance activities.

Subsection 8.6.3. Government Resources

At the federal level, the EPA and the FEMA have both developed programs to help local planning agencies and others implementing EPCRA. These resources can be found by contacting the agency. However, these assistance programs have received only limited funding. Given these limited resources, the EPA and the FEMA have used most of their funds to develop printed materials for implementers.

States have also developed programs to assist constituents. The SERC can direct planners to these resources. Other state assistance may be found at colleges and universities involved in training and education programs for handling of hazardous materials.

Subsection 8.6.4. Marketplace Resources

There are many firms in the health and safety services and product markets that offer EPCRA compliance materials. These include newsletters, educational materials, video and audiovisual training aids, safety products such as respirators and protective clothing, and computer programs. These products and services should be chosen carefully, since the price does not always reflect the quality. A good rule of thumb is to consider the age and reputation of the firm. A new group entering the marketplace may not have sufficient background and experience in the health and safety field. Checking the references provided by service organizations can be informative for anyone making a purchasing decision.

(1) Identification of facilities subject to the requirements of this subtitle that are within the emergency planning district, identification of routes likely to be used for the transportation of substances on the list of extremely hazardous substances referred to in section 302(a), and identification of additional facilities contributing or subjected to additional risk due to their proximity to facilities subject to the requirements of this subtitle, such as hospitals or natural gas facilities.

(2) Methods and procedures to be followed by facility owners and operators and local emergency and medical personnel to respond to any release of such substances.

(3) Designation of a community emergency coordinator and facility emergency coordinators, who shall make determinations necessary to implement the plan.

(4) Procedures providing reliable, effective, and timely notification by the facility emergency coordinators and the community emergency coordinator to persons designated in the emergency plan, and to the public, that a release has occurred (consistent with the emergency notification requirements of section 304).

(5) Methods for determining the occurrence of a release, and the area or population likely to be affected by such release.

(6) A description of emergency equipment and facilities in the community and at each facility in the community subject to the requirements of this subtitle, and an identification of the persons responsible for such equipment and facilities.

(7) Evacuation plans, including provisions for a precautionary evacuation and alternative traffic routes.

(8) Training programs, including schedules for training of local emergency response and medical personnel.

(9) Methods and schedules for exercising the emergency plan.

(d) PROVIDING OF INFORMATION.—For each facility subject to the requirements of this subtitle:

(1) Within 30 days after establishment of a local emergency planning committee for the emergency planning district in which such facility is located, or within 11 months (9/17/87) after the date of the enactment of this title, whichever is earlier, the owner or operator of the facility shall notify the emergency planning committee (or the Governor if there is no committee) of a facility representative who will participate in the emergency planning process as a facility emergency coordinator.

(2) The owner or operator of the facility shall promptly inform the emergency planning committee of any relevant changes occurring at such facility as such changes occur or are expected to occur.

(3) Upon request from the emergency planning committee, the owner or operator of the facility shall promptly provide information to such committee necessary for developing and implementing the emergency plan.

(e) REVIEW BY THE STATE EMERGENCY RESPONSE COMMISSION.—After completion of an emergency plan under subsection (a) for an emergency planning district, the local emergency planning committee shall submit a copy of the plan to the State emergency response commission of each State in which such district is located. The commission shall review the plan and make recommendations to the committee on revisions of the plan that may be necessary to ensure coordination of such plan with emergency response plans of other emergency planning district. To the maximum extent practicable, such review shall not delay implementation of such plan.

(f) GUIDANCE DOCUMENTS.—The national response team, as established pursuant to the National Contingency Plan as established under section 105 of the Comprehensive Environmental Response, Compensation, and Liability Act of 1980 (42 U.S.C. 9601 et seq.), shall publish guidance documents for preparation and implementation of emergency plans. Such documents shall be published not later than five months after the date of the enactment of this title.

(g) REVIEW OF PLANS BY REGIONAL RESPONSE TEAMS.—The regional response teams, as established pursuant to the National Contingency Plan as established under section 105 of the Comprehensive Environmental Response, Compensation, and Liability Act of 1980 (42 U.S.C. 9601 et seq.), may review and comment upon an emergency plan or other issues related to preparation, implementation, or exercise of such a plan upon request of a local emergency planning committee. Such review shall not delay implementation of the plan.

SEC. 304. EMERGENCY NOTIFICATION.

(a) TYPES OF RELEASES.—

(1) 302(a) SUBSTANCE WHICH REQUIRES CERCLA NOTICE.—If a release of an extremely hazardous substance referred to in section 302(a) occurs from a facility at which a hazardous chemical is produced, used, or stored, and such release requires a notification under section 103(a) of the Comprehensive Environmental Response, Compensation, and Liability Act of 1980 (hereafter in this section referred to as "CERCLA")(42 U.S.C. 9601 et seq.), the owner or operator of the facility shall immediately provide notice as described in subsection(b).

(2) OTHER 302(a) SUBSTANCE.—If a release of an extremely hazardous substance referred to in section 302(a) occurs from a facility at which a hazardous chemical is produced, used, or stored, and such release is not subject to the notification requirements under section 103(a) of CERCLA, the owner or operator of the facility shall immediately provide notice as described in subsection (b), but only if the release—

(A) is not a federally permitted release as defined in section 101(10) of CERCLA,

(B) is in an amount in excess of a quantity which the Administrator has determined (by regulation) requires notice, and

(C) occurs in a manner which would require notification under section 103(a) of CERCLA.

(3) NON-302(a) SUBSTANCE WHICH REQUIRES CERCLA NOTICE.—If a release of a substance which is not on the list referred to in section 302(a) occurs at a facility at which a hazardous chemical is produced, used, or stored,

and such release requires notification under section 103(a) of CERCLA, the owner or operator shall provide notice as follows:

(A) If the substance is one for which a reportable quantity has been established under section 102(a) of CERCLA, the owner or operator shall provide notice as described in subsection (b).

(B) If the substance is one for which a reportable quantity has not been established under section 102(a) of CERCLA—

(i) Until April 30, 1988, the owner or operator shall provide, for releases of one pound or more of the substance, the same notice to the community emergency coordinator for the local emergency planning committee, at the same time and in the same form, as notice is provided to the National Response Center under section 103(a) of CERCLA.

(ii) On and after April, 1988, the owner or operator shall provide, for releases of one pound or more of the substance, the notice as described in subsection (b).

(4) EXEMPTED RELEASES.—This section does not apply to any release which results in exposure to persons solely within the site or sites on which a facility is located.

(b) NOTIFICATION.—

(1) RECIPIENTS OF NOTICE.—Notice required under subsection (a) shall be given immediately after the release by the owner or operator of a facility (by such means as telephone, radio, or in person) to the community emergency coordinator for the local emergency planning committees, if established pursuant to section 301(c), for any area likely to be affected by the release and to the State emergency planning commission of any State likely to be affected by the release. With respect to transportation of a substance subject to the requirements of this section, or storage incident to such transportation, the notice requirements of this section with respect to a release shall be satisfied by dialing 911 or, in the absence of a 911 emergency telephone number, calling the operator.

(2) CONTENTS.—Notice required under subsection (a) shall include each of the following (to the extent known at the time of the notice and so long as no delay in responding to the emergency results):

(A) The chemical name or identity of any substance involved in the release.

(B) An indication of whether the substance is on the list referred to in section 302(a).

(C) An estimate of the quantity of any such substance that was released into the environment.

(D) The time and duration of the release.

(E) The medium or media into which the release occurred.

(F) Any known or anticipated acute or chronic health risks associated with the emergency and, where appropriate, advice regarding medical attention necessary for exposed individuals.

(G) Proper precautions to take as a result of the release, including evacuation (unless such information is readily available to the community emergency coordinator pursuant to the emergency plan).

(H) The name and telephone number of the person or persons to be contacted for further information.

(c) FOLLOWUP EMERGENCY NOTICE.—As soon as practicable after a release which requires notice under subsection (a), such owner or operator shall provide a written followup emergency notice (or notices, as more information becomes available) setting forth and updating the information required under subsection (b), and including additional information with respect to-

(1) actions taken to respond to and contain the release.

(2) any known or anticipated acute or chronic health risks associated with the release, and

(3) where appropriate, advice regarding medical attention necessary for exposed individuals.

(d) TRANSPORTATION EXEMPTION NOT APPLICABLE.—The exemption provided in section 327 (relating to transportation) does not apply to this section.

SEC. 305. EMERGENCY TRAINING AND REVIEW OF EMERGENCY SYSTEMS.

(a) EMERGENCY TRAINING.—

(1) PROGRAMS.—Officials of the United States Government carrying out existing Federal programs for emergency training are authorized to specifically provide training and education programs for Federal, State, and local personnel in hazard mitigation, emergency preparedness, fire prevention and control, disaster response, long-term disaster recovery, national security, technological and natural hazards, and emergency processes. Such programs shall provide special emphasis for such training and education with respect to hazardous chemicals.

(2) STATE AND LOCAL PROGRAM SUPPORT.—There is authorized to be appropriated to the Federal Emergency Management Agency for each of the fiscal years 1987, 1988, 1989, and 1990, $5,000,000 for making grants to support programs of State and local governments, and to support university-sponsored programs, which are designed to improve emergency planning, preparedness, mitigation, response, and recovery capabilities. Such programs shall provide special emphasis with respect to emergencies associated with hazardous chemicals. Such grants may not exceed 80 percent of the cost of any such program. The remaining 20 percent of such costs shall be funded from non-Federal sources.

(3) OTHER PROGRAMS.—Nothing in this section shall affect the availability of appropriations to the Federal Emergency Management Agency for any programs carried out by such agency other than the programs referred to in paragraph (2).

(b) REVIEW OF EMERGENCY SYSTEMS.—

(1) REVIEW.—The Administrator shall initiate, not later than 30 days (11/16/86) after the date of the enactment of this title, a review of emergency systems for monitoring, detecting, and preventing releases of extremely hazardous substances at representative domestic facilities that produce, use, or store extremely hazardous substances. The Administrator may select representative extremely hazardous substances from the substances on the list referred to in section 302(a) for the

purposes of this review. The Administrator shall report interim findings to the Congress not later than seven months after such date of enactment, and issue a final report of findings and recommendations to the Congress not later than 18 months after such date of enactment. Such report shall be prepared in consultation with the States and appropriate Federal agencies.

(2) REPORT.—The report required by this subsection shall include the Administrator's findings regarding each of the following:

(A) The status of current technological capabilities to (i) monitor, detect, and prevent, in a timely manner, significant releases of extremely hazardous substances, (ii) determine the magnitude and direction of the hazard posed by each release, (iii) identify specific substances, (iv) provide data on the specific chemical composition of such releases, and (v) determine the relative concentrations of the constituent substances.

(B) The status of public emergency alert devices or systems for providing timely and effective public warning of an accidental release of extremely hazardous substances into the environment, including releases into the atmosphere, surface water, or groundwater from facilities that produce, store, or use significant quantities of such extremely hazardous substances.

(C) The technical and economic feasibility of establishing, maintaining, and operating perimeter alert systems for detecting releases of such extremely hazardous substances into the atmosphere, surface water, or groundwater at facilities that manufacture, use, or store significant quantities of such substances.

(3) RECOMMENDATIONS.—The report required by this subsection shall also include the Administrator's recommendations for—

(A) initiatives to support the development of new or improved technologies or systems that would facilitate the timely monitoring, detection, and prevention of releases of extremely hazardous substances, and

(B) improving devices or systems for effectively alerting the public in a timely manner, in the event of an accidental release of such extremely hazardous substances.

SUBTITLE B—REPORTING REQUIREMENTS

SEC. 311. MATERIAL SAFETY DATA SHEETS.

(a) BASIC REQUIREMENT.—

(1) SUBMISSION OF MSDS OR LIST.—The owner or operator of any facility which is required to prepare or have available a material safety data sheet for a hazardous chemical under the Occupational Safety and Health Act of 1970 and regulations promulgated under Act (15 U.S.C. 651 et seq.) shall submit a material safety data sheet for each such chemical, or a list of such chemicals as described in paragraph (2), to each of the following.

(A) The appropriate local emergency planning committee.

(B) The State emergency response commission.

(C) The fire department with jurisdiction over the facility.

(2) CONTENTS OF LIST.—(A)The list of chemicals referred to in paragraph (1) shall include each of the following:

(i) A list of hazardous chemical for which a material safety data sheet is required under the Occupational Safety and Health Act of 1970 and regulations promulgated under that Act, grouped in categories of health and physical hazards as set forth under such Act and regulations promulgated under such Act, or in such other categories as the Administrator may prescribe under subparagraph (B).

(ii) The chemical name or the common name of each such chemical as provided on the material safety data sheet.

(iii) Any hazardous component of each such chemical as provided on the material safety data sheet.

(B) For purposes of the list under this paragraph, the Administrator may modify the categories of health and physical hazards as set forth under the Occupational Safety and Health Act of 1970 and regulations promulgated under that Act by requiring information to be reported in terms of groups of hazardous chemicals which present similar hazards in an emergency.

(3) TREATMENT OF MIXTURES.—An owner or operator may meet the requirements of this section with respect to a hazardous chemical which is a mixture by doing one of the following:

(A) Submitting a material safety data sheet for, or identifying on a list, each element or compound in the mixture which is a hazardous chemical. If more than one mixture has the same element or compound, only one material safety data sheet, or one listing, of the element or compound is necessary.

(B) Submitting a material safety data sheet for, or identifying on a list, the mixture itself.

(b) THRESHOLDS.—The Administrator may establish threshold quantities for hazardous chemicals below which no facility shall be subject to the provisions of this section. The threshold quantities may, in the Administrator's discretion, be based on classes of chemicals or categories of facilities.

(c) AVAILABILITY OF MSDS ON REQUEST.—

(1) TO LOCAL EMERGENCY PLANNING COMMITTEE.—If an owner or operator of a facility submits a list of chemicals under subsection (a)(1), the owner or operator, upon request by the local emergency planning committee, shall submit the material safety data sheet.

(2) TO PUBLIC.—A local emergency planning committee, upon request by any person, shall make available a material safety data sheet to the person in accordance with section 324. If the local emergency planning committee does not have the requested material safety data sheet, the committee shall request the sheet from the facility owner or operator and then make the sheet available to the person in accordance with section 324.

(d) INITIAL SUBMISSION AND UPDATING.—(1) The initial material safety data sheet or list required under this section with respect to a hazardous chemical shall be provided before the later of-

(A) 12 months (10/17/87) after the date of the enactment of this title, or

(B) 3 months after the owner or operator of a facility is required to prepare or have available a material safety data sheet for the chemical under the Occupational Safety and Health Act for the chemical under the Occupational Safety and Health Act.

(2) Within 3 months following discovery by an owner or operator of significant new information concerning an aspect of a hazardous chemical for which a material safety data sheet was previously submitted to the local emergency planning committee under subsection (a), a revised sheet shall be provided to such person.

(e) HAZARDOUS CHEMICAL DEFINED.—For purposes of this section, the term "hazardous chemical" has the meaning given such term by section 1910.1200(c) of title 29 of the Code of Federal Regulations, except that such term does not include the following:

(1) Any food, food additive, color additive, drug, or cosmetic regulated by the Food and Drug Administration.

(2) Any substance to the extent it is used for personal, family, or household purposes, or is present in the same form and concentration as a product packaged for distribution and use by the general public.

(3) Any substance to the extent it is used for personal, family, or household purposes, or is present in the same form and concentration as a product packaged for distribution and use by the general public.

(4) Any substance to the extent it is used in a research laboratory or a hospital or other medical facility under the direct supervision of a technically qualified individual.

(5) Any substance to the extent it is used in routine agricultural operations or is a fertilizer held for sale by a retailer to the ultimate customer.

SEC. 312. EMERGENCY AND HAZARDOUS CHEMICAL INVENTORY FORMS.

(a) BASIC REQUIREMENT.—

(1) The owner or operator of any facility which is required to prepare or have available a material safety data sheet for a hazardous chemical under the Occupational Safety and Health Act of 1970 and regulations promulgated under that Act shall prepare and submit an emergency and hazardous chemical inventory form (hereafter in this title referred to as an "inventory form") to each of the following:

(A) The appropriate local emergency planning committee.

(B) The State emergency response commission.

(C) The fire department with jurisdiction over the facility.

(2) The inventory form containing tier I information (as described in subsection (d)(1)) shall be submitted on or before March 1, 1988, and annually thereafter on March 1, and shall contain data with respect to the preceding calendar year. The preceding sentence does not apply if an owner or operator provides, by

the same deadline and with respect to the same calendar year, tier II information (as described in subsection (d)(2) to the recipients described in paragraph (1)).

(3) An owner or operator may meet the requirements of this section with respect to a hazardous chemical which is a mixture by doing one of the following:

(A) Providing information on the inventory form on each element or compound in the mixture which is a hazardous chemical. If more than one mixture has the same element or compound, only one listing on the inventory form for the element or compound at the facility is necessary.

(B) Providing information on the inventory form on the mixture itself.

(b) THRESHOLDS.—The Administrator may establish threshold quantities for hazardous chemicals covered by this section below which no facility shall be subject to the provisions of this section. The threshold quantities may, in the Administrator's discretion, be based on classes of chemicals or categories of facilities.

(c) HAZARDOUS CHEMICALS COVERED.—A hazardous chemical subject to the requirements of this section is any hazardous chemical for which a material safety data sheet or a listing is required under section 311.

(d) CONTENTS OF FORM.—

(1) TIER I INFORMATION.—

(A) AGGREGATE INFORMATION BY CATEGORY.—An inventory form shall provide the information described in subparagraph (B) in aggregate terms for hazardous chemicals in categories of health and physical hazards as set forth under the Occupational Safety and health Act of 1970 and regulations promulgated under that Act.

(B) REQUIRED INFORMATION.—The information referred to in subparagraph (A) is the following:

(i) An estimate (in ranges) of the maximum amount of hazardous chemicals in each category present at the facility at any time during the preceding calendar year.

(ii) An estimate (in ranges) of the average daily amount of hazardous chemicals in each category present at the facility during the preceding calendar year.

(iii) The general location of hazardous chemicals in each category.

(C) MODIFICATIONS.—For purposes of reporting information under this paragraph, the Administrator may-

(i) modify the categories of health and physical hazards as set forth under the Occupational Safety and Health Act of 1970 and regulations promulgated under that Act by requiring information to be reported in terms of groups of hazardous chemicals which present similar hazards in an emergency, or

(ii) require reporting on individual hazardous chemicals of special concern to emergency response personnel.

(2) TIER TWO INFORMATION.—An inventory form shall provide the following additional information for each hazardous chemical present at the facility, but only upon request and in accordance with subsection (e):

(A) The chemical name or the common name of the chemical as provided on the material safety data sheet.

(B) An estimate (in ranges) of the maximum amount of the hazardous chemical present at the facility at any time during the preceding calendar year.

(C) An estimate (in ranges) of the average daily amount of the hazardous chemical present at the facility during the preceding calendar year.

(D) A brief description of the manner of storage of the hazardous chemical.

(E) The location at the facility of the hazardous chemical.

(F) An indication of whether the owner elects to withhold location information of a specific hazardous chemical from disclosure to the public under section 324.

(e) AVAILABILITY OF TIER II INFORMATION.—

(1) AVAILABILITY TO STATE COMMISSIONS, LOCAL COMMITTEES, AND FIRE DEPARTMENTS.—Upon request by a State emergency planning commission, a local emergency planning committee, or a fire department with jurisdiction over the facility, the owner or operator of a facility shall provide tier II information, as described in subsection (d), to the person making the request. Any such request shall be with respect to a specific facility.

(2) AVAILABILITY TO OTHER STATE AND LOCAL OFFICIALS.—A State or local official acting in his or her official capacity may have access to tier II information by submitting a request to the State emergency response commission or the local emergency planning committee. Upon receipt of a request for tier II information, the State commission or local committee shall, pursuant to paragraph (1), request the facility owner or operator for the tier II information and make available such information to the official.

(3) AVAILABILITY TO PUBLIC.—

(A) IN GENERAL.—Any person may request a State emergency response commission or local emergency planning committee for tier II information relating to the preceding calendar year with respect to a facility. Any such request shall be in writing and shall be with respect to a specific facility.

(B) AUTOMATIC PROVISION OF INFORMATION TO PUBLIC.—Any tier II information which a State emergency response commission or local emergency planning committee has in its possession shall be made available to a person making a request under this paragraph in accordance with section 324. If the State emergency response commission or local emergency planning committee does not have tier II information the State emergency response commission or local emergency planning committee shall, pursuant to paragraph (1), request the facility owner or operator for tier II information with respect to a hazardous chemical which a facility has stored in an amount in excess of 10,000 pounds present at the facility at any time during the preceding calendar year and make such information available in accordance with section 324 to the person making the request.

(C) DISCRETIONARY PROVISION OF INFORMATION TO PUBLIC.—In the case of tier II information which is not in the possession of a State emergency response commission or local emergency planning committee and which is with respect to a hazardous chemical which a facility has stored in an amount less than 10,000 pounds present at the facility at any time during the preceding calendar year, a request from a person must include the general need for the information. The State emergency response commission or local emergency planning committee may, pursuant to paragraph (1), request the facility owner or operator for the tier II information on behalf of the person making the request. Upon receipt of any information requested on behalf of such person, the State emergency response commission or local emergency planning committee shall make the information available in accordance with section 324 to the person.

(D) RESPONSE IN 45 DAYS.—A State emergency response commission or local emergency planning committee shall respond to a request for tier II information under this paragraph no later than 45 days after the date of receipt of the request.

(f) FIRE DEPARTMENT ACCESS.—Upon request to an owner or operator of a facility which files an inventory form under this section by the fire department with jurisdiction over the facility, the owner or operator of the facility shall allow the fire department to conduct an on-site inspection of the facility and shall provide to the fire department specific location information on hazardous chemicals at the facility.

(g) FORMAT OF FORMS.—The Administrator shall publish a uniform format for inventory forms within three months (1/17/87) after the date of the enactment of this title. If the Administrator does not publish such forms, owners and operators of facilities subject to the requirements of this section shall provide the information required under this section by letter.

SEC. 313. TOXIC CHEMICAL RELEASE FORMS.

(a) BASIC REQUIREMENT.—The owner or operator of a facility subject to the requirements of this section shall complete a toxic chemical release form as published under subsection (g) for each toxic chemical listed under subsection (c) that was manufactured, processed, or otherwise used in quantities exceeding the toxic chemical threshold quantity established by subsection (f) during the preceding calendar year at such facility. Such form shall be submitted to the Administrator and to an official or officials of the State designated by the Governor on or before July 1, 1988, and annually thereafter on July 1 and shall contain data reflecting releases during the preceding calendar year.

(b) COVERED OWNERS AND OPERATORS OF FACILITIES.—

(1) IN GENERAL.—(A) The requirements of this section shall apply to owners and operators of facilities that have 10 or more full-time employees and that are in Standard Industrial Classification Codes 20 through 39 (as in effect on July 1, 1985) and that manufactured, processed, or otherwise used a toxic chemical listed under subsection (c) in excess of the quantity of that toxic chemical established under subsection (f) during the calendar year for which a release form is required under this section.

(B) The Administrator may add or delete Standard Industrial Classification Codes for purposes of subparagraph (A), but only to the extent necessary to provide that each Standard Industrial Code to which this section applies is relevant to the purposes of this section.

(C) For purposes of this section-
(i) The term "manufacture" means to produce, prepare, import, or compound a toxic chemical.
(ii) The term "process" means the preparation of a toxic chemical, after its manufacture, for distribution in commerce-
(I) in the same for or physical state as, or in a different form or physical state from, that in which it was received by the person so preparing such chemical, or
(II) as part of an article containing the toxic chemical.
(2) DISCRETIONARY APPLICATION TO ADDITIONAL FACILITIES.— The Administrator, on his own motion or at the request of a Governor of a State (with regard to facilities located in that State), may apply the requirements of this section to the owners and operators of any particular facility that manufactures, processes, or otherwise uses a toxic chemical listed under subsection (c) if the Administrator determines that such action is warranted on the basis of toxicity of the toxic chemical, proximity to other facilities that release the toxic chemical or to population centers, the history of releases of such chemical at such facility, or such other factors as the Administrator deems appropriate.
(c) TOXIC CHEMICALS COVERED.—The toxic chemicals subject to the requirements of this section are those chemicals on the list on Committee Print Number 99-169 of the Senate Committee on Environment and Public Works, titled "Toxic Chemicals Subject to Section 313 of the Emergency Planning and Community Right-To-Know Act of 1986" (including any revised version of the list as may be made pursuant to subsection (d) or (e).
(d) REVISIONS BY ADMINISTRATOR.—
(1) IN GENERAL.—The Administrator may by rule add or delete a chemical from the list described in subsection (c) at any time.
(2) ADDITIONS.—A chemical may be added if the Administrator determines, in his judgment, that there is sufficient evidence to establish any one of the following:
(A) The chemical is known to cause or can reasonably be anticipated to cause significant adverse acute human health effects at concentration levels that are reasonably likely to exist beyond facility site boundaries as a result of continuous, or frequently recurring, releases.
(B) The chemical is known to cause or can reasonably be anticipated to cause in humans-
(i) cancer or teratogenic effects, or
(ii) serious or irreversible-
(I) reproductive dysfunctions,
(II) neurological disorders,
(III) heritable genetic mutations, or
(IV) other chronic health effects.
(C) The chemical is known to cause or can reasonably be anticipated to cause, because of-
(i) its toxicity,

(ii) its toxicity and persistence in the environment, or

(iii) its toxicity and tendency to bioaccumulate in the environment, a significant adverse effect on the environment of sufficient seriousness, in the judgment of the Administrator, to warrant reporting under this section. The number of chemicals included on the list described in subsection (c) on the basis of the preceding sentence may constitute in the aggregate no more than 25 percent of the total number of chemicals on the list.

A determination under this paragraph shall be based on generally accepted scientific principles or laboratory tests, or appropriately designed and conducted epidemiological or other population studies, available to the Administrator.

(3) DELETIONS.—A chemical may be deleted if the Administrator determines there is not sufficient evidence to establish any of the criteria described in paragraph (2).

(4) EFFECTIVE DATE.—Any revision made on or after January 1 and before December 1 of any calendar year shall take effect beginning with the next calendar year. Any revision made on or after December 1 of any calendar year and before January 1 of the next calendar year shall take effect beginning with the calendar year following such next calendar year.

(e) PETITIONS.—

(1) IN GENERAL.—Any person may petition the Administrator to add or delete a chemical from the list described in subsection (c) on the basis of the criteria in subparagraph (A) or (B) of subsection (d)(2). Within 180 days after receipt of a petition, the Administrator shall take one of the following actions:

(A) Initiate a rulemaking to add or delete the chemical to the list, in accordance with subsection (d)(2) or (d)(3).

(B) Publish an explanation of why the petition is denied.

(2) GOVERNOR PETITIONS.—A State Governor may petition the Administrator to add or delete a chemical from the list described in subsection (c) on the basis of the criteria in subparagraph (A), (B), or (C) of subsection (d)(2). In the case of such a petition from a State Governor to add a chemical, the chemical will be added to the list within 180 days after receipt of the petition, unless the Administrator-

(A) initiates a rulemaking to add the chemical to the list, in accordance with subsection (d)(2), or

(B) publishes an explanation of why the Administrator believes the petition does not meet the requirements of subsection (d)(2) for adding a chemical to the list.

(f) THRESHOLD FOR REPORTING.—

(1) TOXIC CHEMICAL THRESHOLD AMOUNT.—The threshold amounts for purposes of reporting toxic chemicals under this section are as follows:

(A) With respect to a toxic chemical used at a facility, 10,000 pounds of the toxic chemical per year.

(B) With respect to a toxic chemical manufactured or processed at a facility-

(i) For the toxic chemical release form required to be submitted under this section on or before July 1, 1988, 75,000 pounds of the toxic chemical per year.

(ii) For the form required to be submitted on or before July 1, 1989, 50,000 pounds of the toxic chemical per year.

(iii) For the form required to be submitted on or before July 1, 1990, and for each form thereafter, 25,000 pounds of the toxic chemical per year.

(2) REVISIONS.—The Administrator may establish a threshold amount for a toxic chemical different from the amount established by paragraph (1). Such revised threshold shall obtain reporting on a substantial majority of total releases of the chemical at all facilities subject to the requirements of this section. The amounts established under this paragraph may, at the Administrator's discretion, be based on classes of chemicals or categories of facilities.

(g) FORM.—

(1) INFORMATION REQUIRED.—Not later than June 1, 1987, the Administrator shall publish a uniform toxic chemical release form for facilities covered by this section. If the Administrator does not publish such a form, owners and operators of facilities subject to the requirements of this section shall provide the information required under this subsection by letter postmarked on or before the date on which the form is due. Such form shall-

(A) provide for the name and location of, and principal business activities at, the facility;

(B) include an appropriate certification, signed by a senior official with management responsibility for the person or persons completing the report, regarding the accuracy and completeness of the report; and

(C) provide for submission of each of the following items of information for each listed toxic chemical known to be present at the facility:

(i) Whether the toxic chemical at the facility is manufactured, processed, or otherwise used, and the general category or categories of use of the chemical.

(ii) An estimate of the maximum amounts (in ranges) of the toxic chemical present at the facility at any time during the preceding calendar year.

(iii) For each waste stream, the waste treatment or disposal methods employed, and an estimate of the treatment efficiency typically achieved by such methods for that waste stream.

(iv) The annual quantity of the toxic chemical entering each environmental medium.

(2) USE OF AVAILABLE DATA.—In order to provide the information required under this section, the owner or operator of a facility may use readily available data (including monitoring data) collected pursuant to other provisions of law, or, where such data are not readily available, reasonable estimates of the amounts involved. Nothing in this section requires the monitoring or measurement of the quantities, concentration, or frequency of any toxic chemical released into the environment beyond that monitoring and measurement required under other provisions of law or regulation. In order to assure consistency, the Administrator shall require that data be expressed in common units.

(h) USE OF RELEASE FORM.—The release forms required under this section are intended to provide information to the Federal, State, and local governments and the public, including citizens of communities surrounding covered facilities. The release form shall be available, consistent with section 324(a), to inform persons about releases of toxic chemicals to the environment; to assist governmental agencies, researchers, and other persons in the conduct of research and data gathering; to aid in the development of appropriate regulations, guidelines, and standards; and for other similar purposes.

(i) MODIFICATIONS IN REPORTING FREQUENCY.—

(1) IN GENERAL.—The Administrator may modify the frequency of submitting a report under this section, but the Administrator may not modify the frequency to be any more often than annually. A modification may apply, either nationally or in a specific geographic area, to the following:

(A) All toxic chemical release forms required under this section.

(B) A class of toxic chemicals or a category of facilities.

(C) A specific toxic chemical.

(D) A specific facility.

(2) REQUIREMENTS.—A modification may be made under paragraph (1) only if the Administrator—

(A) makes a finding that the modification is consistent with the provisions of subsection (h), based on—

(i) experience from previously submitted toxic chemical release forms, and

(ii) determinations made under paragraph (3), and

(B) the finding is made by a rulemaking in accordance with section 553 of title 5, United States Code.

(3) DETERMINATIONS.—The Administrator shall make the following determinations with respect to a proposed modification before making a modification under paragraph (1):

(A) The extent to which information relating to the proposed modification provided on the toxic chemical release forms has been used by the Administrator or other agencies of the Federal Government, States, local governments, health professionals, and the public.

(B) The extent to which the information is (i) readily available to potential users from other sources, such as State reporting programs, and (ii) provided to the Administrator under another Federal law or through a State program.

(C) The extent to which the modification would impose additional and unreasonable burdens on facilities subject to the reporting requirements under this section.

(4) 5-YEAR REVIEW.—Any modification made under this subsection shall be reviewed at least once every 5 years. Such review shall examine the modification and ensure that the requirements of paragraphs (2) and (3) still justify continuation of the modification. Any change to a modification reviewed under this paragraph shall be made in accordance with this subsection.

(5) NOTIFICATION TO CONGRESS.—The Administrator shall notify Congress of an intention to initiate a rulemaking for a modification under this subsection. After such notification, the Administrator shall delay initiation of the rulemaking for at least 12 months, but no more than 24 months, after the date of such notification.

(6) JUDICIAL REVIEW.—In any judicial review of a rulemaking which

establishes a modification under this subsection, a court may hold unlawful and set aside agency action, findings, and conclusions found to be unsupported by substantial evidence.

(7) APPLICABILITY.—A modification under this subsection may apply to a calendar year or other reporting period beginning no earlier than January 1, 1993.

(8) EFFECTIVE DATE.—Any modification made on or after January 1 and before December 1 of any calendar year shall take effect beginning with the next calendar year. Any modification made on or after December 1 of any calendar year and before January 1 of the next calendar year shall take effect beginning with the calendar year following such next calendar year.

(j) EPA MANAGEMENT OF DATA.—The Administrator shall establish and maintain in a computer data base a national toxic chemical inventory based on data submitted to the Administrator under this section. The Administrator shall make these data accessible by computer telecommunication and other means to any person on a cost reimbursable basis.

(k) REPORT.—Not later than June 30, 1991, the Comptroller General, in consultation with the Administrator and appropriate officials in the States, shall submit to the Congress a report including each of the following:

(1) A description of the steps taken by the Administrator and the States to implement the requirements of this section, including steps taken to make information collected under this section available to and accessible by the public.

(2) A description of the extent to which the information collected under this section has been used by the Environmental Protection Agency, other Federal agencies, the States, and the public, and the purposes for which the information has been used.

(3) An identification and evaluation of options for modifications to the requirements of this section for the purpose of making information collected under this section more useful.

(l) MASS BALANCE STUDY.—

(1) IN GENERAL.—The Administrator shall arrange for a mass balance study to be carried out by the National Academy of Sciences using mass balance information collected by the Administrator under paragraph (3). The Administrator shall submit to Congress a report on such study no later than 5 years (10/17/91) after the date of the enactment of this title.

(2) PURPOSES.—The purposes of the study are as follows:

(A) To assess the value of mass balance analysis in determining the accuracy of information on toxic chemical releases.

(B) To assess the value of obtaining mass balance information, or portions thereof, to determine the waste reduction efficiency of different facilities, or categories of facilities, including the effectiveness of toxic chemical regulations promulgated under laws other than this title.

(C) To assess the utility of such information for evaluating toxic chemical management practices at facilities, or categories of facilities, covered by this section.

(D) To determine the implications of mass balance information collection on a national scale similar to the mass balance information collection carried out by the Administrator under paragraph (3), including implications of the use of such collection as part of a national annual quantity toxic chemical release program.

(3) INFORMATION COLLECTION.—

(A) The Administrator shall acquire available mass balance information from States which currently conduct (or during the 5 years after the date of enactment of this title initiate) a mass balance oriented annual quantity toxic chemical release program. If information from such States provides an inadequate representation of industry classes and categories to carry out the purposes of the study, the Administrator also may acquire mass balance information necessary for the study from a representative number of facilities in other States.

(B) Any information acquired under this section shall be available to the public, except that upon a showing satisfactory to the Administrator by any person that the information (or a particular part thereof) to which the Administrator or any officer, employee, or representative has access under this section if made public would divulge information entitled to protection under section 1905 of title 18. United States Code, such information or part shall be considered confidential in accordance with the purposes of that section, except that such information or part may be disclosed to other officers, employees, or authorized representatives of the United States concerned with carrying out this section.

(C) The Administrator may promulgate regulations prescribing procedures for collecting mass balance information under this paragraph.

(D) For purposes of collecting mass balance information under subparagraph (A), the Administrator may require the submission of information by a State of facility.

(4) MASS BALANCE DEFINITION.—For purposes of this subsection, the term "mass balance" means an accumulation of the annual quantities of chemicals transported to a facility, produced at a facility, consumed at a facility, used at a facility, accumulated at a facility, released from a facility, and transported from a facility as a waste or as a commercial product or byproduct or component of a commercial product or byproduct.

SUBTITLE C-GENERAL PROVISIONS

SEC. 321. RELATIONSHIP TO OTHER LAW.

(a) IN GENERAL.—Nothing in this title shall-

(1) preempt any State or local law,

(2) except as provided in subsection (b), otherwise affect any State or local law or the authority of any State or local government to adopt or enforce any State or local law, or

(3) affect or modify in any way the obligations or liabilities of any person under other Federal law.

(b) EFFECT ON MSDS REQUIREMENTS.—Any State or local law enacted after August 1, 1985, which requires the submission of a material safety data sheet from facility owners or operators shall require that the data sheet be identical in content and format to the data sheet required under subsection (a) of section 311. In addition, a State or locality may require the submission of information which is supplemental to the information required on the data sheet (including information on the location and quantity of hazardous chemicals present at the facility), through additional sheets attached to the data sheet or such other means as the State or locality considers appropriate.

SEC. 322. TRADE SECRETS.

(a) AUTHORITY TO WITHHOLD INFORMATION.—
    (1) GENERAL AUTHORITY.—
        (A) With regard to a hazardous chemical, an extremely hazardous substance, or a toxic chemical, any person required under section 303(d)(2), 303(d((3), 311, 312, or 313 to submit information to any other person may withhold from such submittal the specific identification), as defined in regulations prescribed by the Administrator under Administrator under subsection (c), if the person complies with paragraph (2).
        (B) Any person withholding the specific chemical identity shall, in the place on the submittal where the chemical identity would normally be included, include the generic class or category of the hazardous chemical, extremely hazardous substance, or toxic chemical (as the case may be).
    (2) REQUIREMENTS.—(A)A person is entitled to withhold information under paragraph (1) if such person-
        (i) claims that such information is a trade secret, on the basis of the factors enumerated in subsection (b)
        (ii) includes in the submittal referred to in paragraph (1) an explanation of the reasons why such information is claimed to be a trade secret, based on the factors enumerated in subsection (b), including a specific description of why such factors apply, and
        (iii) submits to the Administrator a copy of such submittal, and the information withheld from such submittal.
        (B) LIMITATION.—The authority under this subsection to withhold information shall not apply to information which the Administrator has determined, in accordance with subsection (c), is not a trade secret.
(b) TRADE SECRET FACTORS.—No person required to provide information under this title may claim that the information is entitled to protection as a trade secret under subsection (a) unless such person shows each of the following:
    (1) Such person has not disclosed the information to any other person, other than a member of a local emergency planning committee, an officer or employee of the United States or a State or local government, an employee of such person, or a person who is bound by a confidentiality agreement, and such person has

taken reasonable measures to protect the confidentiality of such information and intends to continue to take such measures.

(2) The information is not required to be disclosed, or otherwise made available, to the public under any other Federal or State law.

(3) Disclosure of the information is likely to cause substantial harm to the competitive position of such person.

(4) The chemical identity is not readily discoverable through reverse engineering.

(c) TRADE SECRET REGULATIONS.—As soon as practicable after the date of enactment of this title, the Administrator shall prescribe regulations to implement this section. With respect to subsection (b)(4), such regulations shall be equivalent to comparable provisions in the Occupational Safety and Health Administration Hazard Communication Standard (29 CFR 1910.1200) and any revisions of such standard prescribed by the Secretary of Labor in accordance with the final ruling of the courts of the United States in United Steelworkers of America, AFL-CIO-CLC v. Thorne G. Auchter.

(d) PETITION FOR REVIEW.—

(1) IN GENERAL.—Any person may petition the Administrator for the disclosure of the specific chemical identity of a hazardous chemical, an extremely hazardous substance, or a toxic chemical which is claimed as a trade secret under this section. The Administrator may, in the absence of a petition under this paragraph, initiate a determination, to be carried out in accordance with this subsection, as to whether information withheld constitutes a trade secret.

(2) INITIAL REVIEW.—Within 30 days after the date of receipt of a petition under paragraph (1)(or upon the Administrator's initiative), the Administrator shall review the explanation filed by a trade secret claimant under subsection (a)(2) and determine whether the explanation presents assertions which, if true, are sufficient to support a finding that the specific chemical identity is a trade secret.

(3) FINDING OF SUFFICIENT ASSERTIONS.—

(A) If the Administrator determines pursuant to paragraph (2) that the explanation presents sufficient assertions to support a finding that the specific chemical identity is a trade secret, the Administrator shall notify the trade secret claimant that he has 30 days to supplement the explanation with detailed information to support the assertions.

(B) If the Administrator determines, after receipt of any supplemental supporting detailed information under subparagraph (A), that the assertions in the explanation are true and that the specific chemical identity is a trade secret, the Administrator shall so notify the petitioner and the petitioner may seek judicial review of the determination.

(C) If the Administrator determines, after receipt of any supplemental supporting detailed information under subparagraph (A), that the assertions in the explanation are not true and that the specific chemical identity is not a trade secret, the Administrator shall notify the trade secret claimant that the Administrator intends to release the specific chemical identity. The trade secret claimant has 30 days in which he may appeal the Administrator's determination under this subparagraph to the Administrator. If the Administrator does not reverse his determination under this subparagraph in such an appeal by the trade secret claimant, the trade secret claimant may seek judicial review of the determination.

(4) FINDING OF INSUFFICIENT ASSERTIONS.—

(A) If the Administrator determines pursuant to paragraph (2) that the explanation presents insufficient assertions to support a finding that the specific chemical identity is a trade secret, the Administrator shall notify the trade secret claimant that he has 30 days to appeal the determination to the Administrator, or, upon a showing of good cause, amend the original explanation by providing supplementary assertions to support the trade secret claim.

(B) If the Administrator does not reverse his determination under subparagraph (A) after an appeal or an examination of any supplementary assertions under subparagraph (A), the Administrator shall so notify the trade secret claimant and the trade secret claimant may seek judicial review of the determination.

(C) If the Administrator reverses his determination under subparagraph (A) after an appeal or an examination of any supplementary assertions under subparagraph (A), the procedures under paragraph (3) of this subsection apply.

(e) EXCEPTION FOR INFORMATION PROVIDED TO HEALTH PROFESSIONALS.—Nothing in this section, or regulations adopted pursuant to this section, shall authorize any person to withhold information which is required to be provided to a health professional, a doctor, or a nurse in accordance with section 323.

(f) PROVIDING INFORMATION TO THE ADMINISTRATOR; AVAILABILITY TO PUBLIC.—Any information submitted to the Administrator under subsection (a)(2) or subsection (d)(3) (except a specific chemical identity) shall be available to the public, except that upon a showing satisfactory to the Administrator by any person that the information (or a particular part thereof) to which the Administrator has access under this section if made public would divulge information entitled to protection under section 1905 of title 18, United States Code, such information or part shall be considered confidential in accordance with the purposes of that section, except that such information or part may be disclosed to other officers, employees, or authorized representatives of the United States concerned with carrying out this title.

(g) INFORMATION PROVIDED TO STATE.—Upon request by a State, acting through the Governor of the State, the Administrator shall provide to the State any information obtained under subsection (a)(2) and subsection (d)(3).

(h) INFORMATION ON ADVERSE EFFECTS.—

(1) In any case in which the identity of a hazardous chemical or an extremely hazardous substance is claimed as a trade secret, the Governor or State emergency response commission established under section 301 shall identify the adverse health effects associated with the hazardous chemical or extremely hazardous substance and shall assure that such information is provided to any person requesting information about such hazardous chemical or extremely hazardous substance.

(2) In any case in which the identity of a toxic chemical is claimed as a trade secret, the Administrator shall identify the adverse health and environmental effects associated with the toxic chemical and shall assure that such information

is included in the computer database required by section 313(j) and is provided to any person requesting information about such toxic chemical.

(i) INFORMATION PROVIDED TO CONGRESS.—Notwithstanding any limitation contained in this section or any other provision of law, all information reported to or otherwise obtained by the Administrator (or any representative of the Administrator) under this title shall be made available to a duly authorized committee of the Congress upon written request by such a committee.

SEC. 323. PROVISION OF INFORMATION TO HEALTH PROFESSIONALS, DOCTORS, AND NURSES.

(a) DIAGNOSIS OR TREATMENT BY HEALTH PROFESSIONAL.—An owner or operator of a facility which is subject to the requirements of section 311, 312, or 313 shall provide the specific chemical identity, if known, of a hazardous chemical, extremely hazardous substance, or a toxic chemical to any health professional who requests such information in writing if the health professional provides a written statement of need under this subsection and a written confidentiality agreement under subsection (d). The written statement of need shall be a statement that the health professional has a reasonable basis to suspect that-

(1) the information is needed for purposes of diagnosis or treatment of an individual,

(2) the individual or individuals being diagnosed or treated have been exposed to the chemical concerned, and

(3) knowledge of the specific chemical identity of such chemical will assist in diagnosis or treatment.

Following such a written request, the owner or operator to whom such request is made shall promptly provide the requested information to the health professional. The authority to withhold the specific chemical identity of a chemical under section 322 when such information is a trade secret shall not apply to information required to be provided under this subsection, subject to the provisions of subsection (d).

(b) MEDICAL EMERGENCY.—An owner or operator of a facility which is subject to the requirements of section 311, 312, or 313 shall provide a copy of a material safety data sheet, an inventory form, or a toxic chemical release form, including the specific chemical identity, if known, of a hazardous chemical, extremely hazardous substance, or a toxic chemical, to any treating physician or nurse who requests such information if such physician or nurse determines that-

(1) a medical emergency exists,

(2) the specific chemical identity of the chemical concerned is necessary for or will assist in emergency or first-aid diagnosis or treatment, and

(3) the individual or individuals being diagnosed or treated have been exposed to the chemical concerned.

Immediately following such a request, the owner or operator to whom such requests made shall provide the requested information to the physician or nurse. The authority to withhold the specific chemical identity of a chemical from a material safety data sheet, an inventory form, or a toxic chemical release form under section 322 when such information is a trade secret shall not apply to information required to be provided to a treating physician or nurse under this subsection. No written confidentiality agreement or statement of need shall be required as a precondition of such disclosure, both the owner or operator disclosing such information may require a written confidentiality agreement in accordance with subsection (d) and a statement setting forth the items listed in paragraphs (1) through (3) as soon as circumstances permit.

(c) PREVENTIVE MEASURES BY LOCAL HEALTH PROFESSIONALS.—
(1) PROVISION OF INFORMATION.—An owner or operator of a facility subject to the requirements of section 311, 312, or 313 shall provide the specific chemical identity, if known, of a hazardous chemical, an extremely hazardous substance, or a toxic chemical to any health professional (such as a physician, toxicologist, or epidemiologist)-

(A) who is a local government employee or a person under contract with the local government, and

(B) who requests such information in writing and provides a written statement of need under paragraph (2) and a written confidentiality agreement under subsection (d).

Following such a written request, the owner or operator to whom such request is made shall promptly provide the requested information to the local health professional. The authority to withhold the specific chemical identity of a chemical under section 322 when such information is a trade secret shall not apply to information required to be provided under this subsection, subject to the provisions of subsection (d).

(2) WRITTEN STATEMENT OF NEED.—The written statement of need shall be a statement that describes with reasonable detail one or more of the following health needs for the information:

(A) To assess exposure of persons living in a local community to the hazards of the chemical concerned.

(B) To conduct or assess sampling to determine exposure levels of various population groups.

(C) To conduct periodic medical surveillance of exposed population groups.

(D) To provide medical treatment to exposed individuals or population groups.

(E) To conduct studies to determine the health effects of exposure.

(F) To conduct studies to aid in the identification of a chemical that may reasonably be anticipated to cause an observed health effect.

(d) CONFIDENTIALITY AGREEMENT.—Any person obtaining information under subsection (a) or (c) shall, in accordance with such subsection (a) or (c), be required to agree in a written confidentiality agreement that he will not use the information for any purpose other than the health needs asserted in the statement of need, except as may otherwise be authorized by the terms of the agreement or by the person providing such information. Nothing in this subsection shall preclude the parties to a confidentiality agreement from pursuing any remedies to the extent permitted by law.

(e) REGULATIONS.—As soon as practicable after the date of the enactment of this title, the Administrator shall promulgate regulations describing criteria and parameters for the statement of need under subsection (a) and (c) and the confidentiality agreement under subsection (d).

SEC. 324. PUBLIC AVAILABILITY OF PLANS, DATA SHEETS, FORMS, AND FOLLOWUP NOTICES.

(a) AVAILABILITY TO PUBLIC.—Each emergency response plan, material safety data sheet, list described in section 311 (a)(2), inventory form, toxic chemical release form, and followup emergency notice shall be made available to the general public, consistent with section 322, during normal working hours at the location or locations designated by the Administrator, Governor, State emergency response commission, or local emergency planning committee, as appropriate. Upon request by an owner or operator of a facility subject to the requirements of section 312, the State emergency response commission and the appropriate local emergency planning committee shall withhold from disclosure under this section the location of any specific chemical required by section 312(d)(2) to be contained in an inventory form as tier II information.

(b) NOTICE OF PUBLIC AVAILABILITY.—Each local emergency planning committee shall annually publish a notice in local newspapers that the emergency response plan, material safety data sheets, and inventory forms have been submitted under this section. The notice shall state that followup emergency notices may subsequently be issued. Such notice shall announce that members of the public who wish to review any such plan, sheet, form, or followup notice may do so at the location designated under subsection (a).

SEC. 325. ENFORCEMENT.

(a) CIVIL PENALTIES FOR EMERGENCY PLANNING.—The Administrator may order a facility owner or operator (except an owner or operator of a facility designated under section 302(b)(2) to comply with section 302(c) and section 303(d). The United States district court for the district in which the facility is located shall have jurisdiction to enforce the order, and any person who violates or fails to obey such an order shall be liable to the United States for a civil penalty of not more than $25,000 for each day in which such violation occurs or such failure to comply continues.

(b) CIVIL, ADMINISTRATIVE, AND CRIMINAL PENALTIES FOR EMERGENCY NOTIFICATION

(1) CLASS I ADMINISTRATIVE PENALTY.—(A) A civil penalty of not more than $25,000 per violation may be assessed by the Administrator in the case of a violation of the requirements of section 304.

(B) No civil penalty may be assessed under this subsection unless the person accused of the violation is given notice and opportunity for a hearing with respect to the violation.

(C) In determining the amount of any penalty assessed pursuant to this subsection, the Administrator shall take into account the nature, circumstances, extent and gravity of the violation or violations and, with respect to the violator, ability to pay, any prior history of such violations, the degree of culpability, economic benefit or savings (if any) resulting from the violation, and such other matters as justice may require.

(2) CLASS II ADMINISTRATIVE PENALTY.—A civil penalty of not more

than $25,000 per day for each day during which the violation continues may be assessed by the Administrator in the case of a violation of the requirements of section 304. In the case of a second or subsequent violation the amount of such penalty may be not more than $75,000 for each day during which the violation continues. Any civil penalty under this subsection shall be assessed and collected in the same manner, and subject to the same provisions, as in the case of civil penalties assessed and collected under section 16 of the Toxic Substances Control Act. In any proceeding for the assessment of a civil penalty under this subsection the Administrator may issue subpoenas for the attendance and testimony of witnesses and the production of relevant papers, books, and documents and may promulgate rules for discovery procedures.

(3) JUDICIAL ASSESSMENT.—The Administrator may bring an action in the United States district court for the appropriate district to assess and collect a penalty of not more than $25,000 per day for each day during which the violation continues in the case of a second or subsequent violation, the amount of such penalty may be not more than $75,000 for each day during which the violation continues.

(4) CRIMINAL PENALTIES.—Any person who knowingly and willfully fails to provide notice in accordance with section 304 shall, upon conviction, be fined not more than $25,000 or imprisoned for not more than two years, or both (or in the case of a second or subsequent conviction, shall be fined not more than $50,000 or imprisoned for not more than five years, or both).

(c) CIVIL AND ADMINISTRATIVE PENALTIES FOR REPORTING REQUIRE-MENTS.—

(1) Any person (other than a governmental entity) who violates any requirement of section 312 or 313 shall be liable to the United States for a civil penalty in an amount not to exceed $25,000 for each such violation.

(2) Any person (other than a governmental entity) who violates any requirement of section 311 or 323(b), and any person who fails to furnish to the Administrator information required under section 322(a)(2) shall be liable to the United States for a civil penalty in an amount not to exceed $10,000 for each such violation.

(3) Each day a violation described in paragraph (1) or (2) continues shall, for purposes of this subsection, constitute a separate violation.

(4) The Administrator may assess any civil penalty for which a person is liable under this subsection by administrative order or may bring an action to assess and collect the penalty in the United States district court for the district in which the person from whom the penalty is sought resides or in which such person's principal place of business is located.

(d) CIVIL, ADMINISTRATIVE, AND CRIMINAL PENALTIES WITH RESPECT TO TRADE SECRETS.—

(1) CIVIL AND ADMINISTRATIVE PENALTY FOR FRIVOLOUS CLAIMS.—If the Administrator determines-

(A)(i) under section 322(d)(4) that an explanation submitted by a trade secret claimant presents insufficient assertions to support a finding that a specific chemical identity is a trade secret, or (ii) after receiving supplemental supporting detailed information under section 322(d)(3)(A), that the specific chemical identity is not a trade secret, and

(B) that the trade secret claim is frivolous, the trade secret claimant is liable for a penalty of $25,000 per claim. The Administrator may assess the penalty by administrative order or may bring an action in the appropriate district court of the United States to assess and collect the penalty.

(2) CRIMINAL PENALTY FOR DISCLOSURE OF TRADE SECRET INFORMATION. Any person who knowingly and willfully divulges or discloses any information entitled to protection under section 322 shall, upon conviction, be subject to a fine of not more than $20,000 or to imprisonment not to exceed one year, or both.

(e) SPECIAL ENFORCEMENT PROVISIONS FOR SECTION 323.—Whenever any facility owner or operator required to provide information under section 323 to a health professional who has requested such information fails or refuses to provide such information in accordance with such section, such health professional may bring an action in the appropriate United States district court to require such facility owner or operator to provide the information. Such court shall have jurisdiction to issue such orders and take such other action as may be necessary to enforce the requirements of section 323.

(f) PROCEDURES FOR ADMINISTRATIVE PENALTIES.—

(1) Any person against whom a civil penalty is assessed under this section may obtain review thereof in the appropriate district court of the United States by filing a notice of appeal in such court within 30 days after the date of such order and by simultaneously sending a copy of such notice by certified mail to the Administrator. The Administrator shall promptly file in such court a certified copy of the record upon which such violation was found or such penalty imposed. If any person fails to pay an assessment of a civil penalty after it has become a final and unappealable order or after the appropriate court has entered final judgment in favor of the United States, the Administrator may request the Attorney General of the United States to institute a civil action in an appropriate district court of the United States to collect the penalty, and such court shall have jurisdiction to hear and decide any such action. In hearing such action, the court shall have authority to review the violation and the assessment of the civil penalty on the record.

(2) The Administrator may issue subpoenas for the attendance and testimony of witnesses and the production of relevant papers, book, or documents in connection with hearings under this section. In case of contumacy or refusal to obey a subpoena issued pursuant to this paragraph and served upon any person, the district court of the United States for any district in which such person is found, resides, or transacts business, upon application by the United States and after notice to such person, shall have jurisdiction to issue an order requiring such person to appear and give testimony before the administrative law judge appear or to appear and produce documents before the administrative law judge, or both, and any failure to obey such order of the court may be punished by such court as a contempt thereof.

SEC. 326. CIVIL ACTIONS.

(a) AUTHORITY TO BRING CIVIL ACTIONS.—
  (1) CITIZEN SUITS.—Except as provided in subsection (e), any person may commence a civil action on his own behalf against the following:
    (A) An owner or operator of a facility for failure to do any of the following:
      (i) Submit a followup emergency notice under section 304(c).
      (ii) Submit a material safety data sheet or a list under section 311(a).
      (iii) Complete and submit an inventory form under section 312(a) containing tier I information as described in section 312(d)(1) unless such requirement does not apply by reason of the second sentence of section 312(a)(2).
      (iv) Complete and submit a toxic chemical release from under section 313(a).
    (B) The Administrator for failure to do any of the following:
      (i) Publish inventory forms under section 312(g).
      (ii) Respond to a petition to add or delete a chemical under section 313(e)(1) within 180 days after receipt of the petition.
      (iii) Publish a toxic chemical release form under 313(g).
      (iv) Establish a computer database in accordance with section 313(j).
      (v) Promulgate trade secret regulations under section 322(c).
      (vi) Render a decision in response to a petition under section 322(d) within 9 months after receipt of the petition.
    (C) The Administrator, a State Governor, or a State emergency response commission, for failure to provide a mechanism for public availability of information in accordance with section 324(a).
    (D) A State Governor or a State emergency response commission for failure to respond to a request for tier Ii information under section 312(e)(3) within 120 days after the date of receipt of the request.
  (2) STATE OR LOCAL SUITS.—
    (A) Any State or local government may commence a civil action against an owner or operator of a facility for failure to do any of the following:
      (i) Provide notification to the emergency response commission in the State under section 302(c).
      (ii) Submit a material safety data sheet or a list under section 311(a).
      (iii) Make available information requested under section 311(c).
      (iv) Complete and submit an inventory form under section 312(a) containing tier I information unless such requirement does not apply by reason of the second sentence of section 312(a)(2).
    (B) Any State emergency response commission or local emergency planning committee may commence a civil action against an owner or operator of a facility for failure to provide information under section 303(d) or for failure to submit tier II information under section 312(e)(1).
    (C) Any state may commence a civil action against the Administrator for failure to provide information to the State under section 322(g).

(b) VENUE.—

(1) Any action under subsection (a) against an owner or operator of a facility shall be brought in the district court for the district in which the alleged violation occurred.

(2) Any action under subsection (a) against the Administrator may be brought in the United States District Court for the District of Columbia.

(c) RELIEF.—The district court shall have jurisdiction in actions brought under subsection (a) against an owner or operator of a facility to enforce the requirement concerned and to impose any civil penalty provided for violation of that requirement. The district court shall have jurisdiction in actions brought under subsection (a) against the Administrator to order the Administrator to perform the act or duty concerned.

(d) NOTICE.—

(1) No action may be commenced under subsection (a)(1)(A) prior to 60 days after the plaintiff has given notice of the alleged violation to the Administrator, the State in which the alleged violation occurs, and the alleged violator. Notice under this paragraph shall be given in such manner as the Administrator shall prescribe by regulation.

(2) No action may be commenced under subsection (a)(1)(B) or (a)(1)(C) prior to 60 days after the date on which the plaintiff gives notice to the Administrator, State Governor, or State emergency response commission (as the case may be) that the plaintiff will commence the action. Notice under this paragraph shall be given in such manner as the Administrator shall prescribe by regulation.

(e) LIMITATION.—No action may be commenced under subsection (a) against an owner or operator of a facility if the Administrator has commenced and is diligently pursuing an administrative order or civil action to enforce the requirement concerned or to impose a civil penalty under this Act with respect to the violation of the requirement.

(f) COSTS.—The court, in issuing any final order in any action brought pursuant to this section, may award costs of litigation (including reasonable attorney and expert witness fees) to the prevailing or the substantially prevailing party whenever the court determines such an award is appropriate. The court may, if a temporary restraining order or preliminary injunction is sought, require the filing of a bond or equivalent security in accordance with the Federal Rules of Civil Procedure.

(g) OTHER RIGHTS.—Nothing in this section shall restrict or expand any right which any person (or class of persons) may have under any Federal or State statute or common law to seek enforcement of any requirement or to seek any other relief (including relief against the Administrator or a State agency).

(h) INTERVENTION.—

(1) BY THE UNITED STATES.—In any action under this section the United States or the State, or both, if not a party, may intervene as a matter of right.

(2) BY PERSONS.—In any action under this section, any person may intervene as a matter of right when such person has a direct interest which is or may be adversely affected by the action and the disposition of the action may, as a practical matter, impair or impede the person's ability to protect that interest

unless the Administrator or the State shows that the person's interest is adequately represented by existing parties in the action.

SEC. 327. EXEMPTION.

Except as provided in section 304, this title does not apply to the transportation, including the storage incident to such transportation, of any substance or chemical subject to the requirements of this title, including the transportation and distribution of natural gas.

SEC. 328. REGULATIONS.

The Administrator may prescribe such regulations as may be necessary to carry out this title.

SEC. 329. DEFINITIONS. (See Appendix B)

SEC. 330. AUTHORIZATION OF APPROPRIATIONS.

There are authorized to be appropriated for fiscal years beginning after September 30, 1986, such sums as may be necessary to carry out this title.

Appendix B
GLOSSARY

The purpose of this glossary is to provide definitions of the terms presented in the various rules and regulations generated as a result of this law. Each glossary entry ends with its source number. The sources are listed below. [Like this sentence, commentary about these definitions appears in brackets.] Some glossary items appear in more than one standard. When this is the case, the entry is preceded by a number in parenthesis, such as (1) (2) (3), to indicate that another definition follows. There are also entries into this glossary that do not appear in the documents listed below. These items appear without reference numbers.

SOURCE FOR DEFINITIONS
1. OSHA Hazard Communication Standard, 29 CFR 1910.1200
2. Emergency Planning and Release Notification Requirements, Final Rule 40 CFR 355
3. Trade Secret Claims for Emergency Planning and Community Right-to-Know Information, Proposed—40 CFR 350
4. Toxic Chemical Release Reporting; Community Right-to-Know, 40 CFR 372
5. OSHA Hazardous Waste Operations and Emergency Response Worker Protection Standard, 29 CFR 1910.120
6. Title III—Emergency Planning and Community Right-to-Know Act

Acute Effect—A health effect which usually occurs rapidly after a short exposure to a hazardous chemical and is of short duration.[1]

Administrator—The Administrator of the Environmental Protection Agency.[6]

Administrator and General Counsel—The EPA officers or employees occupying the positions so titled.[3]

Article—A manufactured item which is formed to a specific shape or design during manufacture, which has end use function(s) dependent in whole or in part upon its shape or design during end use, and which has either no change in chemical composition during its end use or only those changes of composition which have no commercial purpose separate from that of the article, and that result from a chemical reaction that occurs upon end use of other chemical substances, mixtures, or articles; except that fluids and particles are not considered articles regardless of shape or design.[4] [The purpose of this definition is to exempt furniture and fixture that contain hazardous chemicals that are not released during their use.]

174

Buddy System—A system of organizing employees into work groups in such a manner that each employee of the work group is designated to observe the activities of at least one other employee in the work group. The purpose of the buddy system is to provide quick assistance to those other employees in the event of an emergency.[5]

Business Confidentiality—Includes the concept of trade secrecy and other related legal concepts which give (or may give) a business the right to preserve the confidentiality of business information and to limit its use or disclosure by others in order that the business may obtain or retain business advantages it derives from its right in the information. The definition is meant to encompass any concept which authorizes a Federal agency to withhold business information under 5 U.S.C. 552(b)(4), as well as any concept which requires EPA to withhold information from the public for the benefit of a business under 18 U.S.C. 1905.[3]

Carcinogen—Any cancer-producing agent.[1]

Chemical Manufacturer—For the federal standard, an employer in SIC codes 20 through 39 where chemical(s) are produced for use or distribution. Individual states may have an expanded definition of this term.[1]

Chemical Name—The scientific designation of a chemical in accordance with the nomenclature system developed by the International Union of Pure and Applied Chemistry or the Chemical Abstracts Service.[1]

Chronic Effect—A health effect which generally occurs as a result of long-term exposure to a health hazard and is of long duration.[1]

Commission—The emergency response commission, or the Governor if there is no commission, for the State in which the facility is located.[2] [This is commonly known as the SERC.]

Common Name—Any designation or identification such as code name, code number, trade name, brand name, or generic name used to identify a chemical other than by its chemical name.[1]

Customs Territory of the United States—The 50 States, the District of Columbia, and Puerto Rico.[4]

Decontamination—The removal of hazardous substances from employees and their equipment to the extent necessary to preclude the occurrence of foreseeable adverse health effects.[5]

Distributor—A business, other than a chemical manufacturer or importer, which supplies hazardous chemicals to other distributors or to manufacturing purchasers.[1]

Emergency Response—Response to any occurrence which results, or is likely to result, in a release of a hazardous substance due to an unforeseen event.[5]

Employee—A worker who may be exposed to hazardous chemicals under normal operating conditions or foreseeable emergencies, including but not limited to production workers, line supervisors, and repair or maintenance personnel.[1]

Employer—For the federal standard, a person engaged in a business where chemicals are either used or are produced for use or distribution.[1]

Environment—Includes water, air, and land and the interrelationship which exists among and between water, air, and land and all living things.[2]

EPCRA—Emergency Planning and Community Right-to-Know Act.

Established Permissible Exposure Limit—The inhalation or dermal permissible exposure limit specified in 29 CFR Part 1910, Subpart Z, or if none is specified, the exposure limits in "NIOSH Recommendations for Occupational Health Standards" dated September 1986 incorporated by reference, or if neither of the above is specified, the standards specified by the American Conference of Governmental Industrial Hygienists in their publication "Threshold Limit Values and Biological Exposure Indices for 1986–87" dated 1986 incorporated by reference, or if none of the above is specified, a limit based upon a published study or manufacturer's safety data sheet brought to the employer's attention.[5]

Exposure—Subjection to hazardous chemical in the course of employment through any route of entry (inhalation, ingestion, skin contact or absorption), including potential exposure.[1]

(1) Extremely Hazardous Substance—A substance listed in Appendices A and B of 40 CFR 355.[2] [This is the list specified in Section 302 of EPCRA.]

(2) Extremely Hazardous Substance—A substance on the list described in section 302(a)(2).[6] [Resulting in serious health effects following short-term exposure from accidental release.]

(1) Facility—All buildings, equipment, structures, and other stationary items which are located on a single site or on contiguous or adjacent sites and which are owned or operated by the same person (or by any person which controls, is controlled by or under common control with, such person).[4]

(2) Facility—All buildings, equipment, structures, and other stationary items which are located on a single site or on contiguous or adjacent sites and which are owned or operated by the same person (or by any person which controls, is controlled by or under common control with, such person). For purposes of section 304, the term includes motor vehicles, rolling stock, and aircraft.[2 & 6]

(1) Hazardous Chemical—Any chemical which is a physical hazard or a health hazard.[1]

(2) Hazardous Chemical—Any hazardous chemical as defined under section 1910.1200(c) of Title 29 of the Code of Federal Regulations (the OSHA Hazard Communication Standard), except that such term does not include the following substances:

   (1) Any food, food additive, color additive, drug, or cosmetic regulated by the Food and Drug Administration.

   (2) Any substance present as a solid in any manufactured item to the extent exposure to the substance does not occur under normal conditions of use.

(3) Any substance to the extent it is used for personal, family, or household purposes, or is present in the same form and concentration as a product packaged for distribution and use by the general public.

(4) Any substance to the extent it is used in a research laboratory or a hospital or other medical facility under the direct supervision of a technically qualified individual.

(5) Any substance to the extent it is used in routine agricultural operations or is a fertilizer held for sale by a retailer to the ultimate customer.[2]

Hazardous Substance—Any substance designated or listed under (i) through (iv) below, exposure to which results or may result in adverse effects on the health or safety of employees:

(i) Any substance defined under section 101(14) of CERCLA.

(ii) Any biological agent and other disease-causing agent as defined in section 104(a)(2) of CERCLA.

(iii) Any substance listed by the U.S. Department of Transportation and regulated as hazardous materials under 49 CFR 172.101 and appendices.

(iv) Hazardous waste.[5]

(1) Health Hazard—[There are two different definitions for this term. The second one follows.] A chemical for which there is statistically significant evidence based on at least one study conducted in accordance with established scientific principles that acute or chronic health effects may occur in exposed employees; includes carcinogens, toxins, reproductive hazards, sensitizers, and agents which damage the skin, blood, lungs, eyes, nervous system or mucous membranes.[1] [Note that the definition below is more specific.]

(2) Health Hazard—A chemical, mixture of chemicals or a pathogen for which there is statistically significant evidence based on at least one study conducted in accordance with established scientific principles that acute or chronic health effects may occur in exposed employees. The term "health hazard" includes chemicals which are carcinogens, toxic or highly toxic agents, reproductive toxins, irritants, corrosives, sensitizers, hepatotoxins, nephrotoxins, neurotoxins, agents which act on the hematopoietic system, and agents which damage the lungs, skin, eyes, or mucous membranes. Further definition of the terms used above can be found in Appendix A to 29 CFR 1910.1200.[5] [Note the difference in this definition from the one above. This definition include additionally listed possible effects. However, both accept substances as health hazards if *one* scientific study identifies potential health effect.]

Identity—Any chemical or common name which is indicated on the material safety data sheet (MSDS) for the chemical. The identity used shall permit cross-references to be made among the required list of hazardous chemicals, the label, and the MSDS.[1]

IDLH or Immediately Dangerous to Life or Health—Any condition that poses an immediate threat to life, or which is likely to result in acute or immediate severe health effects. This includes oxygen deficiency conditions.[5]

Immediate Severe Health Effects—Any acute clinical sign or symptom of a serious, exposure-related reaction manifested within 72 hours after exposure to a hazardous substance.[5]

Import—To import a chemical substance into the customs territory of the United States.[4]

Importer—The first business with employees with the Customs Territory of the United States which receives hazardous chemicals produced in other countries for the purpose of supplying them to distributors or manufacturing purchasers within the United States.[1]

Label—Any written, printed, or graphic material displayed on or affixed to containers of hazardous chemicals.[1]

LEPC—the local emergency planning committee.

Manufacture—To produce, prepare, import, or compound a toxic chemical. Manufacture also applies to substances that are produced coincidentally during the manufacture, processing, use, or disposal of another substance or mixture, including byproducts and coproducts that are separated from that other substance or mixture, and impurities that remain in that substance or mixture. "Otherwise use" or "otherwise used" means any use of a toxic chemical that is not covered by the terms "manufacture" or "process" and includes use of a toxic chemical contained in a mixture or trade name product.[4]

Manufacturing Purchaser—An employer with a workplace classified in SIC Codes 20 through 39 who purchases a hazardous chemical for use within that workplace.[1]

(1) Material Safety Data Sheet—Written or printed material concerning a hazardous chemical which is prepared in accordance with paragraph (g) of the OSHA standard, 29 CFR, 1910.1200.[1]

(2) Material Safety Data Sheet—The sheet required to be developed under section 1910.1200(g) of title 29 of the Code of Federal Regulations, as that section may be amended from time to time.[6] [The definition of an MSDS is based on the OSHA hazard communication standard listed in (1).]

(1) Mixture—Any combination of two or more chemicals if the combination is not, in whole or in part, the result of a chemical reaction.[1]

(2) Mixture—A heterogenous association of substances where the various individual substances retain their identities and can usually be separated by mechanical means. Includes solutions or compounds but does not include alloys or amalgams.[2] [Note here that this definition is more descriptive than the original OSHA definition.]

Mutagen—A chemical or physical agent that induces genetic mutations.[1]

Oxygen Deficiency—That concentration of oxygen by volume below which air supplying respiratory protection must be provided. It exists in atmospheres where the percentage of oxygen by volume is less than 19.5 percent oxygen.[5]

Permissible Exposure Limit—(PEL) The legal limit of allowable exposure to a chemical on the basis of an eight-hour workday in a 40-hour week, as developed by OSHA.[1]

Petitioner—Any person who submits a petition under this regulation requesting disclosure of a chemical identity claimed as trade secret.[3]

Physical Hazard—A chemical for which there is scientifically valid evidence that it is a combustible liquid, a compressed gas, an explosive, a flammable, an organic peroxide, an oxidizer, a pyrophoric, an unstable (reactive) or a water-reactive chemical.[1]

Point Source Contamination—Contamination of the environment from a known single source such as an effluent pipe or smokestack.

Process—The preparation of a toxic chemical, after its manufacture, for distribution in commerce:

(1) In the same form or physical state as, or in a different form or physical state from, that in which it was received by the person so preparing such substance, or

(2) As part of an article containing the toxic chemical.

"Process" also applies to the processing of a toxic chemical contained in a mixture or trade name product.[4]

(1) Release—Any spilling, leaking, pumping, pouring, emitting, emptying, discharging, injecting, escaping, leaching, dumping, or disposing into the environment (including the abandonment or discarding of barrels, containers, and other closed receptacles) of any hazardous chemical, extremely hazardous substance, or CERCLA hazardous substance.[2]

(2) Release—Any spilling, leaking, pumping, pouring, emitting, emptying, discharging, injecting, escaping, leaching, dumping, or disposing into the environment (including the abandonment or discarding of barrels, containers, and other closed receptacles) of any toxic chemical.[4] [Note here the interchangeable use of the words hazardous and toxic in this definition and the definition above.]

Reportable Quantity—For any CERCLA hazardous substance, the reportable quantity established in Table 302.4 of 40 CFR Part 302, for such substance, for any other substance, the reportable quantity is one pound.[2]

Reproductive Hazard—A chemical which is capable of affecting the fertility of the parents or offspring or the production of offspring, including the causing of chromosomal damage, mutations, and harmful effects on fetuses.[1]

Route of Entry—The means by which hazardous chemicals can get into the body; specifically, the respiratory system, the digestive system, and the skin.[1]

SERC—State Emergency Response Commission.

Site Safety and Health Officer—The individual located on a hazardous waste site who is responsible to the employer and has the authority and knowledge necessary to implement the site safety and health plan and verify compliance with applicable safety and health requirements.[5]

Specific Chemical Identity—The chemical name, Chemical Abstracts Service (CAS) Registry Number, or any other information that reveals the precise chemical designation of the substance. Where the trade name will be treated as the specific chemical identity for purposes of this part.[3]

Submitter—Any person submitting a trade secret claim under sections 303(d)(2) and (d)(3), 311, 312 and 313 of Title III.[3]

Substance—Any chemical, element, compound, or mixture.[1]

Substantiation—The written answers submitted to EPA by a submitter to the specific questions set forth in this regulation in support of a claim that a chemical identity is a trade secret.[3]

Teratogen—An agent or factor that causes the production of physical or functional defects in the developing embryo.[1]

Threshold Limit Value—(TLV) An exposure level under which most people can work for 8 hours a day, day after day, with no harmful effects, as determined by the American Conference of Governmental Industrial Hygienists.[1]

Threshold Planning Quantity—For a substance listed in Appendices A and B of 40 CFR 355, the quantity listed in the column "threshold planning quantity" for that substance.[2]

Toxic—Harmful to living organisms.[1]

(1) Toxic chemical—A substance on the list described in section 313(c).[6] [of the EPCRA Law.]

(2) Toxic chemical—A chemical or chemical category listed in section 372.45.[4] [These are the regulations associated with Section 313 of EPCRA.]

(1) Trade Secret—Any confidential formula, pattern, process, device, information, or compilation of information (including chemical name or other unique chemical identifier) that is used in an employer's business, and that gives the employer an opportunity to obtain an advantage over competitors who do not know or use it.[1] [This definition and the one below are meant to be the same. The first one is specific for the OSHA hazard communication standard. The one below refers to submissions to EPA under EPCRA.]

(2) Trade Secret—Any confidential formula, pattern, process, device, information, or compilation of information that is used in submitter's business, and that gives the submitter an opportunity to obtain an advantage over competitors who do not know or use it.[3]

Trade Secrecy Claim—A submittal under sections 303(d)(2) or (d)(3), 311, 312 or 313 in which a chemical identity is claimed as trade secret, and is accompanied by a substantiation in support of the claim of trade secrecy for chemical identity.[3]

Appendix C
TIER ONE AND TIER TWO FORMS

Tier One EMERGENCY AND HAZARDOUS CHEMICAL INVENTORY
Aggregate Information by Hazard Type

FOR OFFICIAL USE ONLY

ID #
Date Received

Important: Read instructions before completing form

Reporting Period From January 1 to December 31, 19_____

Facility Identification

Name _____
Street Address _____
City _____ State _____ Zip _____
SIC Code [ ][ ][ ][ ]   Dun & Brad Number [ ][ ]-[ ][ ][ ]-[ ][ ][ ]

Owner/Operator

Name _____
Mail Address _____
Phone ( )

Emergency Contacts

Name _____
Title _____
Phone ( )
24 Hour Phone ( )

Name _____
Title _____
Phone ( )
24 Hour Phone ( )

☐ Check if site plan is attached

Hazard Type	Max Amount*	Average Daily Amount*	Number of Days On-Site	General Location
Physical Hazards				
Fire	[ ][ ]	[ ][ ]	[ ][ ]	
Sudden Release of Pressure	[ ][ ]	[ ][ ]	[ ][ ]	
Reactivity	[ ][ ]	[ ][ ]	[ ][ ]	
Health Hazards				
Immediate (acute)	[ ][ ]	[ ][ ]	[ ][ ]	
Delayed (Chronic)	[ ][ ]	[ ][ ]	[ ][ ]	

Certification (Read and sign after completing all sections)

I certify under penalty of law that I have personally examined and am familiar with the information submitted in this and all attached documents, and that based on my inquiry of those individuals responsible for obtaining the information, I believe that the submitted information is true, accurate and complete.

_____
Name and official title of owner/operator OR owner/operator's authorized representative

_____   _____
Signature   Date signed

* Reporting Ranges	Range Value	Weight Range in Pounds From...	To...
	00	0	99
	01	100	999
	02	1000	9,999
	03	10,000	99,999
	04	100,000	999,999
	05	1,000,000	9,999,999
	06	10,000,000	49,999,999
	07	50,000,000	99,999,999
	08	100,000,000	499,999,999
	09	500,000,000	999,999,999
	10	1 billion	higher than 1 billion

181

TIER ONE INSTRUCTIONS

GENERAL INFORMATION

Submission of this form is required by Title III of the Superfund Amendments and Reauthorization Act of 1986, Section 312, Public Law 99–499.

The purpose of this form is to provide State and local officials and the public with information on the general types and locations of hazardous chemicals present at your facility during the past year.

YOU MUST PROVIDE ALL INFORMATION REQUESTED ON THIS FORM.

You may substitute the Tier Two form for this Tier One form. (The Tier Two form provides detailed information and must be submitted in response to a specific request from State or local officials.)

WHO MUST SUBMIT THIS FORM

Section 312 of Title III requires that the owner or operator of a facility submit this form if, under regulations implementing the Occupational Safety and Health Act of 1970, the owner or operator is required to prepare or have available Material Safety Data Sheets (MSDS) for hazardous chemicals present at the facility. MSDS requirements are specified in the Occupational Safety and Health Administration (OSHA) Hazard Communication Standard, found in Title 29 of the Code of Federal Regulations at §1910.1200.

WHAT CHEMICALS ARE INCLUDED

You must report the information required on this form for every hazardous chemical for which you are required to prepare or have available an MSDS under the Hazard Communication Standard. However, OSHA regulations and Title III exempt some chemicals from reporting.

Section 1910.1200(b) of the OSHA regulations currently provides the following exemptions:

(i) Any hazardous waste as such term is defined by the Solid Waste Disposal Act, as amended (42 U.S.C. 6901 et seq.) when subject to regulations issued under that Act;

(ii) Tobacco or tobacco products;

(iii) Wood or wood products;

(iv) "Articles"– defined under §1910.1200 (b) as a manufactured item:

● Which is formed to a specific shape or design during manufacture;

● Which has end use function(s) dependent in whole or in part upon the shape or design during end use; and

● Which does not release, or otherwise result in exposure to a hazardous chemical under normal conditions of use.

(v) Food, drugs, cosmetics or alcoholic beverages in a retail establishment which are packaged for sale to consumers;

(vi) Foods, drugs, or cosmetics intended for personal consumption by employees while in the workplace;

(vii) Any consumer product or hazardous substance, as those terms are defined in the Consumer Product Safety Act (15 U.S.C. 1251 *et seq.*) respectively, where the employer can demonstrate it is used in the workplace in the same manner as normal consumer use, and which use results in a duration and frequency of exposure which is not greater than exposures experienced by consumers; and

(viii) Any drug, as that term is defined in the Federal Food, Drug, and Cosmetic Act (21 U.S.C. 301 *et seq.*), when it is in solid, final form for direct administration to the patient (i.e., tablets or pills).

In addition, Section 311(e) of Title III excludes the following substances:

(i) Any food, food additive, color additive, drug, or cosmetic regulated by the Food and Drug Administration;

(ii) Any substance present as a solid in any manufactured item to the extent exposure to the substance does not occur under normal conditions of use;

(iii) Any substance to the extent it is used for personal, family, or household purposes, or is present in the same form and concentration as a product packaged for distribution and use by the general public;

(iv) Any substance to the extent it is used in a research laboratory or a hospital or other medical facility under the direct supervision of a technically qualified individual;

(v) Any substance to the extent it is used in routine agricultural operations or is a fertilizer held for sale by a retailer to the ultimate customer.

Also, minimum reporting thresholds have been established under Title III, Section 312. You need to report only those hazardous chemicals that were present at your facility at any time during the preceding calendar year at or above the levels listed below:

● January to December 1987 (or first year of reporting) ...10,000 lbs.

● January to December 1988 (or second year of reporting) ...10,000 lbs.

● January to December 1989 (or third year of reporting) ...zero lbs. *

　* EPA will publish the final threshold, effective in the third year, after additional analysis.

● For extremely hazardous substances...500 lbs. or the threshold planning quantity, whichever is less, from the first year of reporting and thereafter.

WHEN TO SUBMIT THIS FORM

Beginning March 1, 1988, owners or operators must submit the Tier One form (or substitute the Tier Two form) on or before March 1 of every year.

1

INSTRUCTIONS

Please read these instructions carefully. Print or type all responses.

WHERE TO SUBMIT THIS FORM
Send one completed inventory form to each of the following organizations:

1. Your State emergency planning commission

2. Your local emergency planning committee

3. The fire department with jurisdiction over your facility.

PENALTIES
Any owner or operator of a facility who fails to submit or supplies false Tier One information shall be liable to the United States for a civil penalty of up to $25,000 for each such violation. Each day a violation continues shall constitute a separate violation. In addition, any citizen may commence a civil action on his or her own behalf against any owner or operator who fails to submit Tier One information.

> You may use the Tier Two form as a worksheet for completing Tier One. Filling in the Tier Two chemical information section should help you assemble your Tier One responses.

If your responses require more than one page, fill in the page number at the top of the form.

REPORTING PERIOD
Enter the appropriate calendar year, beginning January 1 and ending December 31.

FACILITY IDENTIFICATION
Enter the complete name of your facility (and company identifier where appropriate).

Enter the full street address or state road. If a street address is not available, enter other appropriate identifiers that describe the physical location of your facility (e.g., longitude and latitude). Include city, state, and zip code.

Enter the primary Standard Industrial Classification (SIC) code and the Dun & Bradstreet number for your facility. The financial officer of your facility should be able to provide the Dun & Bradstreet number. If your firm does not have this information, contact the state or regional office of Dun & Bradstreet to obtain your facility number or have one assigned.

OWNER/OPERATOR
Enter the owner's or operator's full name, mailing address, and phone number.

EMERGENCY CONTACT
Enter the name, title, and work phone number of at least one local person or office that can act as a referral if emergency responders need assistance in responding to a chemical accident at the facility.

Provide an emergency phone number where such emergency information will be available 24 hours a day, every day.

PHYSICAL AND HEALTH HAZARDS
Descriptions, Amounts, and Locations
This section requires aggregate information on chemicals by hazard categories as defined in 40 CFR 370.3. The two health hazard categories and three physical hazard categories are a consolidation of the 23 hazard categories defined in the OSHA Hazard Communication Standard, 29 CFR 1910.1200. For each hazard type, indicate the total amounts and general locations of all applicable chemicals present at your facility during the past year.

- What units should I use?

  Calculate all amounts as *weight in pounds*. To convert gas or liquid volume to weight in pounds, multiply by an appropriate density factor.

- What about mixtures?

  If a chemical is part of a mixture, *you have the option* of reporting either the weight of the entire mixture or only the portion of the mixture that is a particular hazardous chemical (e.g., if a hazardous solution weighs 100 lbs. but is composed of only 5% of a particular hazardous chemical, you can indicate either 100 lbs. of the mixture or 5 lbs. of the chemical).

  Select the option consistent with your Section 311 reporting of the chemical on the MSDS or list of MSDS chemicals.

- Where do I count a chemical that is a fire reactivity physical hazard and an immediate (acute) health hazard?

  Add the chemical's weight to your totals for all three hazard categories and include its location in all three categories. Many chemicals fall into more than one hazard category, which results in double-counting.

MAXIMUM AMOUNT
The amounts of chemicals you have on hand may vary throughout the year. The peak weights -- greatest single-day weights during the year -- are added together in this column to determine the maximum weight for each hazard type. Since the peaks for different chemicals often occur on different days, this maximum amount will seem artificially high.

> To complete this and the following sections, you may choose to use the Tier Two form as a worksheet.

To determine the Maximum Amount:

1. List all of your hazardous chemicals individually.

2. For each chemical...

   a. Indicate all physical and health hazards that the chemical presents. Include all chemicals, even if they are present for only a short period of time during the year.

2

b. Estimate the maximum weight in pounds that was present at your facility on any single day of the reporting period.

3. For each hazard type -- beginning with Fire and repeating for all physical and health hazard types...

   a. Add the maximum weights of all chemicals you indicated as the particular hazard type.

   b. Look at the Reporting Ranges at the bottom of the Tier One form. Find the appropriate range value code.

   c. Enter this range value as the Maximum Amount.

EXAMPLE:

You are using the Tier Two form as a worksheet and have listed raw weights in pounds for each of your hazardous chemicals. You have marked an X in the Immediate (acute) hazard column for phenol and sulfuric acid. The maximum amount raw weight you listed were 10,000 lbs. and 50 lbs. respectively. You add these together to reach a total of 10,050 lbs. Then you look at the Reporting Range at the bottom of your Tier One form and find that the value of 03 corresponds to 10,050 lbs. Enter 03 as your Maximum Amount for Immediate (acute) materials.

You also marked an X in the Fire hazard box for phenol. When you calculate your Maximum Amount totals for fire hazards, add the 10,000 lb. weight again.

AVERAGE DAILY AMOUNT
This column should represent the average daily amount of chemicals *of each hazard type* that were present at your facility at any point during the year.

To determine this amount:

1. List all of your hazardous chemicals individually (same as for Maximum Amount).

2. For each chemical...

   a. Indicate all physical and health hazards that the chemical presents (same as for Maximum Amount).

   b. Estimate the average weight in pounds that was present at your facility throughout the year. To do this, total all daily weights and divide by the number of days the chemical was present on the site.

3. For each hazard type -- beginning with Fire and repeating for all physical and health hazard types...

   a. Add the average weights of all chemicals you indicated for the particular hazard type.

   b. Look at the Reporting Ranges at the bottom of the Tier One form. Find the appropriate range value code.

   c. Enter this range value as the Average Daily Amount.

EXAMPLE:

You are using the Tier Two form, and have marked an X in the Immediate (acute) hazard column for nicotine and phenol. Nicotine is present at your facility 100 days during the year, and the sum of the daily weights is 100,000 lbs. By dividing 100,000 lbs. by 100 days on-site, you calculate an Average Daily Amount of 1,000 lbs. for nicotine. Phenol is present at your facility 50 days during the year, and the sum of the daily weights is 10,000 lbs. By dividing 10,000 lbs. by 50 days on-site, you calculate an Average Daily Amount of 200 lbs. for phenol. You then add the two average daily amounts together to reach a total of 1,200 lbs. Then you look at the Reporting Range on your Tier One form and find that the value 02 corresponds to 1,200 lbs. Enter 02 as your Average Daily Amount for Immediate (acute) Hazard.

You also marked an X in the Fire hazard column for phenol. When you calculate your Average Daily Amount for fire hazards, use the 200 lb. weight again.

NUMBER OF DAYS ON-SITE
Enter the greatest number of days that a single chemical within that hazard category was present on-site.

EXAMPLE:

At your facility, nicotine is present for 100 days and phosgene is present for 150 days. Enter 150 in the space provided.

GENERAL LOCATION
Enter the general location within your facility where each hazard may be found. General locations should include the names or identifications of buildings, tank fields, lots, sheds, or other such areas.

For each hazard type, list the locations of all applicable chemicals. As an alternative you may also attach a site plan and list the site coordinates related to the appropriate locations. If you do so, check the Site Plan box.

EXAMPLE:

On your worksheet you have marked an X in the Fire hazard column for acetone and butane. You noted that these are kept in steel drums in Room C of the Main Building, and in pressurized cylinders in Storage Shed 13, respectively. You could enter Main Building and Storage Shed 13 as the General Locations of your fire hazards. However, you choose to attach a site plan and list coordinates. Check the Site Plan box at the top of the column and enter site coordinates for the Main Building and Storage Shed 13 under General Locations.

If you need more space to list locations, attach an additional Tier One form and continue your list on the proper line. Number all pages.

CERTIFICATION
This must be completed by the owner or operator or the officially designated representative of the owner or operator. Enter your full name and official title. Sign your name and enter the current date.

Tier Two

EMERGENCY AND HAZARDOUS CHEMICAL INVENTORY

Specific Information by Chemical

Facility Identification

Name _____

Street Address _____

City _____ State _____ Zip _____

SIC Code ☐☐☐☐   Dun & Brad Number ☐☐☐☐-☐☐☐☐-☐

FOR OFFICIAL USE ONLY   ID # _____ Date Received _____

Owner/Operator Name

Name _____

Mail Address _____

Phone ( ) _____

Emergency Contact

Name _____ Title _____

Phone ( ) _____ 24 Hr. Phone ( ) _____

Name _____ Title _____

Phone ( ) _____ 24 Hr. Phone ( ) _____

Important: Read all instructions before completing form   Reporting Period From January 1 to December 31, 19___

Chemical Description	Physical and Health Hazards (check all that apply)	Inventory			Storage Codes and Locations (Non-Confidential)	
		Max. Daily Amount (code)	Avg. Daily Amount (code)	No. of Days On-site (days)	Storage Code	Storage Locations
CAS ☐☐☐☐☐☐ ☐ Trade Secret Chem. Name _____ Check all that apply: ☐ Pure ☐ Mix ☐ Solid ☐ Liquid ☐ Gas	☐ Fire ☐ Sudden Release of Pressure ☐ Reactivity ☐ Immediate (acute) ☐ Delayed (chronic)	☐	☐	☐	☐☐☐ ☐☐☐	
CAS ☐☐☐☐☐☐ ☐ Trade Secret Chem. Name _____ Check all that apply: ☐ Pure ☐ Mix ☐ Solid ☐ Liquid ☐ Gas	☐ Fire ☐ Sudden Release of Pressure ☐ Reactivity ☐ Immediate (acute) ☐ Delayed (chronic)	☐	☐	☐	☐☐☐ ☐☐☐	
CAS ☐☐☐☐☐☐ ☐ Trade Secret Chem. Name _____ Check all that apply: ☐ Pure ☐ Mix ☐ Solid ☐ Liquid ☐ Gas	☐ Fire ☐ Sudden Release of Pressure ☐ Reactivity ☐ Immediate (acute) ☐ Delayed (chronic)	☐	☐	☐	☐☐☐ ☐☐☐	

Certification *(Read and sign after completing all sections)*

I certify under penalty of law that I have personally examined and am familiar with the information submitted in this and all attached documents, and that based on my inquiry of those individuals responsible for obtaining the information, I believe that the submitted information is true, accurate, and complete.

Name and official title of owner/operator OR owner/operator's authorized representative

Signature _____ Date signed _____

Optional Attachments *(Check one)*

☐ I have attached a site plan

☐ I have attached a list of site coordinate abbreviations

Page _____ of _____ pages
Form Approved OMB No. 2050-0072

Tier Two

EMERGENCY AND HAZARDOUS CHEMICAL INVENTORY

Specific Information by Chemical

Facility Identification

Name _____

Street Address _____

City _____ State ____ Zip ____

SIC Code ____ Dun & Brad Number ____

FOR OFFICIAL USE ONLY   ID # ____   Date Received ____

Owner/Operator Name

Name _____

Mail Address _____

Phone ( )

Emergency Contact

Name _____ Title _____

Phone ( ) ____ 24 Hr. Phone ( )

Name _____ Title _____

Phone ( ) ____ 24 Hr. Phone ( )

Reporting Period From January 1 to December 31, 19__

Important: Read all instructions before completing form

Confidential Location Information Sheet

Storage Codes and Locations
(Confidential)

Storage Codes	Storage Locations

CAS # ____   Chem. Name ____

CAS # ____   Chem. Name ____

CAS # ____   Chem. Name ____

Certification *(Read and sign after completing all sections)*

I certify under penalty of law that I have personally examined and am familiar with the information submitted in this and all attached documents, and that based on my inquiry of those individuals responsible for obtaining the information, I believe that the submitted information is true, accurate, and complete.

Name and official title of owner/operator OR owner/operator's authorized representative ____ Signature ____ Date signed ____

Optional Attachments *(Check one)*

☐ I have attached a site plan

☐ I have attached a list of site coordinate abbreviations

TIER TWO INSTRUCTIONS

GENERAL INFORMATION

Submission of this Tier Two form (when requested) is required by Title III of the Superfund Amendments and Reauthorization Act of 1986, Section 312, Public Law 99-499. The purpose of this Tier Two form is to provide State and local officials and the public with specific information on hazardous chemicals present at your facility during the past year.

YOU MUST PROVIDE ALL INFORMATION REQUESTED ON THIS FORM TO FULFILL TIER TWO REPORTING REQUIREMENTS.

This form may also be used as a worksheet for completing the Tier One form or may be submitted in place of the Tier One form.

WHO MUST SUBMIT THIS FORM

Section 312 of Title III requires that the owner or operator of a facility submit this Tier Two form if so requested by a State emergency planning commission, a local emergency planning committee, or a fire department with jurisdiction over the facility.

This request may apply to the owner or operator of any facility that is required, under regulations implementing the Occupational Safety and Health Act of 1970, to prepare or have available a Material Safety Data Sheet (MSDS) for a hazardous chemical present at the facility. MSDS requirements are specified in the Occupational Safety and Health Administration (OSHA) Hazard Communications Standard, found in Title 29 of the Code of Federal Regulations at §1910.1200.

WHAT CHEMICALS ARE INCLUDED

You must report the information required on this form for each hazardous chemical for which Tier Two information is requested. However, OSHA regulations and Title III exempt some chemicals from reporting.

Section 1910.1200(b) of the OSHA regulations currently provides the following exemptions:

(i) Any hazardous waste as such term is defined by the Solid Waste Disposal Act as amended (42 U.S.C. 6901 et seq.) when subject to regulations issued under that Act;

(ii) Tobacco or tobacco products;

(iii) Wood or wood products;

(iv) "Articles" – defined under §1910.1200(b) as a manufactured item:

- Which is formed to a specific shape or design during manufacture;
- Which has end use function(s) dependent in whole or in part upon the shape or design during end use; and
- Which does not release, or otherwise result in exposure to a hazardous chemical under normal conditions of use.

(v) Food, drugs, cosmetics or alcoholic beverages in a retail establishment which are packaged for sale to consumers;

(vi) Foods, drugs, or cosmetics intended for personal consumption by employees while in the workplace.

(vii) Any consumer product or hazardous substance, as those terms are defined in the Consumer Product Safety Act (15 U.S.C. 1251 et seq.) respectively, where the employer can demonstrate it is used in the workplace in the same manner as normal consumer use, and which use results in a duration and frequency of exposure which is not greater than exposures experienced by consumers

(viii) Any drug, as that term is defined in the Federal Food, Drug, and Cosmetic Act (21 U.S.C. 301 et seq.), when it is in solid, final form for direct administration to the patient (i.e., tablets or pills).

In addition, Section 311(e) of Title III excludes the following substances:

(i) Any food, food additive, color additive, drug, or cosmetic regulated by the Food and Drug Administration;

(ii) Any substance present as a solid in any manufactured item to the extent exposure to the substance does not occur under normal conditions of use;

(iii) Any substance to the extent it is used for personal, family, or household purposes, or is present in the same form and concentration as a product packaged for distribution and use by the general public;

(iv) Any substance to the extent it is used in a research laboratory or a hospital or other medical facility under the direct supervision of a technically qualified individual;

(v) Any substance to the extent it is used in routine agricultural operations or is a fertilizer held for sale by a retailer to the ultimate customer.

Also, minimum reporting thresholds have been established for Tier One under Title III, Section 312. You need to report only those hazardous chemicals that were present at your facility at any time during the preceding calendar year at or above the levels listed below:

- January to December 1987
  (or first year of reporting) ...10,000 lbs.
- January to December 1988
  (or second year of reporting) ...10,000 lbs.
- January to December 1989
  (or third year of reporting) ...zero lbs. *
  * EPA will publish the final threshold, effective in the third year, after additional analysis.
- For extremely hazardous substances...500 lbs. or the threshold planning quantity, whichever is less, from the first year of reporting and thereafter.

A requesting official may limit the responses required under Tier Two by specifying particular chemicals or groups of chemicals. Such requests apply to hazardous chemicals regardless of established thresholds.

1

INSTRUCTIONS

Please read these instructions carefully. Print or type all responses.

WHEN TO SUBMIT THIS FORM

Owners or operators must submit the Tier Two form to the requesting agency within 30 days of receipt of a written request from an authorized official.

WHERE TO SUBMIT THIS FORM

Send the completed Tier Two form to the requesting agency.

PENALTIES

Any owner or operator who violates any Tier Two reporting requirements shall be liable to the United States for a civil penalty of up to $25,000 for each such violation. Each day a violation continues shall constitute a separate violation.

> You may use the Tier Two form as a worksheet for completing the Tier One form. Filling in the Tier Two Chemical Information section should help you assemble your Tier One responses.

If your responses require more than one page, fill in the page number at the top of the form.

REPORTING PERIOD

Enter the appropriate calendar year, beginning January 1 and ending December 31.

FACILITY IDENTIFICATION

Enter the full name of your facility (and company identifier where appropriate).

Enter the full street address or state road. If a street address is not available, enter other appropriate identifiers that describe the physical location of your facility (e.g., longitude and latitude). Include city, state, and zip code.

Enter the primary Standard Industrial Classification (SIC) code and the Dun & Bradstreet number for your facility. The financial officer of your facility should be able to provide the Dun & Bradstreet number. If your firm does not have this information, contact the state or regional office of Dun & Bradstreet to obtain your facility number or have one assigned.

OWNER/OPERATOR

Enter the owner's or operator's full name, mailing address, and phone number.

EMERGENCY CONTACT

Enter the name, title, and work phone number of at least one local person or office who can act as a referral if emergency responders need assistance in responding to a chemical accident at the facility.

Provide an emergency phone number where such emergency chemical information will be available 24 hours a day, every day.

CHEMICAL INFORMATION: Description, Hazards, Amounts, and Locations

The main section of the Tier Two form requires specific information on amounts and locations of hazardous chemicals, as defined in the OSHA Hazard Communication Standard.

- **What units should I use?**

  Calculate all amounts as *weight in pounds.* To convert gas or liquid volume to weight in pounds, multiply by an appropriate density factor.

- **What about mixtures?**

  If a chemical is part of a mixture, *you have the option* of reporting either the weight of the entire mixture or only the portion of the mixture that is a particular hazardous chemical (e.g., if a hazardous solution weighs 100 lbs. but is composed of only 5% of a particular hazardous chemical, you can indicate either 100 lbs. of the mixture *or* 5 lbs. of the chemical).

  Select the option consistent with your Section 311 reporting of the chemical on the MSDS or list of MSDS chemicals.

CHEMICAL DESCRIPTION

1. Enter the Chemical Abstract Service number (CAS#).

   For mixtures, enter the CAS number of the mixture as a whole if it has been assigned a number distinct from its components. For a mixture that has no CAS number, leave this item blank or report the CAS numbers of as many constituent chemicals as possible.

   > If you are withholding the name of a chemical in accordance with criteria specified in Title III, Section 322, enter the generic chemical class (e.g., list toluene disocynate as organic isocynate) and check the box marked Trade Secret. Trade secret information should be submitted to EPA and must include a substantiation. Please refer to Section 322 of Title III for detailed information on how to comply with trade secret requests.

2. Enter the chemical name or common name of each hazardous chemical.

3. Circle *ALL* applicable descriptors: pure or mixture, *and* solid, liquid, or gas.

> **EXAMPLE:**
>
> You have pure chlorine gas on hand, as well as two mixtures that contain liquid chlorine. You write "chlorine" and enter the CAS#. Then you circle "pure" *and* "mix" -- as well as "liq" *and* "gas".

PHYSICAL AND HEALTH HAZARDS

For each chemical you have listed, check all the physical and health hazard boxes that apply. These hazard categories are defined in 40 CFR 370.3. The two health hazard categories and three physical hazard categories are a consolidation of the 23 hazard categories defined in the OSHA Hazard Communication Standard, 29 CFR 1910.1200.

MAXIMUM AMOUNT

1. For each hazardous chemical, estimate the greatest amount present at your facility on any single day during the reporting period.
2. Find the appropriate range value code in Table I.
3. Enter this range value as the Maximum Amount.

Table I   REPORTING RANGES

Range Value	Weight Range in Pounds From...	To...
00	0	99
01	100	999
02	1,000	9,999
03	10,000	99,999
04	100,000	999,999
05	1,000,000	9,999,999
06	10,000,000	49,999,999
07	50,000,000	99,999,999
08	100,000,000	499,999,999
09	500,000,000	999,999,999
10	1 billion	higher than 1 billion

If you are using this form as a worksheet for completing Tier One, enter the actual weight in pounds in the shaded space below the response blocks. Do this for both Maximum Amount and Average Daily Amount.

EXAMPLE:

You received one large shipment of a solvent mixture last year. The shipment filled your 5,000-gallon storage tank. You know that the solvent contains 10% benzene, which is a hazardous chemical.

You figure that 10% of 5,000 gallons is 500 gallons. You also know that the density of benzene is 7.29 pounds per gallon, so you multiply 500 by 7.29 to get a weight of 3,645 pounds.

Then you look at Table I and find that the range value 02 corresponds to 3,645. You enter 02 as the Maximum Amount.

(If you are using the form as a worksheet for completing a Tier One form, you should write 3,645 in the shaded area.)

AVERAGE DAILY AMOUNT

1. For each hazardous chemical, estimate the average weight in pounds that was present at your facility during the year.

   To do this, total all daily weights and divide by the number of days the chemical was present on the site.
2. Find the appropriate range value in Table I.
3. Enter this range value as the Average Daily Amount.

EXAMPLE:

The 5,000-gallon shipment of solvent you received last year was gradually used up and completely gone in 315 days. The sum of the daily volume levels in the tank is 929,250 gallons. By dividing 929,250 gallons by 315 days on-site, you calculate an average daily amount of 2,950 gallons.

You already know that the solvent contains 10% benzene, which is a hazardous chemical. Since 10% of 2,950 is 295, you figure that you had an average of 295 gallons of benzene. You also know that the density of benzene is 7.29 pounds per gallon, so you multiply 295 by 7.29 to get a weight of 2,150 pounds.

Then you look at Table I and find that the range value 02 correponds to 2,150. You enter 02 as the Average Daily Amount.

(If you are using the form as a worksheet for completing a Tier One form, you should write 2,150 in the shaded area.)

NUMBER OF DAYS ON-SITE

Enter the number of days that the hazardous chemical was found on-site.

EXAMPLE:

The solvent composed of 10% benzene was present for 315 days at your facility. Enter 315 in the space provided.

STORAGE CODES AND STORAGE LOCATIONS

List all non-confidential chemical locations in this column, along with storage types/conditions associated with each location.

Storage Codes: Indicate the types and conditions of storage present.

   a. *Look at Table II.* For each location, find the appropriate storage type(s). Enter the corresponding code(s) in front of the parentheses.
   b. *Look at Table III.* For each storage type, find the temperature and pressure conditions. Enter the applicable pressure code in the first space within the parentheses. Enter the applicable temperature code in the last space within the parentheses.

3

Table II – STORAGE TYPES

CODES	Types of Storage
A	Above ground tank
B	Below ground tank
C	Tank inside building
D	Steel drum
E	Plastic or non-metallic drum
F	Can
G	Carboy
H	Silo
I	Fiber drum
J	Bag
K	Box
L	Cylinder
M	Glass bottles or jugs
N	Plastic bottles or jugs
O	Tote bin
P	Tank wagon
Q	Rail car
R	Other

Table III – TEMPERATURE AND PRESSURE CONDITIONS

CODES	Storage Conditions
	(PRESSURE)
1	Ambient pressure
2	Greater than ambient pressure
3	Less than ambient pressure
	(TEMPERATURE)
4	Ambient temperature
5	Greater than ambient temperature
6	Less than ambient temperature but not cryogenic
7	Cryogenic conditions

EXAMPLE:

The benzene in the main building is kept in a tank inside the building, at ambient pressure and less than ambient temperature.

Table II shows you that the code for a tank inside a building is C. Table III shows you that code for ambient pressure is 1, and the code for less than ambient temperature is 6.

You enter: C(1,6)

Storage Locations:

Provide a brief description of the precise location of the chemical, so that emergency responders can locate the area easily. You may find it advantageous to provide the optional site plan or site coordinates as explained below.

For each chemical, indicate at a minimum the building or lot. Additionally, where practical, the room or area may be indicated. You may respond in narrative form with appropriate site coordinates or abbreviations.

If the chemical is present in more than one building, lot, or area location, continue your responses down the page as needed. If the chemical exists everywhere at the plant site simultaneously, you may report that the chemical is ubiquitous at the site.

Optional attachments: If you choose to attach one of the following, check the appropriate Attachments box at the bottom of the Tier Two form.

a. A site plan with site coordinates indicated for buildings, lots, areas, etc. throughout your facility.

b. A list of site coordinate abbreviations that correspond to buildings, lots, areas, etc. throughout your facility.

EXAMPLE:

You have benzene in the main room of the main building, and in tank 2 in tank field 10. You attach a site plan with coordinates as follows: main building = G-2, tank field 10 = B-6. Fill in the Storage Location as follows:

B-6 [Tank 2] G-2 [Main Room]

Under Title III, Section 324, you may elect to withhold location information on a specific chemical from disclosure to the public. If you choose to do so:

● Enter the word "confidential" in the Non-Confidential Location section of the Tier Two form.

● On a separate Tier Two Confidential Location Information Sheet, enter the name and CAS# of each chemical for which you are keeping the location confidential.

● Enter the appropriate location and storage information, as described above for non-confidential locations.

● Attach the Tier Two Confidential Location Information Sheet to the Tier Two form. This separates confidential locations from other information that will be disclosed to the public.

CERTIFICATION.

This must be completed by the owner or operator or the officially designated representative of the owner or operator. Enter your full name and official title. Sign your name and enter the current date.

4

Appendix D
MATERIAL SAFETY DATA SHEETS

Material Safety Data Sheets are formal documents used to transfer information about specific chemicals from chemical producer to chemical user. The information included on these sheets can be quite detailed and often covers a wide range of topics. For example, the physical characteristics of chemicals, any health hazards associated with their use, control technologies and personal protection information are a few of the areas covered.

These documents were developed and used by chemical manufacturers for many years to maintain a written record regarding the chemical properties of materials. One of the purposes of these documents was to establish protection criteria to be followed by anyone who used the substance or compound that the Material Safety Data Sheets covered. Traditionally, they were used by chemists, toxicologists and other technical professionals to exchange information among themselves, and, therefore, were not widely distributed. Starting in the 1960's, when concern about the toxic properties of chemicals increased, the use of Material Safety Data Sheets became more commonplace. However, their distribution remained limited and rarely extended beyond the technical community.

With the advent of OSHA in the early 1970's, the Material Safety Data Sheet increased in popularity as the basis of the information used to design employee protection programs on the job. Here again, however, their distribution was mostly limited to technical and health and safety professionals who designed process control as well as personal protective measures and safety programs.

These early forms of the Material Safety Data Sheet often emphasized acute rather than chronic health hazards. In this context, an acute hazard relates to any chemical whose effects usually occur rapidly, as a result of short-term exposure, and are of short duration. In other words, a chemical substance that can cause immediate danger, such as skin or eye irritation, is considered an acute hazard. Besides acute health hazards, Material Safety Data Sheets most likely contained information regarding physical hazards such as fire and explosion potential. An example of an acute hazard is chlorine or ammonia gas, which create an immediate health problem if overexposure occurs. A physical hazard is a substance such as acetone, which is highly flammable.

When the OSHA Hazard Communication Standard went into effect on May 25, 1985, the Material Safety Data Sheet was codified as the document of record for the transferral of information about hazards associated with chemicals. This OSHA standard clearly specified the kind of information that the Material Safety Data Sheet was to contain. Of particularly importance was the requirement that it include information about chronic health hazards. These hazards relate to long-term health effects from continuous exposure which is also of long duration. Chronic health hazards include substances such as benzene, trichloroethylene, and other solvents where overexposure may cause long-term health hazards such as liver or kidney damage. Chronic health hazards also include those substances which can cause cancer. Asbestos, considered a serious chronic health hazard, may not cause disease in a overexposed person until 10 to 50 years after the initial exposure.

The standard also established that any individual who worked with a hazardous material in the manufacturing sector had the right of access to the Material Safety Data Sheet. The firm using the chemical was also required to provide training to employees about how to read and interpret this document.

This OSHA standard established the requirement that the Material Safety Data Sheet, which is technical in nature, must be made available to lay individuals with little background or understanding of much of the information contained in it. It is interesting to note, in this regard, that many people find the information difficult to understand and, to some extent, frightening. This increased dissemination of Material Safety Data Sheets is another indication of the growing technological sophistication of our society and the increased knowledge required for an individual to participate in the workplace.

The Hazard Communication Standard requires that manufacturers produce this document based on a hazard determination methodology outlined in the standard and described in more detail below. It is the chemical producer's responsibility to provide the Material Safety Data Sheet to the purchaser of the product. This purchaser may, in fact, be a chemical producer as well. For example, a firm may receive a chemical from a manufacturer in its pure state and then formulate or mix that chemical with other chemicals to produce a new substance. It then becomes the responsibility of the second user to incorporate the information provided by the various suppliers into a new Material Safety Data Sheet which describes the properties of the newly created chemical.

The number of chemicals that require Material Safety Data Sheets is quite impressive. *The Registry of Toxic Effects of Chemical Substances (RTECS)*, published by the National Institute of Occupational and Safety and Health,[1] contain approximately 50,000 chemical substances which may be constituents of hundred of thousands of products. Each producer of a product is required to provide a Material Safety Data Sheet. Once a chemical is produced and distributed in the marketplace, it is the responsibility of the supplier to provide the downstream user with a copy of the Material Safety Data Sheet. So, for every facility that uses hazardous chemicals in the United States, Material Safety Data Sheets must be kept on hand. With the expansion of the Hazard Communication Standard to all employers in May 1988, hundreds of thousands of facilities will be receiving Material Safety Data Sheets that will become available to millions of employees.

---

[1] *Registry of Toxic Effects of Chemical Substances,* National Institute of Occupational Safety and Health, Superintendent of Documents, U.S. Government Printing Office, Washington, D.C. 20402.

With the expansion of EPCRA, the distribution of Materials Safety Data Sheets increases even further. These documents will become available to tens of millions of citizen in communities throughout the nation. The increased use of this document to transfer information about chemical hazards make it important for all of those involved in EPCRA implementation to understand.

HAZARD DETERMINATION

The OSHA Hazard Communication Standard puts the responsibility for hazard determination on the chemical producer. The methods prescribe for making such a determination are contained in 29 CFR 1910.1200(D). This section of the regulation or standard states clearly that chemical manufacturers and importers shall evaluate chemicals produced in their workplaces or imported by them to determine if they are hazardous. Employers who use chemicals but do not produce them are not required to evaluate chemicals unless they choose to do so. It is expected that chemical users will rely on the evaluation performed by the manufacturer or importer of the chemical.

Even though it is the responsibility of the manufacturer to determine if the chemical is hazardous, the standard requires any chemical that appears in the following sources to be treated as a hazard:

1. 29 CFR, Part 1910, Subpart Z, "Toxic and Hazardous Substances, Occupational Safety and Health Administration"
2. *Threshold Limit Values for Chemical Substances and Physical Agents in the Work Environment,* American Conference of Government Industrial Hygienists, latest edition

The standard also requires that any chemical for which there is at least one positive scientific study showing a statistically significant health hazard (when the study is conducted in accordance with established scientific principles) is considered to be sufficient to establish a hazardous effect. By including this caveat, OSHA has created a generally inclusive definition for determining a chemical to be a health hazard, greatly expanding the range of possible chemicals covered by the standard.

In addition to the general characteristics of health hazards, the standard specifically requires that chemical manufacturers evaluate each chemical for its potential carcinogenicity, or ability to cause cancer. Here again, OSHA includes a baseline list of references to consider:

1. The *National Toxicological Program Annual Report on Carcinogens,* latest edition
2. The *International Agency for Research on Cancer IARC Monograph,* latest edition

3. 29 CFR, Part 1910, Subpart Z, "Toxic and Hazardous Substances, Occupational Safety and Health Administration"

Another consideration of the standard regarding hazard determination relates to mixtures of chemicals. The standard clearly states that if a mixture has been tested as a whole to determine its hazards, the result of such testing shall be used to determine whether the mixture is hazardous. However, if a mixture has not been tested as a whole to determine its hazards, it shall be assumed to have the same health hazards as its components (if they comprise 1% by weight or volume or greater in the mixture). For carcinogens, the percentage to be considered a hazard is reduced to 0.1% or greater.

With regard to physical hazards, mixtures can pose a difficult problem. The standard does not require that mixtures be tested as a whole. However, it is sometimes difficult to determine from existing information whether the physical hazards remain the same in a mixture.

When a chemical producer makes a hazard determination for a chemical, the kinds of information used must be based on specific criteria outlines in the OSHA standard.

Physical Hazards

The following physical characteristics of chemicals must be considered:

Boiling point
Specific gravity
Vapor density
Percentage of volatiles by volume
Appearance and odor
Melting point
Vapor pressure
Solubility and evaporation rate

Other physical characteristics that are important are chemical reactivity characteristics and fire and explosion hazard information, including incompatible materials, hazardous decomposition products and special precautions in handling. Fire and explosion hazard information includes information such as the flash point, flammability limits in air by percent and by volume, fire extinguishing agents to be used and not used, and special firefighting procedures.

Health Hazards

Regarding health hazard information, the particularly important items are the chemical's method of entry into the body, including inhalation, skin contact, absorption, eye contact and ingestion. Signs and symptoms of acute and chronic exposure must also be included in the Material Safety Data Sheet. Medical conditions aggravated by exposure to the chemical is another required piece of information. Also, OSHA permissible exposure limits and ACGIH threshold limit values, two measurements used to determine the level of exposure, must be recorded on the Material Safety Data Sheet if they have been established.

Emergency Procedures

Another item to be considered by a manufacturer in making a hazard determination are the emergency and first aid procedures to be instituted. This is particularly important with regard to EPCRA compliance, since it is in an emergency situation that local emergency response teams will act on this information.

PROVISIONS OF THE MATERIAL SAFETY DATA SHEET

A sample Material Safety Data Sheet is included at the end of this appendix. Each section is specified by the Hazard Communication Standard; the remainder of this chapter will explain the various sections. In reviewing these documents supplied by manufacturers, one may find a wide variation in the quality and quantity of information provided. Some documents may even be incomplete. If the information on a Material Safety Data Sheet seems, inadequate, the requester should contact the supplier.

SECTION I:
Product
identification

Section I identifies the chemical and specifies who makes it. It provides both the chemical and trade names of the substance, synonyms for these names, the chemical family, and the formula. It also gives the name and address of the manufacturer and an emergency telephone number.

SECTION II:
Hazardous
ingredients

Section II lists the hazardous ingredients that the substance contains, including hazardous mixtures of liquids, solids or gases. It may also indicate the percentage of each ingredient in the substance, and it gives appropriate hazard data as established by scientific research.

Carcinogens

Section II also lists the carcinogen or carcinogenic components of the hazardous chemical. It provides the chemical and common names of the carcinogen, the percentage in which it is present in the substance, and any appropriate data on its carcinogenicity as determined by scientific research.

Mutagens and teratogens

Although the federal rule does not specifically mention mutagens or teratogens, some state laws do require this information on Material Safety Data Sheets. If a chemical has been found to be a mutagen, a substance which may induce genetic mutations, or a teratogen, an agent which causes physical defects in developing embryos, this information may appear under carcinogenic hazard data.

SECTION III: Physical characteristics

Section III provides information about the physical properties of the substance. This section gives the engineering and production staffs the information they need to determine how to work with the chemical safely and how to store it. This section gives the boiling point, flash point, solubility rate and evaporation rate, in addition to other physical characteristics of the substance.

Section IV: Chemical reactivity/ characteristics

Section IV gives reactivity data, including information on stability, incompatibility with other substances, hazardous decomposition products and conditions that should be avoided. This information on chemical properties is essential when substances are to be mixed together.

SECTION V: Fire and explosion hazard information

Section V deals with fire and explosion hazards. This information is especially important in an emergency. The chance of a fire may be small, but one must be prepared. If special firefighting equipment is required, it must be readily available and inspected regularly.

SECTION VI: Health hazard information

Section VI gives health hazard information, including primary routes of entry for the chemical, signs and symptoms of exposure, medical conditions aggravated by exposure, and emergency and first aid procedures to prepare employees and rescue workers to act quickly if an emergency occurs.

Section VI also includes two types of exposure limits. The permissible exposure limit (PEL), as determined by OSHA, describes allowable exposures to a chemical on the basis of an eight hour workday.

The PEL is akin to the threshold limit value (TLV), which is also given in this section but which focuses instead on allowable limits for repeated exposures on a daily basis without special protection. This section may also indicate whether the substance is a carcinogen, a mutagen, a teratogen, or a reproductive hazard, as previously defined.

SECTION VII: Protection and control information	Section VII gives special protection information. It specifies hygiene practices, ventilation in the work area, appropriate personal protective equipment for workers, and engineering controls.
SECTION VIII: Spill or leak procedures	Section VIII specifies how to clean up spills and leaks. It also describes how to dispose of the resulting waste, and describes protective measures needed during the repair and maintenance of contaminated equipment. Spill and leak procedures are often regulated by the U.S. Department of Transportation and by such statutes and laws as the Toxic Substances Control Act (TSCA) and the Resource Conservation and Recovery Act (RCRA). The information in this section is especially important in preparing emergency plans.

INTERPRETING A MATERIAL SAFETY DATA SHEET

It is important to understand that interpreting information on a Material Safety Data Sheet can sometimes be difficult. Since there is often a relationship between exposure limits, health hazards and the particular situation in which the chemical exposure occurs, something may appear more or less hazardous depending upon this relationship. Therefore, understanding the hazards associated with a chemical can be difficult. In these situations, one must rely on experts to interpret these materials. Given this problem, the EPA has begun to generate documents to help communities understand relative hazards; the agency plans to continue to produce these documents.

It is also important to understand that because the Material Safety Data Sheet requirements are based on a performance-oriented standard, manufacturers have a fair amount of latitude in reporting information. There are various incentives for underreporting hazard information, one of which is the fear of future liability. On the other hand, overreporting can also cause market problems and can limit product distribution. All of these issues make the use of Material Safety Data Sheets for public distribution of a difficult challenge for industry.

A MODEL MATERIAL SAFETY DATA SHEET

Following is a copy of a blank Material Safety Data Sheet that will give you some idea of what information it contains.

Material Safety Data Sheet

☐ Initial Preparation

☐ Change

Date of
Preparation/Change _____

Prepared by _____

Please print or type in English

MSDS Design Meets the Criteria of the Federal Hazard Communication Rule
29 CFR Part 1910.1200   Issued Nov. 25, 1983.

(Attention Preparers: Mark N/A (Not Applicable) for Sections
Where No Relevant Information Has Been Found.)

Product Identification

Name on Label

Chemical Name(s)   **CAS No.**

Common Name(s)

Manufacturer's Name:

Address:

Regular Telephone Number: **Emergency Telephone Number:**

Hazardous Ingredients

A. Hazardous Chemical(s) (%)

Chemical name(s)   Common name(s)

B. Carcinogenic Chemical(s) (%)   **Found to be** (state which)
                                            carcinogenic by: NTP, IARC, OSHA

Chemical Name(s)   Common Name(s)

Physical Characteristics

Boiling point, °F (°C) at 760 mmHg	Melting point °F (°C)
Specific gravity (H₂0 = 1)	Vapor pressure, mmHg
Vapor density (Air = 1)	Solubility in H₂0 by Wt.
% Volatiles by Vol.	Evaporation rate (Butyl Acetate = 1)
Appearance and odor	

Single substance ☐   Mixture tested as a whole ☐   Mixture not tested as a whole ☐

Chemical Reactivity/Characteristics

Conditions Contributing to Instability
Reactivity with water
Reactivity with common materials
Potential for polymerization
Inhibitor of polymerization

Incompatible Materials

Hazardous Decomposition Products

Special Precautions in Handling/Storage   **Neutralizing Chemicals**

Fire and Explosion Hazard Information

Flash Point °F (°C) (Test Method)	Autoignition °F(°C) Temperature	
Flammable Limits in Air % by Vol.	Lower Explosive Limit	Upper Explosive Limit

Fire Extinguishing Agents to Be Used/Not to Be Used

Special Fire Fighting Procedures

Unusual Fire and Explosion Hazard
(Including Combustion Products)

Health Hazard Information

Routes of Exposure

Inhalation

Skin Contact/Absorption

Eye Contact

Ingestion

Signs and Symptoms of:

Acute Exposure

Chronic Exposure

Medical Conditions Aggravated by Exposure to the Chemical

OSHA Permissible Exposure Limit (PEL)

ACGIH Threshold Limit Value (TLV)

Other Exposure Limits Used or Recommended

Emergency and First Aid Procedures for Different Routes of Exposure

Inhalation

Skin Contact/Absorption

Eye Contact

Ingestion

*Notes to Physician

Protection and Control Information

Hygienic Practices

Ventilation Requirements

Personal Protective Equipment
Respiratory (Specify in Detail)

Eyes

Gloves

Other Clothing and Equipment

Engineering Controls/Work Practices

Spill or Leak Procedures

Steps to Be Taken If Material Is Released or Spilled

Waste Disposal Method(s)

Hazard Classification

Code of Federal Regulations (CFR)

National Fire Protection Association (NFPA) Hazard Classification

Other

RESOURCES

Printed Works

A list of resources to be used when interpreting the Material Safety Data Sheet follows. These resources are available at university libraries as well as at many firms in the community. The local library may also contain some of these books.

Casarett and Doull's Toxicology: The Basic Science of Poisons, by Doull, Klaasen, and Amdur, Macmillan Publishing Co., 866 Third Avenue, New York, NY 10022.

Chemical Hazards of the Workplace. Nick H. Proctor and James P. Hughes, J.P. Lipincott Co., 6 Winchester Terrace, New York, NY 10022.

Condensed Chemical Dictionary. Van Nostrand Reinhold Co., 115 Fifth Avenue, New York, NY.

Handbook of Chemistry and Physics, Chemical Rubber Company, 18901 Cranwood Parkway, Cleveland, OH 44128.

IARC Monographs on the Evaluation of the Carcinogenic Risk of Chemicals to Man, Geneva: World Health Organization, International Agency for Research on Cancer, 1972-the present (multivolume work). 49 Sheridan Street, Albany, NY.

Industrial Hygiene and Toxicology (5 vols.), by F. A. Patty, John Wiley & Sons, 605 Third Avenue, New York, NY 10158.

Industrial Toxicology, by Alice Hamilton and Harriet L. Hardy, Publishing Sciences Group, Inc., Acton, MA

Recognition of Health Hazards in Industry. William A. Burgess, John Wiley & Sons, 605 Third Avenue, New York, NY 10158.

The Merck Index: An Encyclopedia of Chemicals and Drugs. Merck and Company, Inc., 126 E. Lincoln Avenue, Rahway, NJ 07065.

Threshold Limit Values for Chemical Substances and Physical Agents in the Workroom Environment with Intended Changes, American Conference of Governmental Industrial Hygienists, 6500 Glenway Avenue, Bldg. D-5, Cincinnati, OH 45211.

Note: The following documents are on sale from the Superintendent of Documents, U.S. Government Printing Office, Washington, D.C. 20702:

"NIOSH/OSHA Pocket Guide to Chemical Hazards" (NIOSH Pub. No. 78-210).

"Occupational Health Guidelines," NIOSH/OSHA (NIOSH Pub. No. 81-123).

"Registry of Toxic Effects of Chemical Substances," U.S. Department of Health and Human Services, Public Health Service, Center for Disease Control, National Institute for Occupational Safety and Health (NIOSH Pub. No. 80-102).

"The Industrial Environment—Its Evaluation and Control," U.S. Department of Health and Human Services, Public Health Service, Center for Disease Control, National Institute for Occupational Safety and Health (NIOSH Pub. No. 74-117).

BIBLIOGRAPHIC DATA BASES TO USE FOR COMPUTER SEARCHES

Bibliographic Retrieval Services (BRS), Corporation Park, Bldg. 702, Scotia, NY 12302.

Chemical Information System (CIS), Chemical Information Systems Inc., 7215 Yorke Road, Baltimore MD 21212

Lockheed—DIALOG, Lockheed Missles and Space Company, Inc., P.O. Box 44481, San Francisco, CA 94144.

National Library of Medicine, Department of Health and Human Services, Public Health Service, National Institutes of Health, Bethesda, MD 20209

Toxicology Data Bank (TDB)

INDEX